An Imperial Homeland

THE MAX KADE RESEARCH INSTITUTE SERIES:
GERMANS BEYOND EUROPE

Series Editor   *Founding Editor*
Daniel Purdy   A. Gregg Roeber

The Max Kade Research Institute Series is an outlet for
scholarship that examines the history and culture of
German-speaking communities in America and across the
globe from the early modern period to the present. Books
in this series examine the movements of the German-
speaking diaspora as influenced by forces such as migration,
colonization, war, research, religious missions, or trade.
This series explores the historical and cultural depictions of
the international networks that connect these communities,
as well as linguistic relations between German and other
languages within European global networks.

This series is a project of the Max Kade Research Institute
located on Penn State's campus. It was founded in 1993
thanks to a grant from the Max Kade Foundation, New York.

An Imperial Homeland

FORGING GERMAN IDENTITY IN SOUTHWEST AFRICA

The Pennsylvania State University Press
University Park, Pennsylvania

Adam A. Blackler

Library of Congress Cataloging-in-Publication Data

Names: Blackler, Adam A., author.
Title: An imperial homeland : forging German identity
    in southwest Africa / Adam A. Blackler.
Other titles: Max Kade German-American Research
    Institute series.
Description: University Park, Pennsylvania : The Pennsylvania
    State University Press, [2022] | Series: The Max Kade
    Research Institute series : Germans beyond Europe | Includes
    bibliographical references and index.
Summary: "Examines the relationship between imperial
    Germany and its empire in southwest Africa (present-day
    Namibia), exploring how Africans confronted foreign rule and
    altered German national identity between 1842 and 1915"—
    Provided by publisher.
Identifiers: LCCN 2022019036 | ISBN 9780271092980 (hardback) |
    ISBN 9780271092997 (paper)
Subjects: LCSH: National characteristics, German. | Imperialism.
    | Namibia—History—1884–1915. | Germany—Colonies—
    Africa. | Germany—Relations—Namibia—History—19th
    century. | Namibia—Relations—Germany—History—19th
    century. | Germany—Relations—Namibia—History—20th
    century. | Namibia—Relations—Germany—History—20th
    century. | Germany—Colonies—Race relations.
Classification: LCC DT1603 .B53 2022 | DDC 968.81/00431—
    dc23/eng/20220427
LC record available at https://lccn.loc.gov/2022019036

The Pennsylvania State University Press is a member of the
Association of University Presses.

It is the policy of The Pennsylvania State University Press
to use acid-free paper. Publications on uncoated stock satisfy
the minimum requirements of American National Standard for
Information Sciences—Permanence of Paper for Printed Library
Material, ANSI Z39.48–1992.

For my mother, grandmother, and grandfather,
to whom I owe everything

Contents

Illustrations

Acknowledgments

It is with considerable pleasure that I can finally acknowledge the many individuals and institutions that have supported me and this project. Before I do so, however, I would first like to recognize the countless victims of settler-colonialism. We must never forget their memory, for as the Genocide Memorial in Windhoek reminds us, it is "their blood [that] waters our freedom." *An Imperial Homeland* cannot right the wrongs of the past. I can only aspire for it to engage people in the necessary and uncomfortable conversations that we all so often ignore in our own national histories. In particular, we need greater awareness, most notably in the Global North, of the factors that empowered imperial enthusiasts to marshal communal, financial, and political support in the nineteenth and twentieth centuries. Only then can we begin to undertake the long-overdue work of coming to terms with the inherent violence of colonialism and its systemic legacies. I hope that the following pages give credence to the import of this collective necessity and underscore the dangers that civil exclusion and racism pose in our present-day world.

I had the good fortune to visit multiple repositories and research libraries as I composed this book. My efforts would have fallen short without the help of countless archivists, librarians, and staff at the Bundesarchiv, Berlin-Lichterfelde (BArch); Cape Town Archival Repository (CAR); Freie Universität zu Berlin—Universitätsbibliothek; National Archives of Namibia—Windhoek (NAN); National Archives of Namibia—Central Library (NANL); National Library of South Africa (NLSA); Politisches Archive des Auswärtigen—Amt (PAAA); Staatsbibliothek zu Berlin—Preußischer Kulturbesitz (Stabi); Vereinte Evangelische Mission—Rheinische Missionsgesellschaft (VEM-RMG); and Wilson Library, University of Minnesota, Twin Cities. Sven Schneidereit (BArch), whose assistance and smile welcomed me each day throughout the duration of my research year in Berlin, proved invaluable. He not only helped make Berlin-Lichterfelde an enjoyable place to examine historical sources, but also made sure that the coffee machine remained full in spite of my frequent visits. I thank also Wolfgang Apelt (VEM-RMG), who made my first archival trip in Germany both educational and fruitful. Finally, Albertina Nekongo (NAN) went to great lengths to accommodate my many collection requests during my two-week stay in Namibia.

Given the international scope of this book, I am indebted to numerous organizations whose essential support enabled me to complete archival trips in Germany, Namibia, South Africa, and Botswana. These include the Central European History Society (CEHS); the Deutscher Akademischer Austauschdienst (DAAD); the National Endowment for the Humanities (NEH); the German Historical Institute (GHI); the Center for German and European Studies (CGES); the Center for Holocaust and Genocide Studies (CHGS); the United States Holocaust Memorial Museum (USHMM); the Wyoming Institute for Humanities Research (WIHR); the University of Minnesota, Twin Cities, Black Hills State University; and the University of Wyoming. I am also forever grateful to Prof. Dr. Sebastian Conrad, who kindly sponsored my doctoral research year at the Freie-Universität (FU). I still reflect on the many insights I gained as a participant in his weekly global history colloquium. His own scholarship, moreover, continues to inspire and push me intellectually. I thank also Monika Freier, Mahon Murphy, and Sean A. Wempe, three brilliant scholars who I met at the FU that continue to furnish me with advice, feedback, and unwavering friendship.

My dissertation advisors at the University of Minnesota, Eric D. Weitz and Gary B. Cohen, modeled what it means to be a professional historian. When *An Imperial Homeland* was still in its conceptual stages, first as a dissertation and later as a book monograph, they offered facilitatory critiques that steered my interests in fruitful directions. After I moved to Berlin, they kept a tactful distance that enabled me to undertake archival research in my own unique way. But perhaps most consequently, they taught me the importance of writing and its significance to the disciplinary fabric of history. I will always keep their copious notes on my chapter submissions as guides for how to approach my future research interests, as well as a reminder that the best gifts one can give a student are attention and encouragement. I can say with absolute certainty that I owe all of my academic accomplishments to their patience, supervision, and vast disciplinary knowledge. Eric's untimely passing in 2021 robbed me of the opportunity to share these truths with him in person. May his memory be a blessing.

I thank also Helena Pohlandt-McCormick, Patricia Lorcin, Alejandro Baer, Howard Louthan, Ofer Ashkenazi, Theo Stavrou, Bruno Chaouat, Mary Jo Maynes, Ann Waltner, Robert Swartout Jr., and David Messenger. They dedicated many hours of their own time to my academic pursuits and shared their expertise in graduate seminars, field studies, and workshops. In particular, Helena helped engineer my first trip to South Africa and challenged me to write a book that did not diminish Africa to a static role in an otherwise German history. Eric S. Roubinek and Julie Ault listened to various musings about this project from the beginning. I thank them for their friendship and reassurance over these past ten years. I also wish to thank James Coplin, Heidi Coplin, Andersen Coplin, Steve Bivans, Cameron Bradley, Grace Bradley, Basit Hammad Qureshi, Ann Zimo, Tiffany D. Vann Sprecher, Alex Wisnoski, Alan Fujishin, Caitlin Gallogly, Emily Bruce, Christopher Marshall, Edward Snyder, Jess Farrell, Virgil Slade, Elliot James, David Morton, Bryan Pekel, Katie Lambright, Paul Vig, Elizabeth Williams, Katie McKeown, Elizabeth Venditto, and Jason Herbert. I could not have finished this book without their companionship, especially during the cold Minnesota and Wyoming winters.

An additional network of colleagues read sections of this book either as conference presentations or as contributions to academic programs, edited volumes, and seminar reports. They are Jeremy Best, Sean A. Wempe, Eric S. Roubinek, Sara Pugach, David Pizzo, Michelle Moyd, Matt Fitzpatrick, Jake Short, Stephen Morgan, Willeke Sandler, Matthew Unangst, David Meola, and Jazmine Contreras. Their advice fills the pages of this study and has improved its analysis and arguments in fundamental ways. The same is true of the two anonymous reviewers, whose constructive criticisms and deep engagement elevated the potential of this book significantly. I also wish to acknowledge my two excellent editors, Kathryn Yahner and Daniel Purdy. Their sound advice, dedication, and transparency made for a gratifying publishing experience. John Morris carefully edited every chapter of this study. His careful eye improved the overall quality of this project immensely.

I researched and drafted a majority of this book in my eternal second home—Berlin. While the *Hauptstadt* has much to offer in scholarly colloquia, libraries, museums, and archives, several fellow academics transformed the city into much more than a worksite. In so doing, Julie Ault, Scott

Krause, Laura Yacovone, Scott Harrison, Alex Ruble, Lars Stiglich, Peter Gengler, Robert Terrell, Stephen Morgan, Kathryn Julian, Lauren Stokes, Willeke Sandler, Erin Hochman, Philipp Stelzel, and Andrew Kloiber contributed to this study profoundly. Though the sources that fill this project primarily came from libraries and repositories, it was during our wanderings in Friedenau, Volkspark-Jungfernheide, Köpenick, Wannsee, and other places that they all started to tell a story. In the immortal words of Marlene Dietrich, "I will always keep a suitcase in Berlin."

The faculty and staff at Black Hills State University provided me much joy and professional opportunity during my two years in the History Department. Jason Daniels, most notably, read initial drafts of my book proposal and was always quick to alert me when my arguments did not emphasize African voices forcefully or fully enough. The same is true of my colleagues at the University of Wyoming. It is difficult to imagine a better group of people with whom to share my love of history. In that spirit, I sincerely thank Isadora Helfgott, Alexandra Kelly, Melissa Morris, Peter Walker, Melissa Hampton, Jeff Means, Renee Laegreid, Barbara Logan, Leif Cawley, and Caroline Bragg. I am eager to continue learning from all of them in the coming years.

My mother, Jennifer Blackler, and grandparents, Colleen and John Maricelli, remain my inspiration. Thanks for the tireless support and unapologetic love, most especially during those years when I was too young to realize my good fortune. Finally, Melissa Hampton has endured all that has gone into this book more than any other person. From my various travels and conference presentations to "thinking walks" and late night/early morning writing sessions, she has perhaps looked forward to this day even more than me. But most important, Melissa exhibited considerable patience with me each day as I drafted my first book-length monograph. I am a social person at heart. But my devotion to this study, at times, led me to think about it almost exclusively. She not only tolerated this approach, but also appreciated it as "my way." I look forward to returning the favor as she finishes her own book. Her, CJ, AW, and AS's love sustains all that I do. Here's to our next adventure.

Whatever virtues this book may have are the result of everyone in this acknowledgment. Any errors are, of course, my own.

Abbreviations

AAKA	Auswärtiges Amt—Kolonial Abteilung
ADSV	Allgemeiner Deutscher Sprachverein
DFB	Deutscherkolonialen Frauenbundes
DKG	Deutsche Kolonialgesellschaft
DKGfSWA	Deutsche Kolonialgesellschaft für Südwestafrika
DKZ	*Deutsche Kolonialzeitung*
DOAG	Deutsch Ostafrikansiche Gesellschaft
DSWA	Deutsch Südwestafrika
EMGfDOA	Evangelische Missions Gesellschaft für Deutsch Ostafrika
GfdK	Gesellschaft für deutsche Kolonisation
LMS	London Mission Society
MHAG	Missions Handels Aktien Gesellschaft
MHG	Missions Handelsgesellschaft
NAZ	*Norddeutsche Allgemeine Zeitung*
RKA	*Reichskolonialamt*
RMG	Rheinische Missionsgesellschaft
VEM	*Vereinte Evangelische Mission*
WBMC	Walvis Bay Mining Company
WdVfCE	Westdeutscher Verein für Kolonisation und Export
ZAfA	Zentral Auskunftstelle für Auswanderer

FIG. 1 German Southwest Africa at the height of German imperial authority, 1910. Deutsch-Südwestafrika / Landkarte 1910. Photo: akg-images.

Introduction
National Fantasies—German Identity and the African Heimat

"NO ONE WANDERS BENEATH PALM TREES UNPUNISHED"

In 1857, the popular German periodical *Die Gartenlaube—Illustriertes Familienblatt* (The Garden Arbor—Illustrated Family Journal) extolled the supposed absolute truths of empire to a sympathetic audience. "The natural, uncultivated man," the piece avowed, "is and remains a product of the earth, a product of the climate, of landscapes and scenery. For himself, the educated man requires a meaningful moral strength in order to become master of this dependency. 'No one wanders beneath palm trees unpunished,' said Goethe."[1] The journal's accusation that "uncultivated peoples" were reliant upon their natural surroundings is noteworthy, as it divorced Europeans from those who lived in what *Die Gartenlaube*'s editors considered the global periphery. High *Kultur* was the purview of "civilized" societies, a marriage between moral strength and independence from nature. *Die Gartenlaube*'s review board took care to identify Germans as an especially enlightened community. Their reference to Johann Wolfgang Goethe, the quintessential man of rational virtue, underscored this claim in stark cultural terms. The passage further implied that high *Kultur* was an outgrowth of a diligent work ethic, humanistic education, and social cultivation, shared conditions that did not appear in nature innately. Much to the contrary, a society could only embody *Kultur* after its citizenry underwent a period of communal enrichment and enlightened growth.

Goethe's assertion that "no one wanders beneath palm trees unpunished" certainly exemplified that contention, but it also, importantly, served as a subtle warning to readers. The line first appeared in his *Elective Affinities*, a novel that explored human passion and the scientific affinities of relationships, in a passage that aligned well with contemporary nationalists and others who claimed that Black Africans had not evolved as fully as white Europeans. In the context of *Elective Affinities*, however, the excerpt offered a much deeper lesson: "At times when a longing and curiosity about these strange things has come over me, I have envied the traveler who sees such marvels in living, everyday connection with other marvels. But he, too, becomes another person. No one wanders beneath palm trees unpunished; and attitudes are certain to change in a land where elephants and tigers are at home."[2] In other words, even those of high culture were susceptible to change in a foreign land. "Only the naturalist . . . who remains in his own special element, with all that surrounds him," could observe the world free from its influence.[3]

Elective Affinities and the article that invoked its philosophy are remarkable for two reasons. First, both appeared long before Chancellor Otto von Bismarck joined with liberals, nationalists, and sympathetic conservatives to forge a unified German state in 1871. Though they relied on many of the same figurative and literary elements to construct an image of a supposed primordial and superior identity, Goethe and *Die Gartenlaube*'s editorial staff came to their conclusions without any direct influence from a centralized government. The same was true of their readership. In particular, university-educated, middle-class, and inquisitive German women and men were the principal audience to seize upon information about and from the non-European world. This broad coalition, which this study defines as the imperial consensus, looked upon Africa as a space where its wildest fantasies could find refuge and mature. The imperial consensus generated considerable public interest in the prospect of a German colonial project during the nineteenth century as a result. As a political initiative, colonialism generated turbulent arguments between demographically diverse populations, first throughout the German Confederation and later throughout the Kaiserreich. In so doing, an imperial project, even before 1871, inspired many bourgeois and liberal groups to conflate unification and overseas conquest as constituent elements of the same national enterprise. After Germany joined the "African scramble" in 1884, the colonial domain evolved into a defining element of everyday life for people outside of the imperial consensus as well. Whether in the colonies themselves, or in fairs, museums, zoological displays, and other titillating spectacles in the metropole, Germans could suddenly "wander beneath palm trees" in the real world and not only one of imperial fantasy.

Second, Goethe and *Die Gartenlaube* alluded to the world's so-called peripheries in exotic and harsh terms. Conviction, integrity, and strength were values inherent to Europeans, whereas the places where "palm trees grew" purportedly consisted solely of cultural backwardness and unexploited resources. Many contemporary associations and patriotic factions proliferated these same dogmas. Travel writers, merchants, and missionaries, for instance, regularly cast Africa through simplistic portrayals that followed civilizational worldviews and racist stereotypes. Militarists and aspiring settler colonists similarly envisaged conquest and expansion in glorified terms, while urban working-class citizens and industrial laborers contemplated the fresh air and open spaces that they read about in pro-imperial publications and travel literature. Largely left with only these orientalist accounts, German women, men, and children often accepted as fact narratives that cast Germany as enlightened and the Global South as a place without any tenets of civilization.

At the turn of the twentieth century, depictions of the so-called colonized world and its varied populaces were prevalent throughout the German metropole. Tobacconists catered to the erotic gaze of imperial enthusiasts with images of *Hereromädchen* (Herero girls) in their advertisements.[4] Coffee companies used portraits of Black African women to affirm the quality of their beans.[5] Youth magazines allowed children to escape into "exotic domains" where their imaginations could wander freely, unhindered by "civilized" social expectations.[6] Anthropologists shifted the paradigms of scientific analysis with examinations that looked upon so-called *Naturvölker* (natural peoples) as faceless and static objects.[7] Novelists published highly dramatic and romantic stories of faraway conflicts, a practice that over time made the realities of colonial bloodshed palpable for a continental audience.[8] Trade systems, print media, and imperial conquest shattered Germany's continental seclusion, pressing citizens to consume information from a variety of new sources, including from people in the overseas imperium.[9] Flora, fauna, and natural resources from Africa were at the fingertips of everyone—at least in literary form—as were stories of indigenous polities and their affiliation within Germany's expansive global empire.[10] Though racist theories still underlay a majority of these narratives, the prevalence of colonial imagery in Germany compelled women and men—both implicitly and explicitly—to contemplate the world beyond Europe in more holistic terms.[11]

Germany's colonial occupation of Southwest Africa (DSWA; present-day Namibia) in 1884 proved especially consequential in this process. As the Kaiserreich's first overseas protectorate and only settlement colony, DSWA most directly brought the "land where elephants and tigers are at home" to Central Europe, forever altering how Germans thought about Africans, as well as themselves. The importance of Germany's colonial project and how it affected impressions of national identity are important questions to consider. In particular, they compel us to scrutinize modern German history through a global lens.[12] Though civilizational characterizations like those in *Die Gartenlaube* typified Germans' contemporary discourse on Africa and epitomized Europe's dominance over the continent, they belie the degree to which African societies in turn influenced the evolution of Germany's colonial occupation in DSWA. They also provide a one-dimensional narrative on what is an otherwise diverse network of cultures, religions, and polities. In so doing, such perspectives from the nineteenth and early twentieth centuries ignore Africans and their essential place in German history.

An Imperial Homeland: Forging German Identity in Southwest Africa seeks to reorient our understanding of the relationship between the Kaiserreich and its empire in Southwest Africa. Specifically, it traces the transnational dimensions of colonialism, race, and genocide in DSWA, beginning with the arrival of Protestant missionaries in 1842 and concluding with Germany's imperial forfeiture after World War I. Precolonial and colonial Southwest Africa offer ideal settings to assess how Germans conceptualized the imperial domain in Europe and to analyze the evolution of its significance in the metropole. Due to its size, location, and status as Germany's first colony, DSWA assumed an important role in public discussions on southern Africa and its importance to the German state. A large number of citizens, officials, and volunteer organizations engaged with communities in Africa in a variety of ways during these eras. Rhenish missionaries, for example, contended that Southwest Africa's "heathen populations" were worthy of God's mercy and necessitated a strong missionary presence in the region. Well-propertied nobles, meanwhile, looked to designate Südwest as a suitable place to create plantation-style *latifundia* reminiscent of those that filled the countryside in East Prussia. Moneyed industrial and social elites sought to establish commercial monopolies and trade centers along the coastline, while pan-Germanists and advocates of racial hierarchy dreamed of white farming settlements that could stand as bulwarks of Germandom beyond the political borders of German Central Europe.

Though citizens shared wildly disparate motivations for overseas settlement, as well as numerous opinions on imperialism and its necessity, colonial fantasies inspired fierce interest among metropolitans in Africa.[13] Imperial desires and myths had an especially consequential effect on collective interpretations of the so-called *Heimat* (home/homeland) ideal, a historically elusive perception that conveyed among Germans a sense of place with local landmarks and cultural peculiarities.[14] This book provides *Heimat* greater conceptual and spatial mobility through its focus on DSWA, allowing us to consider for the first time how a distant colony with diverse ecologies, peoples, and social dynamics grew into an extension of German memory and tradition. The evolution of *Heimat* between the start of the *Vormärz* and the conclusion of World War I was principally the result of colonial encounters, which this study defines as the formal occasions when Germans and Africans interacted with one another, such as through treaty negotiations, trade networks, and military conflict. These encounters also comprised informal points of contact, specifically those that correspondence, newspapers, missionary reports, and travel literature generated in German and international media markets. In isolated towns and rural communities, as well as in cosmopolitan cities and industrial districts, these outlets spread information to German women and men who thirsted for news about the colonial empire. Illustrations of supposedly untamed landscapes and self-congratulatory tales of scientific discovery saturated literature, political debates, and raucous discussions in cafés, lecture halls, and town squares. As educational conduits, formal and informal encounters linked colony and metropole together in all aspects of everyday life, enabling citizens who never left the confines of Europe to establish connections with a region far beyond the traditional boundaries of the German state.

This book's focus on colonial encounters further shows that African and non-African populations in DSWA were as integral to Germany's national development as the merchants, soldiers, and settlers who first ventured overseas in the nineteenth century. Such an emphasis exposes the other side of imperial domination, most notably how Black Africans confronted colonial rule and the degree to which transnational entanglements altered German national identity. Precolonial apparitions may have instigated personal curiosities about Africa, but formal and informal encounters with the imperial world inspired detractors and enthusiasts alike to fashion a shared affiliation that extended past the geographical demarcations of Europe. As a result, what started as a small commercial enterprise in a faraway African territory in 1884 grew into an important extension of the German state by the turn of the twentieth century. Africans played a significant role in this political transformation. Their refusal to voluntarily accept German supremacy pressed colonial officers to confront their administrative limitations and to question the purpose behind imperial rule.

Most significantly, however, colonial encounters shattered the illusion of German cultural superiority. After 1884, white settlers and imperial authorities discovered that they could not govern the colony merely on the basis of their nationalist convictions or sense of adventure. The same was true for metropolitans who espoused open support for the colonial project. When the façade of imperial fantasy gave way to colonial reality, German colonists and their compatriots in Europe increasingly sought to fortify their presence in Africa using juridical and physical acts of violence. In addition, once Africans laid bare the mirage of German colonial logic, white settlers embraced eliminatory racism as a solution for their individual failures and collective ills. After the Herero-Nama genocide, race functioned as the only determinative category in imperial society. White settlers seized control over all political and social affairs in the colony and used their newfound power to target African survivors in extraordinarily inhumane ways.

In this manner, "race thinking" surfaced as perhaps the most consequential legacy of Germany's colonial project. As an ideological principle that upheld ethnic purity as the historical driver of national politics, race thinking not only shifted the paradigms of the imperial state but also elevated the exclusionary perspectives of those in the Kaiserreich who framed citizenship along an inflexible color line. Racism begat violence, and annihilatory violence begat an apartheid state in DSWA. While the same dangerous potential existed in every other European imperial project, Black Africans in *Heimat* Südwest saw colonial officials unleash those same violent capabilities in courtrooms, local elections, so-called native reservations, and, most callously, in the Omaheke Desert. This development was not the inevitable result of an instinctive genocidal character but rather the horrific product of settler-colonial logic and practice that continued to find refuge in Germany and elsewhere long after 1919.

GERMANY'S EMPIRE IN GERMAN HISTORY

Scholarly interest in German imperial history has grown considerably in the twenty-five years since Susanne Zantop published her now-classic study on the maturation of colonial fantasies in the eighteenth and nineteenth centuries.[15] She was the first to scrutinize colonialism through a prism of imagined imperial scenarios and how such reveries informed collective views on gender, nation, and race in German-speaking lands in Central Europe. In addition to Zantop's essential research, Horst Drechsler and Helmut Bley were the foremost historians after World War II to provide serious consideration of the colonial empire on its own terms.[16] Though the historiography has evolved considerably since the 1960s, their studies remain foundational reading for any project on Germany's overseas territories. Drechsler was the earliest historian to designate the Herero-Nama massacre as an act of genocide, while Bley dissected the various political and social factors that led DSWA to "cross over into totalitarianism."[17] Though they primarily concentrated on the links between colonialism, Nazi genocide, and "totalitarian" rule, Drechsler and Bley exposed just how entangled Germany and DSWA were in the immediate years before 1914.

Much of the recent scholarship has concentrated on German-imperial violence and its influence on radical-right politics and social movements after World War I.[18] This body of work has raised important questions concerning the inherent role of military aggression in Germany's colonial occupations in Africa and elsewhere throughout the Pacific and Global South. In particular, Isabel Hull, Jürgen Zimmerer, Benjamin Madley, and many others have pointed to the structural continuities that they see as links between the Kaiserreich and Third Reich, such as military personnel, hypernationalism, and romantic notions of conquest. While considerations of such topics as the consequences of Wilhelm II's "polycratic government" or the "Windhoek to Auschwitz" thesis continue to arouse debate among scholars, few historians today question the *general* effect of colonial racism and annihilatory warfare on systemic acts of violence in Europe after 1918.[19]

The intense—albeit necessary—focus on the brutal legacy of the Herero-Nama genocide, however, has in many ways rendered the precolonial and formative colonial periods nothing more than historical footnotes to the so-called Kaiser's Holocaust.[20] While this study does not minimize the exterminatory realities of German colonialism in any way,

An Imperial Homeland chiefly concentrates on formal and informal encounters in the nineteenth century so as to illustrate the evolutionary nature of the Kaiserreich's settler-colonial project in DSWA. Though their motives were manifestly absolute and cruel, German settlers, unlike soldiers in the Wehrmacht in Eastern Europe, did not embark for Southwest Africa with the explicit intention to commit wholesale mass murder.[21] If we recognize the *Vernichtungsbefehl* and its eliminatory consequences as genocide—which this study does emphatically—we must acknowledge that these outcomes were a maturation of violence that started long before Lieutenant General Lothar von Trotha and the *Schutztruppe* (protection force) embarked for the Waterberg in 1904. Such a position does not mean to construct a false hierarchy of mass murder but rather aims to scrutinize the dangerous potentials that helped make settler-colonial genocide possible in the first place. The same capacities that incited the first genocide of the twentieth century in Southwest Africa also existed in every other European imperial project. Historical inquiries that search for a fixed point of exterminatory warfare and its potential Nazi inspiration often overlook this fact. They can also ignore the very populations that suffered the most at the hands of German colonists, officials, and settlers.

Two equally important historiographical developments during this same time frame are the growth of diaspora studies and Black German history, fields that have found considerable prominence in historical analyses on identity and nationality, as well as on German colonialism and postcolonialism. Fatima El-Tayeb's important 2001 study explored the place and evolution of "race" as a concept in Germany between 1890 and 1933.[22] She specifically examined "discourses of the dominant culture" and questions how "images of 'race'" decisively influenced "political, social, economic, and transcendental changes" in German society.[23] El-Tayeb's examination initiated a renewed focus on Black Germans among historians and other scholars, who she rightly observed had ignored the contributions of people of color in German history for decades.[24] Tina M. Campt, Patricia Mazón, Reinhild Steingröver, Mischa Honeck, Martin Klimke, Anne Kuhlmann, Robbie Aitken, Eve Rosenhaft, Theodor Michael, Sara Lennox, Maureen Maisha Eggers, Tiffany N. Florvil, and Vanessa D. Plumly have all since written accounts of Black German experiences in modern German history and have pushed historiographical inquires on these topics forward in a more holistic direction.[25]

In addition to this vital research, historians have increasingly emphasized the transnational character of Germany's global empire.[26] This development has led scholars to consider colonialism's impact on local and federal elections, institutional practices, shared views on "traditional" gender roles, commercial marketing campaigns, the proliferation of travel literature, anthropology and new forms of scientific analysis, the growth of Pan-German leagues, and social rights movements in Europe.[27] In the period between the *Vormärz* and German unification, notions of national belonging galvanized liberal politicians, students, merchants, and indus- trialists to forge a centralized state with expansionist capabilities. As Geoff Eley has recently contended, this geopolitical environment occupied "older established national states, where nationalist ideas were palpably circulat- ing through those Central European lands soon to be remapped into a new state-bounded entity of Germany."[28] In this manner, he avows, the language of transnationalism "already made sense" to national groups long before traders, missionaries, and settlers embarked on an official program of over- seas conquest.[29] Matthew Fitzpatrick and John Phillip Short have also concentrated on so-called outside informers, specifically representatives of the Paulskirche (Frankfurt National Assembly), working-class citizens, and women, and how they helped fashion popular notions of *Deutschtum* (Germanness) in a transnational manner.[30] Sean Andrew Wempe's recent study on Germany's involvement in the formation of international orga- nizations after 1918, moreover, has shed fresh light on how *Kolonialdeutsche* "exploited transnational opportunities to recover, renovate, and market their understandings . . . to re-establish themselves as 'experts' and fellow civilizers'" in the wake of World War I.[31] These examples present nine- teenth- and twentieth-century Germany as a space where identity assumed a fluid nature due to foreign contact, economic trade, and the influence of international organizations in society. One can only hope that historians continue this line of inquiry in the future.

The extent to which globalization transformed the Kaiserreich into a global entity is also at the center of new scholarship on German imperi- alism. Sebastian Conrad, Jürgen Osterhammel, and Andreas Eckert have maintained that transnational networks directly contributed to the popu- larity of national characteristics in the nineteenth century "because [they] created upheavals in the political, economic and discursive orders of the world of nations."[32] Mass mobility "flattened the world" with the spread of people, goods, ideas, and scientific achievement, a phenomenon that both jolted nationalist movements to create inherently sovereign states and more closely entangled colony and metropole together with telegraph lines, postal services, print media, and military conflict.[33] Likewise, Angela

Zimmerman's focus on the complex interrelations between slavery, race, social science, and colonialism has exposed the close ties that existed between Germany, Africa, and the United States.[34] He has proposed that transnational history "allows historians to apply microhistorical cultural methods . . . to macrohistorical political-economic questions," a methodological circumstance that invites scholars to write nationally specific studies of otherwise disparate peoples, communities, and regions.[35]

An Imperial Homeland ultimately follows in the methodological footsteps of these transnational investigations.[36] It contends that colonial encounters both strengthened geographically inclusive conceptions of German identity in the formative imperial era and emboldened racially exclusive definitions of citizenship once white settlers seized total control of DSWA after the Herero-Nama genocide. Through this approach, culturally and ethnically diverse African polities emerge as central protagonists in modern German history. This effort not only emphasizes the inherent malice of imperialism but also reveals how peoples in distant places like Windhoek and Otjimbingwe transformed collective understandings of the Heimat ideal throughout the German metropole.

While places of birth, familial experiences, shared vernaculars and linguistic dialects, and local, regional, and national histories had profound effects on the development of German identity, Deutschtum did not evolve exclusively inside a spatial vacuum. If mass media and modern transit made it possible for Westphalians and Bavarians to forge a common sense of self by the early twentieth century, those same factors also made it possible for peoples in imperial Africa to shape how Germans thought about their station as women and men, citizens and subjects, and colonists and nationalists. A fantasy no more, the Heimat abroad linked women and men, cattle and commodities, fresh air, and genocidal violence in Southwest Africa with café culture, general amusements, political debate, and Wilhelmine notions of patriarchy in Germany. Over time, these encounters enheartened metropolitans to perceive Germany and DSWA as one common entity—as one imperial homeland.

CHAPTER OUTLINE

The six chapters in this book regard modern German history as inextricably tied with the communities, ideas, and landscapes beyond the geographical strictures of Europe. Each section seeks to illustrate that

Germany's imperial presence in DSWA, however short or inglorious, fashioned consequential associations between colony and metropole that tailored the boundaries of Germanness on a global scale. Part 1, "National Aspirations, 1842–1884," focuses on the emergence of common notions of German identity during the precolonial and preunification eras. From liberal-minded nationalists and aristocratic nobles to hopeful merchants and Rhenish missionaries, Germans increasingly regarded the expansionary potential of centralized statecraft as necessary components of Germandom over the course of the nineteenth century.

Chapter 1 explores how after a long history of indifference, skepticism, anxiety, and aristocratic hostility, liberal German views on the potential of territorial expansion grew into a flexible consensus that shaped how they looked upon the world. As women and men imagined their identity in the context of continental Europe and the so-called global periphery, they created an image of themselves as natural colonizers. This chapter emphasizes the rhetoric of notable members of the Frankfurt National Assembly, the popularity of geographic magazines and travel narratives in the 1850s and 1860s, and the political ramifications of the Berlin Conference (1884–85) to underscore how shared impressions of overseas imperialism performed as part of a broad spectrum of dynamics that citizens debated and experimented with between 1848 and 1884. While imperial enthusiasts had a significant effect on German nationhood and its development, impressions of Germanness often varied from region to region and city to city. Among liberal-minded citizens most notably, however, the practice of imagining colonialism instigated common desires about expansionism that eventually made it possible for people to regard German unity and overseas conquest as part of the same national project.

Chapter 2 concentrates on the Rheinische Missionsgesellschaft (Rhenish Mission Society, RMG) after its arrival in Southwest Africa in 1842. At a time when the majority of Germans who fantasized about Africa remained in Central Europe, Rhenish missionaries actually pursued a life overseas. As a Protestant mission society, the RMG aspired above all to spread Christianity to peoples who its members believed lived beyond the reach of God. This chapter considers the RMG's evolution in two entangled contexts: first, as a Westphalian religious society in revolutionary Europe, and second, as a small and isolated institution in Southwest Africa. While they remained first and foremost members of a religious society, Rhenish missionaries frequently modified their proselytization efforts to attract more African converts and followers. The RMG's adoption of religious chauvinism was among the most consequential outcomes of this process. This practice inspired many missionaries to intertwine contemporary nationalist beliefs with foundational Christian philosophies. Over time, religious chauvinism led the RMG to bring not only salvation but also unsolicited advice, "modern" infrastructure, and cultural programs designed to proliferate Christianity throughout southern Africa. If Africans failed to see the so-called benefit of Christian civilization voluntarily, missionaries felt justified in bringing it to them in the form of churches, schools, farms, and commercial marketplaces. In this fashion, the RMG strengthened its institutional influence in southern Africa and also empowered German citizens in Europe to encounter the future colony on an informal basis, most notably through their correspondence and religious sermons. Regardless of their own personal intentions, therefore, Rhenish missionaries increased public awareness about life overseas and also established the RMG as an important German outpost in southern Africa well before the start of the formal colonial era in 1884.

Part 2, "Colonial Encounters, 1884–1904," shifts attention to the official imperial age and the importance of informal and formal colonial encounters in the evolution of German national identity. Chapter 3 examines the relationship between Germany and DSWA through the lens of imperial propaganda, racist testimonials, board games, and ethnographic spectacles. These media and exhibitions most especially affected public interpretations of the *Heimat* ideal. In doing so, they helped to ingrain the lived and exaggerated realities of colonialism into everyday life in the German metropole. Though imperialism was a controversial issue in various bourgeois and other demographic circles, the increased attention on Africa in speeches, tabloid headlines, fairs, museums, and children's amusements elevated the importance of empire in the Kaiserreich. As informational conduits, informal colonial encounters linked colony and metropole together in sustained contact and allowed metropolitans to experience the overseas imperium from the confines of their neighborhoods and market squares. DSWA may have started as nothing more than a fanciful enterprise that several monied investors used to acquire even more wealth, but thanks to these media and mass spectacles, it evolved into something far more significant to a much larger German audience than people like Adolf Lüderitz and Carl Peters.

Chapter 4 reorients what is often our traditional understanding of German imperial rule in Africa. It focuses on formal encounters between the Witbooi Nama and Ovaherero with imperial German officers through the actions and perspectives of Africans themselves. Far more than all other figures, Hendrik Witbooi and Samuel Maharero unmasked the realities of colonial life for both metropolitans and settlers after 1884, primarily through treaty negotiations, trade networks, correspondence, and military engagements with German allies and the imperial government itself. In response, politicians and other procolonial enthusiasts advocated for a greater physical presence in DSWA over the course of the formative period of imperial occupation. As more soldiers and military equipment arrived in Südwest, the role of the colonial administration expanded markedly. Africans played a prominent role in this development. Witbooi and Maharero's refusal to accept German rule pressed the imperial government to respond to *their* actions as opposed to the other way around. An emphasis on the notable place of Africans during this foundational fifteen-year epoch reveals how peoples in places like Windhoek and Okahandja manipulated German efforts to exploit Southwest Africa for their own ends. Colonialism was an inherently brutal enterprise in all of its forms and guises. This chapter, therefore, does not mean to imply that Africans made their own conditions worse through acts of resistance. Much to the contrary, it seeks to counter a still—unfortunately—common narrative that misrepresents Nama and Ovaherero peoples as passive victims in the face of military assaults and violence. Once Africans shattered the foundational myths of European imperial fantasies, German authorities increasingly relied on systemic and physical violence to quell African demands for equality and sovereignty. In this manner, civil and annihilatory acts of aggression emerged as the principal instruments of German authority in *Heimat* Südwest shortly after the start of the twentieth century.

Part 3, "An Imperial Homeland, 1905–1914," centers on the eliminatory transformation of colonial society and its segregatory consequences in DSWA. Chapter 5 shows how state-condoned acts of mass murder and an increased reliance on "race thinking" helped to promote exclusionary notions of citizenship throughout the German Empire. After the Herero-Nama war, *Heimat* Südwest evolved into an apartheid state, where white settlers sought to define imperial and national belonging along a racial color line. Four instances characterize this process: the imperial government's adoption of *Rassentrennung* (racial separation), national efforts to increase the emigration of white women to DSWA, the colonial administration's categorization of Afrikaners in strictly racial terms, and the electoral landscape in Germany, which culminated in the so-called Hottentot elections of 1907. From supporters and white colonists to eager patriots and opportunistic politicians, German women and men used postgenocide Southwest Africa to reflect what they saw as a model national character. After the conclusion of the Herero-Nama genocide, a majority of white Germans—in both colony and metropole—defined that character in racial terms.

Chapter 6 traces the private convictions of white German men in the wake of genocide and how their sentiments about the ideal settler eventually transformed collective impressions of masculinity in the Kaiserreich. Annihilation, forced imprisonment, and the imperial government's enforcement of ethnic apartheid created a setting that championed bravado, self-reliance, and cultural hierarchy as the foundation of Germany's presence in southern Africa. These sentiments arose chiefly among farmers and soldiers, who first experienced armed conflict in DSWA and then secondly wrote about it for public consumption. This chapter also analyzes the emergence of a global *Heimat* ideal in the thousands of colonial *Eingaben* (petitions) that aspiring settlers sent to the Auswärtiges Amt—Kolonial Abteilung (Foreign Office—Colonial Division; AAKA). In remarkable detail, these petitions document the extent to which prospective colonists used *Heimat* rhetoric to justify their involvement in the imperial project. Though colonial *Eingaben* demonstrate a hopeful naïveté about life in DSWA, they illustrate how aspiring imperialists accentuated the cultural, spiritual, and racial qualities of Germandom to support their appeals for settlement, as well as how they used the supposedly heroic experiences they read about in memoirs, letters, and newspapers to define German manhood.

Dreams of empire—and later the loss of a real one—expanded views of Germanness to include Southwest Africa as a formal extension of the German state. The evolution of colonial race policy, most notably, demonstrates how citizens and settlers modified their impressions of imperialism in seismic ways between 1842 and 1915. In this sense, Germany's violent presence in Southwest Africa illustrates colonialism's centrality to German history and also reflects the consequence of its genocidal legacy up to the present day.

PART 1

National Aspirations, 1842–1884

Nothing other than the propagation of
nations and states, and an inability to
colonize means nothing more and nothing less than impotence for a nation.
—Johann Sturz, 1862

CHAPTER 1

"New Worlds of Vitality"

Colonial Aspirations and the German Nation, 1848–1884

CONSENSUS AND IMAGINATION IN PRE-IMPERIAL GERMANY

"All those big beautiful worlds overseas . . . we are allowed to look at them, to look forward to their beautiful sight, and even to exploit them for our own enrichment. But to carry our nationality in proudly, and to create a pertinent state position on the other side of the sea. In one word, to create a respected New Germany—that is and remains for our Teutonic race, as [a participant] in the race for nations' forbidden fruits!"[1] So wrote Ernst von Weber, a self-styled ethnographer from Dresden, after returning from a four-year agriculturist tour of southern Africa in 1875. Though a farmer by training, with no previous experience overseas, Weber embarked on his African sojourn to satisfy an inner longing to "see and sense the vast overseas world" for himself.[2] Upon his return to Germany, Weber moved to advance the cause of German national expansion through his writings and participation in proimperial campaigns.

Weber was a young man who came of age in the *Vormärz* (1815–48), and his views on the German nation evolved in a period of notable political tension. While some of his contemporaries envisaged a united state carefully demarcated along cultural and ethnic lines, many others cast their gaze past the European continent to the so-called exotic peripheries of Africa and Asia. For women and men who shared Weber's imperial fantasies, the German nation could not achieve its full potential without a

colonial empire, most especially in Africa. "The spread of German nationality in overseas continental worlds," Weber asserted, "seems to be especially
important from a patriotic point of view. . . . [The] aspirations of the southern African Huns are particularly significant, for the sympathies of this
powerful and good Teutonic tribe for their German motherland are of great
value to us and would possibly make it easier for us to gain a firm foothold
on the southern African high plateau, as far as it has not yet been seized
by the English."[3] Weber perceived empire and nation as constituent parts
of the same enterprise. They represented a joint aspiration that could unite
all German peoples and simultaneously afford them an occasion to establish a foothold in the so-called empty and undeveloped regions of the globe.

Reveries of colonial conquest manipulated the contours of the "German
question" long before the Kaiserreich formally occupied an overseas empire
in 1884. Though skepticism, social anxiety, aristocratic hostility, and even
general indifference consistently swayed individual opinions about a colonial project's prospects, favorable notions on expansion grew into a general
consensus during the nineteenth century. Not every national activist or
self-described patriot, of course, yearned to control hectares of land and
large herds of cattle in a distant colony. Most German citizens in favor of
unification, notably intellectuals, members of the middle class, and self-
identified liberals, however, did agree that an effective foreign policy
necessitated some form of territorial conquest in Europe and *potentially*
overseas.[4] In that spirit, domestic attitudes regarding Germany's prospective status as a world power before and after 1871—one that was still in
search of its own "place in the sun"—overcame contrary voices and suspicious politicians who asserted that they had arrived too late to the "African
scramble." As German enthusiasts pictured themselves in deserts, jungles,
mountainous terrains, and faraway archipelagos outside of Europe, their
imaginations increasingly fashioned an identity as natural colonizers.

This chapter explores three instances that mark the significance of
empire for liberal nationalists in the precolonial nineteenth century. The
rhetoric of prominent *Vormärz* intellectuals leading up to the Frankfurt
National Assembly (Paulskirche), public consumption of travel literature
and magazines, and the geopolitical ramifications of the Berlin Conference
(1884–85) all exhibit how dreams of colonial expansion shaped the evolution of German nationalism and statecraft before and after German
unification in 1871. Bradley Naranch has shown that "emigration fever"
sparked sharp debate about the necessity of overseas colonies among
nationalist and intellectual audiences during this formative national period.[5]

In disparate cities, regions, and towns in the German Confederation, German-speaking peoples held a variety of opinions on the orientation of the future state as well, ranging from inclusive notions reliant on culture and language to exclusionary perspectives dependent on demarcated borders and race. Apart from Naranch's analysis, however, the historiography has not holistically accounted for *Vormärz* colonialism and the significant ways it informed contemporary discussions on German nationalism and identity.[6]

Conceptualizations of belonging do not occur inside a regional or linguistic vacuum. To the contrary, individuals can also incorporate shared perceptions of the unknown as a means to make the mysterious familiar and the familiar contingent on the mysterious. In order to understand the manner in which German women and men fashioned a national identity, therefore, we must consider *why* so many people adopted sympathetic impressions of overseas conquest and how it evolved into an important element of Germandom during this crucial period of European history. A holistic analysis of this nature invites us to broaden our impression of Germany's national evolution and to recognize the critical role that both imperial fantasies and *Auslandsdeutschen* (overseas Germans) played in the same process. The practice of imagining colonialism, an introspective activity that flourished without formal direction, instigated a pervasive desire among the *Bildungsbürgertum* (educated middle class) and *Wirtschaftsbürgertum* (mercantile middle class), as well as people from all provinces, social classes, and political stations, to establish a national state and global empire. Whether in general discursive practices, in debates in the culture and opinion sections of newspapers, or simply in how women and men conversed about global affairs, dreams of territorial occupation generated imperial desires that eventually culminated in Germany's colonization of Southwest Africa in 1884.

Auslandsdeutschen proved exceptionally influential in the evolution of German imperial consciousness. Rhenish missionaries spoke at length about Africans in their diaries and dispatches, portraying them as "garrulous, trifling, laughing, quarrelsome, boastful, crawling, at one moment in the highest rage and anger, in others brave where there is no resistance."[7] Images of lions, elephants, tigers, ostriches, and marine life helped familiarize students and a curious public with Africa, Asia, and diverse archipelagos in the Pacific Ocean. Merchants, coal miners, and farmers, alongside business owners, aristocrats, and political officials, boasted that the "exploitation of [foreign] soil, its natural resources, flora and fauna, and above all the people" carried the potential to transform Germany into a European and global "great power."[8] Rich descriptions of arid terrain, endless horizons, unexploited resources, and indigenous peoples stimulated deep interest in the world beyond Europe and eventually fashioned a story line that not even a genuine colonial empire could entirely dispel.[9]

Expansionist dreams were part of a broad spectrum of thoughts and experiences that German society experimented with between 1815 and 1884, a period when notions of national identity were fluid, and debates about the German question enlivened cafés, salons, and university lecture halls. Idealistic opinions on conquest and territorial occupation contributed to liberal models of national belonging, social hierarchy, and cultural enlightenment, gradually pushing middle-class citizens to envisage themselves as instinctive global pioneers. In the four decades between the end of the *Vormärz* and Germany's occupation of Southwest Africa, settler-colonial fantasies led to an imperial consensus of largely educated, financially secure, and curious women and men that concealed and produced similarity, generated shared senses of cultural responsibility, and expanded individual perspectives of identity to include territories outside the geographical boundaries of Europe.

VORMÄRZ IMPERIALISM AND THE FRANKFURT NATIONAL ASSEMBLY, 1815–1849

On 16 June 1848, Johann Tellkampf, a liberal national delegate from Bückeburg in Lower Saxony, rose to address his colleagues in the National Assembly about the necessity of establishing a German navy. In his view, a national fleet had the potential to bring a permanent end to regional conflicts between Germany and its European neighbors and afford prospective merchants more favorable trade opportunities with other countries worldwide. As his speech continued, however, Tellkampf gradually directed his words past the walls of the Paulskirche toward posterity and the masses outside. "It is not merely the present war [with Denmark] that we must have before our eyes," he asserted, but also "times of peace. . . . We have seen it everywhere that other nations obtain far more favorable terms . . . where their flag is already known and respected. A fleet is also required for the removal of trade tariffs and for the establishment and maintenance of a colony."[10] At the conclusion of Tellkampf's address, loud applause and good cheer filled the National Assembly's halls.[11] The excited delegates proclaimed that they could now signal to "the world with the clearest proof that the unity of Germany is a reality."[12] While a navy provided national advocates a symbol of strength and cultural unity, the idea gained prominence only because a considerable number of representatives already harbored expansionist views. For many delegates in Frankfurt am Main, national and imperial aspirations were one and the same narrative. Two crucial questions, however, remained up for debate. What exactly was the "German nation," and how essential was imperial expansion to the cultural and political orientation of the future nation-state?

The problem of national definition stood squarely at the forefront of liberal discourse in the *Vormärz*, an epoch when literary censorship, monarchal authority, regional factionalism, and Austro-Prussian dualism guided politics and society in the German Confederation. Though European sovereigns rescinded most of Napoleon's "enlightened reforms" at the Congress of Vienna in 1815, a return to dynastic legitimacy failed to suppress the repercussions of the French Revolution in people's minds.[13] Europe's monarchs may have successfully reoriented their respective governments in an absolutist direction, but they could not mold the way people thought about and perceived the world. Collective consciousness and communal growth thus evolved into cornerstones of liberal-nationalist ideology, as German intellectuals evoked the principles of the Enlightenment and challenged any centralized unification that did not consider the *Volksgeist* (national spirit) of the people.[14]

Nationhood, German liberals maintained, involved more than a simple proclamation from an unassailable monarch or a two-dimensional designation on a map. It originated from public memories, a unique history, and a progressive notion of *Bildung* (self-cultivation), convictions that favored individuality and self-awareness over biological or other exclusionary perceptions of identity.[15] Communal impressions of *Heimat*, therefore, performed a crucial role in their conceptions of national belonging during this period. Distinct customs and recollections afforded women and men opportunities to transcend any potential obstacle that might otherwise impede their creation of an inclusive homeland. When people could relate to a particular countryside or reflexively convey a local landmark's significance to someone they did not know intimately, their shared kinship created a bond along colloquial and emotional lines that permanently linked them to each other and to the region in question. In this way, *Heimat* offered liberal sympathizers a simple yet powerful occasion to unite people who might not otherwise regard themselves as transcendent members of the

German *Volk*. If individuals could imagine a shared association with others whom they had never met in their own hometowns, then over time they had the potential to form a bond with every person in German-speaking Central Europe as well.

While liberal contemporaries and their allies generally agreed on the educative and spiritual composition of a nation, they found less common ground over the future German state's political borders, system of government, and standards for full civil membership. Brian Vick and most recently Erin R. Hochman have shown that social clashes over national identity reflected the seriousness and vibrancy of the matter.[16] Discussions about the German question, in particular, influenced discourses on nationhood more than any other topic between the conclusion of the Napoleonic Wars and the inauguration of the Paulskirche. Among the most contentious issues were whether the new Germany should be *kleindeutsch* (excluding an Austrian Empire), *großdeutsch* (including the Habsburg federal lands), or a "Reich of seventy million" (including all the Habsburg lands in their entirety). After Prussian king Friedrich Wilhelm IV figuratively left the German crown "in the gutter" in 1849, the Austro-Prussian War of 1866 seemingly produced a decisive answer on the battlefield in Königgrätz.[17] Otto von Bismarck's Prussian-dominated solution, however, failed to mollify many liberal nationalists, who alleged that the Kaiserreich did not go far enough to satisfy their idealistic image of nationhood. From Württemberg and Rhenish Pfalz to Budweis and Prague, *Deutschtum* did not inherently emanate from Berlin for everyone. After 1871, the *Hauptstadt* exemplified authority and enjoyed significant influence over every other *Bezirk* as the seat of federal power. Nevertheless, Prussian supremacy did not entice every liberal nationalist and other like-minded citizens to rally behind Bismarck's vision of the nation-state reflexively.

In this manner, the continued reticence of many German citizens after 1871 signified that nationhood was far from a settled question, especially for those who championed the imperialistic ambitions of the 1848 revolution and the Frankfurt National Assembly. Even before the advent of the nineteenth century, Germans enjoyed a long history of cultural interaction with peoples and regions beyond the coastlines of Europe. Susanne Zantop's important analysis of colonial fantasies, for example, has demonstrated how a "colonialist subjectivity" emerged in Germany as early as the 1770s and grew into a "collective obsession" by the late 1880s. Stories of territorial and sexual conquest "made the strange familiar" and enabled citizens to generate new identities along national and imperial lines.[18] Matthew Fitzpatrick and John Phillip Short have also convincingly argued that German liberals drew upon "heterogeneous imperialist theoretics" from the eighteenth century to assemble an imperialist foreign policy agenda.[19] While elite and intellectual circles sculpted the "official mind" of colonialism and its place in German society, an imperial drive from below flourished in unofficial venues as well.[20]

Although debates on colonial expansion did not create the same social unrest in German-speaking communities as questions over the ideal state, public fascination with the colonial realm nevertheless manipulated the German question's evolution profoundly. From commercial amusements and public spectacles to private clubs and grassroots organizations, urban laborers and rural farmers gave voice to the potential of empire. In the context of the *Vormärz*, therefore, the most significant aspect of public conversations on colonialism is that they happened at all. Our recognition that imperial sympathizers, regardless of their class or education, shared a common belief in expansionism allows us to trace how romantic notions of colonialism influenced protonationalist debates over the structure of the German state. Perhaps even more importantly, it presses us to interrogate why communal exchanges on conquest and its potential stimulated the emergence of an imperial consensus in German lands in the first place.

As a political idea, imperialism inspired fierce arguments between liberals, nobles, and reform-minded citizens about its prospective opportunities and shortcomings. Fredrich List, a liberal economist from Württemberg, for instance, promoted overseas conquest as an entrepreneurial initiative that could benefit a united German nation economically and geopolitically. "Colonies are the lifeblood of manufacturing strength, and the related growth in domestic and foreign trade, of meaningful coastal and open sea maritime travel and of large ocean fisheries and at some point of significant naval power," List wrote in his 1841 *The National System of Political Economy*.[21] "The surplus strength of the mother nation in terms of populations, capital and entrepreneurial spirit," he continued, "gains a positive channel through colonization, the return on which is paid with interest. . . . If European nations other than Britain wish to take part in the very profitable business of cultivating wild lands or civilizing barbaric nations . . . they must begin to develop their domestic manufacturing strength, their maritime capacity, and their naval strength."[22] List's arguments inspired many nationalists as they promoted territorial expansion as a necessity to a wider German public.

Intellectuals often justified the need for colonialism in other ways during the era as well. Friedrich Hundeshagen, a prominent liberal theorist, promoted empire as a solution for population surpluses and as spaces for lower-class citizens who faced the worst effects of industrialization and urbanization.[23] "The question of emigration," Hundeshagen began his 1849 *German Emigration as a National Matter, Especially the Emigration of the Proletariat*, "has long been the subject of serious statesmanship, but in the fragmentation and isolation of the various German lands, there has never been much talk of foreign affairs abroad."[24] This issue, he continued, "can only be apprehended with the hope of finding a suitable solution to the national question, for only by a strong unified representation abroad, and by the foundation of German naval power, is it possible to guide and protect emigrants to overseas states."[25] Though these imperial enthusiasts did not speak for every proponent of German nationhood, List, Hundeshagen, and others characterized the widespread social impact of colonialism and how it might benefit all adherents of nationhood. *Bürgerlich* expansionist dreams proved so palpable among German polities, in fact, that they continued to shape discourses on nationalism long after the dissolution of the Paulskirche in 1849.[26]

The Frankfurt National Assembly's failure to create a unified state is well known. While the end result did not lead to a *großdeutsch* or *kleindeutsch* solution, the Paulskirche was nevertheless the first civil forum in modern German history where imperial and national exponents ratified constitutional measures designed to transform their fantasies into realities. After an initial period of collective protest and social unrest, regional leaders in each of the thirty-nine German-speaking states established a *Vorparlament* (interim parliament) to oversee an election of delegates to the National Assembly, which was officially inaugurated in Saint Paul's Church in Frankfurt am Main on 18 May 1848. The representatives who convened the Paulskirche embodied the vanguard of the post-*Vormärz* era. Of the 830 delegates who gathered in the National Assembly, over six hundred had a university education and worked either in the civil service or as university teachers and professors, while only sixty-five members, about 10 percent of the total parliamentary delegation, were from the nobility. There were also sixty delegates who represented commerce and trade, forty-six agriculturists, and four members who advocated for craftsmen and small shop owners.[27] Though constituent blocs were not monoliths,

intellectuals, scholars, and other representatives of the German bourgeoi-
sie comprised a significant majority in the Paulskirche.

This political alignment exemplified the relative egalitarian nature of
the *Vorparlament* electoral process as well as the hierarchical composition
of those who sought a position in the National Assembly. Due to the Frankfurt Parliament's configuration and the political objectives of its participants,
the Paulskirche quickly evolved into a liberal experiment that tested the
boundaries of the German Confederation's social order. In spite of the regional
differences that often divided them during the *Vormärz*, parliamentarians
found considerable agreement on the necessity of a unified German state—
even if they disagreed on its ideal form—as well as the prospective benefits
of an overseas imperium. Ironically, the lack of both entities in 1848 led
many delegates to focus on romantic portrayals of nationhood rather than
actual legislative outcomes. As a result, proponents of unification who
espoused exclusionary views on the German question often found common
ground with members who championed more inclusive ideas of civil
belonging, as well as the importance of a colonial empire.

Prussian prince Heinrich Adalbert, cousin to King Friedrich Wilhelm
IV, in many ways personified this phenomenon. A fierce advocate of a
German navy, Adalbert maintained that continental affairs made it a necessity. In his 1848 *Memorandum on the Formation of a German Navy*, Adalbert
cited Prussia's ongoing war with Denmark. "If we wanted to be on an equal
footing with the Danes," he wrote, "and be able to obtain the Sound and
the Great Belt at any time, we would [need] to procure five to six ships
of the line . . . and construct naval ports [on the northern coast]."[28] Germany,
he went on, is "tightly wedged between the three great sea powers of
England, France, and Russia, its squadrons can hardly evade a decisive
battle as they are either half or completely enclosed in the [Baltic] gulf."[29]
Earlier in the same publication, however, he asserted that the future of any
unified state lay in lands beyond the borders of Central Europe. "During
times of peace," Adalbert avowed, "Germany could be in the Mediterranean, in the West Indies and North America, in South America and the
Pacific Ocean, in the Chinese and East Indian waters, and on the coasts of
Africa—in a word, wherever naval powers maintain stations." Such an
outcome, he concluded, was "the destiny of a naval squadron."[30] German
continentalists could justify the need for a German navy on the basis of
regional security, while hopeful colonists could support its formation as
an essential instrument for imperial conquest in the future. One vision
favored German Central Europe's demarcated integrity; the other looked

to posterity and the foreign shores that awaited them. As Prince Adalbert exemplified, what brought both sides together was a shared discourse on territorial expansion and integrity, not a unified viewpoint of nationhood. Distinct interpretations certainly existed in the Paulskirche, but they were primarily variations on the same theme.

Emigration also received considerable attention in the National Assembly. Section VI, clause 136 of the Constitution of the German Empire established that all Germans had the right to travel freely and without interference from the state. "The liberty of emigration is not restricted by the state," the clause asserted; "exit fees may not be applicable. The emigration matter is under the protection and welfare of the German Empire."[31] While collective travel rights might seem unrelated to national unification and its outcome, emigration was in fact a central issue for contemporary sponsors of imperialism and nationhood. In particular, supporters feared that a rise in emigration might weaken the German state's cultural and intellectual prospects. Though their embrace of economic liberalism and the tenets of the Enlightenment led a majority of delegates to affirm prospective emigrants' rights, they nevertheless sought legislative outcomes to address emigration's domestic consequences.

Tellkampf, for example, promoted a plan that extended rights and privileges to overseas Germans, arguing that it guaranteed the maintenance of a national bond between citizens abroad and the German state. "If we were to now extend our German emigrants protection, we would win the adoration of all emigrants; they would then be more favorably disposed toward supporting trading regulations that were equally advantageous to North America and Germany through their votes. As we unfortunately do not have any colonies, this would be for our nature a use for emigration that is not to be overlooked."[32] In the absence of a formal empire, Tellkampf argued that emigration could actually serve a useful purpose, supplementing the nation's economic capacities in exchange for specific civil guarantees for emigrants overseas. Tellkampf's pronouncement also afforded him occasion to remind his colleagues of the fantastic riches that a colony offered those bold enough to seize them. "The youth overseas, in the colonies, in the to-be-cultivated lands," he contended, "find free room for the development of their energy, that possibly could have been ruined by the overpopulated Fatherland. Overseas these energies are developed and a free, worthwhile field of activity is offered, along with the way to prosperity and respectability."[33] The *Constitution of the German Empire*, therefore, embodied a discourse that promoted national unity and domestic sovereignty, as well as the expectation of imperial conquest.

Friedrich Schulz, a publisher and radical democrat from Hesse, gave voice to this actuality one week before his colleagues voted to ratify the Frankfurt Constitution in March 1849. "On the great ocean a powerful, ruling New Germany can blossom," he wrote, "which will significantly strengthen the natural friendship with the United States. However, if we do not hurry, we will also come to Western America too late."[34] Schulz professed Germany's right to engage diplomatically with the United States as equals, a claim that first required Frankfurt delegates to summon the necessary courage to unite the German lands into one centralized nation-state. Schulz also pleaded for swift action. If his fellow parliamentarians did not commit themselves to this great national enterprise, he warned, Germany might "not be in a position to exercise an independent influence" over the United States and German emigrants abroad. After his assessment of foreign diplomacy, Schulz turned his attention to colonialism and the German question: "There on our border is our Texas, our Mexico. . . . I hope that the Foreign Office, as soon as relations allow, will come to an understanding with the Austrian government about a regulated system of colonization for the Danube regions."[35] Schulz believed that Germany, much like the United States in the Mexican-American War, could use colonial expansion as a means to address domestic challenges and imperial desires simultaneously. Just as that war, he wrote, had resolved the slavery question in the United States, foreign conquest in the "Danube regions" could settle the German question.

Schulz's arguments unquestionably helped further the imperial orientation of the Frankfurt Constitution. As a political mechanism, expansion afforded parliamentarians a means to unite Germans from different religious backgrounds or residing in culturally distinct provinces behind a shared national agenda. Most significantly, liberal sentiments on the German question fused even more closely with those of contemporary allies who sought to control spaces outside Central Europe. The realities of emigration, foreign travel, and international trade, together with the growth of popular geographic magazines and procolonial literature, helped fuel this agenda's proliferation throughout German society. While the *Bildungsbürgertum* primarily concerned itself with German-speaking Europe, that did not prevent a consensus of intellectuals, liberals, protocapitalists, and reform-minded nobles from fashioning a national identity that also included territories on the world's "margins." A considerable segment of German society, as a result, continued to struggle for a state that had the capacity to both defend its sovereignty in Europe and reap the benefits of empire overseas. As interest in an imperial project grew in the minds of citizens, so, too, did their geographic impressions of Germany.

The political collapse of the Paulskirche only intensified the desires of liberal nationalists and their supporters to define nationhood in imperial terms. Adherents of *Bildung* had fused self-cultivation and personal curiosity with spiritual perceptions of nationhood, and supporters of colonialism increasingly came to do the same. Though the imperial consensus's prospects temporarily lay dormant in the aftermath of 1848, its sympathizers continued to articulate their goals in venues that enhanced their public celebrity and profile, most especially in literary chronicles, periodicals, and family magazines.

POPULARIZING THE NATION: COLONIAL LITERATURE AND THE IMPERIAL IMAGINATION

After the breakdown of the Paulskirche, national enthusiasts lacked both a unified state and a colonial empire upon which to test their imperial fantasies. But despite the setback for supporters of German statehood, other sources emerged to carry the "spirit of 1848" into a new era. The most successful were of a literary variety, notably geographic magazines, travel literature, and popularized accounts from German explorers overseas. These outlets operated as unofficial mouthpieces for liberal activists and sustained the romantic expectations of German expansionists in an era of political retrenchment.

The principal consumers of these media were initially literate members of society who found common cause with the imperial consensus: erudite women and men who enjoyed some degree of financial flexibility and championed liberal sentiments such as individual civil rights and the unification of the German people. As members of a growing segment of the population, middle-class citizens increasingly used these inexpensive media to find common cause with other like-minded individuals. The most successful publications typically used dramatized and fictional accounts to generate wide domestic appeal, especially among families and urban households. Editors believed that if they could gain access to the intimacy of familial life, their thematic aims might permeate throughout the German lands regardless of official censorship campaigns. Over time, liberal-imperial authors who promoted national expansion with colorful illustrations and inviting prose were able to expand their readership to a broad spectrum of people in German Central Europe. While women and men from academic, middle-class, and mercantile backgrounds continued to make up a majority of the imperial consensus's members during the precolonial era, liberal-oriented literature did more to define collective national identities than any other factor.

As Benedict Anderson and other scholars have argued, print media's proliferation in the nineteenth century fashioned constellations of "imagined communities" that transcended customary social boundaries, most commonly along cultural and linguistic lines.[36] While high literacy rates and subscription statistics do not elucidate every facet of Germany's national development, they do reveal what audiences frequently read about and the topics they engaged with on a regular basis. In this case, the abundance and popularity of globally themed periodicals, picture books, and scientific journals allow us to discern precisely how aspiring colonialists enveloped their sympathies together with national campaigns for German statehood. Whether at work or during times of leisure, at home or in lively cafés and raucous market squares, women, men, and even children engaged the possibility of colonial conquest through media that stoked their imagination and spurred their desire to see the world for themselves.

How people determine the parameters of collective belonging is neither a monolithic nor a universal process. In the circumstance of Germany's imperial consensus, stories about Africa and Asia fostered the growth of a socially diverse class of individuals who deemed colonialism an essential feature of national unification. For them, geographic space and dialectical similarity did not bind the German "national community" to the confines of Central Europe exclusively. To the contrary, any unified state, they believed, was as dependent on their establishment of a global imperium as it was on the cultural ambiguities that demarcated its people as unique. In their estimation, therefore, advocates of colonial conquest could reasonably claim that empire was integral to their desired national homeland and still regard Germany as an "inherently limited and sovereign" state.[37] The growth and distribution of prominent liberal publications after 1848 demonstrates the stubborn appeal of narratives that featured the world's "peripheries" in literary detail. These media also illustrate how supporters of an expansionist agenda often relied on hierarchical and racist tropes to convey their ideas to audiences who remained skeptical about the collective necessity of a nationally oriented colonial project.

Die Gartenlaube—Illustriertes Familienblatt, for instance, tantalized its readers with vivid accounts of adventure, discovery, and romance in treacherous landscapes and ocean expanses. Ernst Keil, a successful bookseller and ardent nationalist from Bad Langensalza, founded the popular periodical in January 1853.[38] Previously, Keil had edited a small monthly pamphlet in Leipzig entitled Der Leuchtthurm: Monatsschrift zur Unterhaltung und Belehrung für das deutsche Volk (The Lighthouse: Monthly Entertainment and Instruction for the German People).[39] With The Lighthouse, which he characterized as the "magazine for politics, literature, and social life," he sought to capture the fascination of sympathizers as the Vormärz transitioned into its final revolutionary phase. Keil's writing staff contributed to the periodical's initial success. He employed an array of well-known liberal authors, including Robert Blum, Johann Jacoby, Leberecht Uhlich, Ernst Dronke, and Gustav Adolf Wislicenus, to inject nationalist sentiments into the public sphere.[40] By appealing to the mercantile and self-reliant ambitions of the Bildungsbürgertum, The Lighthouse enabled Keil to influence liberal discourses considerably in the leadup to 1848.[41]

In the aftermath of the Paulskirche, postrevolutionary forces heavily censored The Lighthouse and closely monitored Keil's activities. Authorities later arrested him for his refusal to abide by their censorship protocols and sentenced him to nine months in prison.[42] After his release, Keil founded Die Gartenlaube with the aim of continuing to give voice to revolutionary ideals, but in a manner that was more "culturally educational" and not explicitly antimonarchical.[43] As an 1855 article later put it, a truly free state could only exist "in a uniformly educated, uniformly virtuous society with equal interests."[44] Keil sought to reach as wide an audience as possible to meet this objective, collecting dramatic accounts and pictures that could "interest and teach in an entertaining way."[45] Die Gartenlaube presented factual and fictional anecdotes of human bravery, love, mystery, and emotional struggle so its editors could animate what they regarded as positive features of life overseas. In this way, Die Gartenlaube catered to liberal enthusiasts who envisaged a national identity without geographical limitations, as well as to citizens who previously had little or no interest in events beyond their own city or town. Even more importantly, it introduced readers to global themes on a personal and familial level.[46] At the start of *Die Gartenlaube*'s publication in 1853, Keil printed 5,000 copies.[47] Within only ten years, however, public interest pressed him to increase his publication numbers dramatically. In 1863, *Die Gartenlaube*'s annual subscriptions expanded to 180,000, and four years later reached over 230,000.[48] By 1875, four years after German unification, *Die Gartenlaube* reached its peak circulation at 382,000, making it the only magazine in the Kaiserreich capable of reaching 5 percent of the total population.[49]

Though the pages of each edition were filled with a wide range of stories, it primarily featured narratives about European pioneers and German communities overseas. In 1869, for instance, *Die Gartenlaube* greeted its readership with a "smiling beautiful bright spring morning" from atop the Acropolis in Athens.[50] The article, entitled "A Morning in the Athenian Castle of the Gods," traces the experiences of a German family living in Greece. Its opening paragraph describes a "cloudless sky, the transparent southern air, the outlines of the objects from afar as completely clear to the naked eye."[51] After this rich presentation, "A Morning" profiles the historic countryside in the distance: "the hill in the middle of the landscape, with its hall and temple ruins, which looks so proud and stoic, is the Acropolis of Athens, the castle of Theseus's city, the capital of its supreme gods, the naval capital and the embodiment of [posterity's] noblest artistic ideas, now a place of ruin, but the proudest and richest in the whole of Greece" (see fig. 2).[52] The article's prose pulses with nostalgia and wanderlust, encouraging readers to reflect on Athens's status in antiquity. Such dynamic language, moreover, inspired citizens to visit the Hellenistic world for themselves. The central German protagonists in the story likely heightened the latter aspiration, a marketing strategy that Keil utilized throughout his career. Curiosity was a natural emotion that united members of the imperial consensus and allowed periodicals like *Die Gartenlaube* to use romantic notions of antiquity, patriotism, and history as vehicles for editors' expansionary ambitions.

In a subsequent issue, *Die Gartenlaube* introduced its large circulation to a German settler in South America. Entitled "Robinson's Island: A German Settlement," the piece emphasized themes of adventure, freedom, and opportunity in an attempt to raise awareness about the conditions of German-speaking communities overseas. "Hardly three days' journey from Valparaiso in Chile and almost at the same latitude with this central port on the west coast of South America," the article began, "lies the island of Juan Fernandez [i.e., Robinson Crusoe Island], where Alexander Selkirk collected the materials for Defoe's 'Robinson Crusoe' during his four years

FIG. 2 The Acropolis, from "Ein Morgen auf der Götterburg der Athener," *Die Gartenlaube*, no. 8 (1869): 126. Note how the artist sought to portray a tranquil scene that both exoticized and normalized Greek antiquity. Photo: Wikimedia Commons / Joergens.mi.

in exile."[53] The island, "which the trade-zealous inhabitants off the Chilean coast pay little attention, has in recent times earned, given its importance and history, much attention from us Germans since the famous Saxon engineer Robert Wehrhan leased it in December." Subscribers followed along as Wehrhan affirmed their imperial fantasies about the Chilean landscape. "We have found European fruit trees such as sour cherry, peaches, plum, and even grapevines, and vegetables such as cabbage, potatoes, corn, onions, lettuce, and several types of beets. The few houses still standing were in a very dilapidated state, but have since been made more or less inhabitable. We also visited Robinson's cave, [which is] high and vaulted, but not deep and about sixty steps away for the seashore."[54] Wehrhan casts Robinson Crusoe Island as a place of mystery and tranquility, a realm of endless resources, fruits, vegetables, striking landscapes, and majestic coastlines. In the infinite expanses of the imagination, German women and men found adventure and solace, stimulating their own desires to travel to the world's unknown places. They also found reason to hope. Robinson's Island, after all, now represented an extension of German nationhood, a reality that Wehrhan shared with his sympathizers in vivid terms: "And so the fertile Germania has once again spread a seed for the future! Small and remote, but it nevertheless represents a deep meaning and great diligence [to the German nation]. May God let it grow!"[55]

Keil also circulated accounts from geographers, surveyors, and other purportedly heroic individuals who claimed to illuminate the "dark regions" of the globe for European society. In 1855, for instance, a cover story praised two German-born pioneers as the first travelers to spread civilization in Africa. "While the lion as king of the desert roars through the night, and by day the Black and brown tribes rob, steal, and trade from each other, half a hundred Europeans have forged the first avenues of culture [*Kulturstraßen*] through the desert toward the interior."[56] Later on, the piece claimed that "soon the Bible and the cotton bales, the missionary and the palm oil travelers will follow and offer the spirit of sailing and of the steamship, so that new and inquisitive strains of culture may improve native lives and develop their human dignity."[57] Valiant accounts of discovery symbolized how all German women and men might benefit culturally and scientifically from colonial expansion. "The German expedition," Keil declared in a subsequent article, "is a German affair. It will be a fine victory in a field in which we have never been surpassed; in addition, it will contribute to Germany attaining new honor and glory abroad."[58]

Die Gartenlaube was not the only contemporary magazine to inspire German liberals to envisage the world beyond Central Europe. *Globus: Illustrierte Zeitschrift für Länder- und Völkerkunde* also advanced a romanticized image of empire at a time when neither a unified state nor a formal colonial project could satisfy the desires of their supporters. Colorful illustrations and striking details about Africa, Asia, and Latin America filled the weekly's pages to dramatize protagonists' experiences in hostile settings such as deserts or dense jungles. The next page might then trace animal migration patterns in Equatorial Guinea, or showcase an advertisement for consumer products from Sumatra or the Caribbean. Karl Andree, a journalist from Braunschweig, founded *Globus* in Dresden in 1862. Andree's life paralleled Keil's revolutionary background in many ways. Before he moved to Dresden, Andree studied geography in Jena and Tübingen, where he acquainted himself with the works of Alexander von Humboldt, the famous Prussian explorer and romantic philosopher, and Carl Ritter, who established the first chair in geography at the University of Berlin.[59] Though he never lost his interest in geography, Andree's nationalist sympathies

FIG. 3 Dr. Julius Ferdinand Berini, a German immigrant in Australia, with five indigenous men in Brisbane, from "Ein deutscher gruss von Australien her," *Die Gartenlaube*, no. 44 (1868): 699–700. This image is an example of Ernst Keil's regular use of racist imagery to contrast so-called barbaric and civilized societies in his articles. Dr. Berini fancied himself an amateur anthropologist and took several photographs of regional polities that eventually found their way to the *Berliner Anthropologische Gesellschaft*. Photo: Wikimedia Commons / Jowinix.

eventually led him to embark on a journalistic career. His outspoken liberal views regularly attracted the attention of authorities and censors, and Andree was obliged to move frequently throughout the 1840s. He eventually settled in Dresden in the immediate aftermath of the 1848 revolution. In 1859, Andree published a two-volume work on contemporary geographic and political issues, entitled *Geographical Walks*, in which he devoted significant negative attention to the abolitionist movement in the United States. An outspoken racist with deep-seated civilizational views, Andree later admitted that he wrote it to discourage similar efforts from emerging elsewhere in the world.[60]

After he established *Globus* in 1862, Andree concentrated on international exploration and technology as the magazine's primary thematic content. He consistently used *Globus*, however, as a vehicle to advocate for a German colonial project. In the foreword of *Globus*'s first volume, Andree stated that he wanted to present the total picture of world travel in an intimate manner. Though maps and vivid artwork sold magazines, Andree believed that ethnological stories offered the best way to encourage people to view the world holistically. "Ethnology, in particular," he wrote, "gives important clues to the correct assessment of historical and political phenomena. It shows that the great differences and deviations which emerge in bodily, spiritual, and moral relation among the various great human families, and which through the whole course of history and anthropological observations prove to be indisputable, are not the consequences of chance or external circumstances; they are the achievements of international psychology."[61] In a subsequent issue, Andree stated proudly that "we take the reader to those continents, to which one already has been accustomed for more than two thousand years, to learn something 'new.'"[62] Each edition strove to teach Germans about ancient cultures and "unexploited" landscapes in order to facilitate collective desires to experience something that was larger than themselves.

An 1870 article entitled "The Bushmen: A Contribution to South African Ethnology," exemplifies this effort in several notable ways. "It is wonderful: that part of the world," the piece began, "in the north, under the Pharaohs, developed a rich civilization, so that it even transplanted the first seeds of human civilization to Greece, from whose bosom we drink nourishment for our spirit daily. [Africa], however, is still to a large extent a 'veiled image.' Do there still yet prevail stranger conceptions concerning people's geography on the continent?"[63] The author starts with a broad reference to ancient antiquity and the origins of so-called enlightened

civilization. A gesture to Egypt gives the reader both context and familiarity, due in large part to the orientalist imaginaries that circulated throughout
Western Europe during the period.[64] Greece represented European culture
and provided subscribers a way to relate to the Hellenistic world. The
passage then shifts its focus to the "veiled" peripheries of Africa, arousing
those with an adventurous spirit to push forward and discover new regions
in a still unknown land. In doing so, the article invokes the image of the
natural German colonizer, a cultured and capable man with the moral fortitude to see his task to a victorious conclusion. It also proliferates racist
perceptions of Africa that sympathizers of imperial expansion used to fabri-
cate hierarchical divisions between the Global North and Global South.

Globus followed this thematic pattern throughout the remainder of
the nineteenth century. Germans read "that in Africa, both north and south
of the equator, large tracts of land suitable for the cultivation of [cotton]
existed, and that the Negro used cotton for his own needs."[65] They discovered that "their compatriots in California [enjoyed] a magnificent selection
of Christmas trees . . . in more than thirty species of evergreen" and that
"Chinese people love to reflect their traditions in novels as much as we
do."[66] Globus appealed to a large German readership precisely because it
consistently offered an account of the "exotic" in a manner that was immediately recognizable. Over time, the prospect of German expansion overseas
evolved from an outlandish fantasy into a prospective national ambition.
From the "Cape of Good Hope" and "Goldmines in Finland" to the "Bengal
Province of Assam" and "Mountain Railroads in Chile," Germans appro-
priated knowledge of the world while sipping coffee in salons or in the
confines of their homes.[67] Colonialism was something that everyone could
suddenly imagine, even if they did not support the effort personally.

Historians can never precisely know Globus's impact on public and
private impressions of the German question in the nineteenth century.
Nevertheless, we can still recognize it as an influential contemporary force,
for two central reasons. First, Globus enjoyed a broad readership with a
large base of subscribers; only Die Gartenlaube had a greater circulation
in the 1870s.[68] The consistent and seemingly instantaneous availability of
the magazine both created and satiated a public desire to read about the
world beyond Europe. Globus thus acted as a disseminator of real and
sensationalized stories about life overseas and afforded its readers a means
to participate in the construction of a global German identity. Second,
Andree and subsequent editors never deviated from the thematic narrative they first adopted in 1862. Page after page, issue after issue, Globus

presented its audience with illustrations of distant regions and "mysterious" animals, thrilling tales of exploration, ethnographic descriptions of "backwards" societies, and self-congratulatory accounts of historic discoveries. In a relatively short period of time, readers became acquainted with *Globus*'s content almost instinctively. Accessibility to travel literature and familiarity with common literary protagonists kindled a desire among a diverse populace to think as a unified citizenry.

A variety of other publications also introduced Germans to the non-European world. Travel narratives, missionary reports, and novels about German explorers attracted a substantial audience throughout the precolonial era.[69] Friedrich Gerhard Rohlfs's *Across Africa: Journey from the Mediterranean to Lake Chad and the Gulf of Guinea*, for instance, enthralled readers with evocative accounts of his extensive travels throughout northern Africa.[70] Rohlfs grew up in Bremen and studied medicine in Heidelberg and Göttingen in the early 1850s. After finishing his studies, he joined the French Foreign Legion in 1856 and participated in several notable campaigns in northern Africa. Upon the conclusion of his service, Rohlfs completed a general survey of the Moroccan oases. He later expanded his analysis to include all of the territory between the Atlas Mountains and Tuat. Rohlfs's scholarly assessment was the first of its kind and earned him significant fame in Great Britain and Prussia, most notably among various geographic associations.[71] At the order of Prussian king Wilhelm I, he joined a British expedition to Abyssinia (Ethiopia) in 1867 and completed a second journey to the Siwah oasis (in present-day Egypt) in 1869.

After a brief stay in Weimar, Rohlfs returned to Africa in 1873, this time at the behest of Isma'il Pasha, the viceroy of Egypt. Over the next two years, Rohlfs explored the Libyan Desert west of the Nile Valley while dressed as a Bedouin traveler. Bringing with him over one hundred camels and ninety men, he navigated from the Dakhla Oasis to within approximately ninety kilometers of Kufra.[72] After returning to Germany in 1874, Rohlfs published his notes under the title *Across Africa*. Even though the two volumes amounted to almost seven hundred pages, Rohlfs's tales of adventure found a ready audience in Germany. In contrast to Andree, he abhorred slavery and argued vociferously against its practice and trade. Rohlfs did, however, maintain a strong belief in European cultural superiority and cited "evidence" of his civilizational beliefs throughout *Across Africa*. "After two short hours," began one entry, "[I] reached the eastern border of the Mschia-Oasis, in the vicinity of the city of Tripoli, which is sharply delimited by the sea in the north and a ring of dunes in the south. . . .

The Mschia like the Tadjura are a sedentary population."[73] Rohlfs assumed the position of enlightened observer, depicting his hierarchical conclusions on the Mschia and Tadjura as points of fact. On another occasion, he bade a temporary farewell to Western culture after his expedition departed from Tripoli: "As I was wandering away from [Tripoli] late in the evening, melodies from the 'White Lady' rang out across the palm forest which a French Spahi [Algerian] officer elicited from a horn."[74] Rohlfs's purposeful contrast between "white civilization" and the "primitive dark continent" presented his cultural viewpoint in stark terms. As the central protagonist, Rohlfs enabled his readership to assume the identity of an intrepid traveler on the cusp of historic discovery. *Across Africa*, moreover, offered its audience a supposedly neutral perspective of the colonial world. From their orientalist vantage point, German readers could either confirm or revise their imperial fantasies in real time based on Rohlfs's detailed study.

Friedrich Wilhelm Gerstäcker's works also advanced discussions on colonial expansion throughout the post-1848 era. A child of a famous opera singer in Hamburg, Gerstäcker labored as a farmer for a small commercial house in Saxony. In 1837, however, curiosity led him to travel to the United States, where he worked in a variety of professions—fireman, deck hand, farmer, silversmith, and merchant—to support his six-year sojourn.[75] He traveled on foot from New York to Niagara Falls, Cleveland, Cincinnati, Illinois, St. Louis, Little Rock, and Shreveport and Natchitoches, Louisiana, and then back up the Mississippi River.[76] After his return to Europe, Gerstäcker learned that he was already somewhat famous in northern Germany, as his mother had sent all of his journal entries and letters to a family friend, who then submitted them to Robert Heller's journal *Rosen*.[77] Heller eventually went on to serve as a reporter in the Paulskirche. Gerstäcker, like a majority of his fellow national-liberals, surmised that citizens could only have a greater voice in government if the various German states forged a unified nation.

In March 1849, the Frankfurt Assembly financed a new expedition for Gerstäcker to examine the conditions of overseas Germans in Brazil, Argentina, and Chile. Over the next three years, Gerstäcker traversed the world, participating in the California gold rush, working as a whaler on a ship in the South Sea Islands and off the coast of Australia, and traveling across much of Java.[78] When Gerstäcker returned to Europe in February 1852, he had a wealth of material from which to write travel narratives, short stories, and novels. His various works soon satisfied Germans' desire to learn about faraway places, and he would become one of the most popular writers of the nineteenth century.[79] Though he wrote extensively about regions and peoples in foreign countries, most notably the United States, Gerstäcker also used his stories to promote emigration and the necessity of a German colonial project. In *Among the Penhuenchen*, for example, Gerstäcker underscored this assertion in clear terms. "No other nation," he proclaimed, "gains such attachment to the soil it cultivates as the German, none is so hard working and tireless in its work. . . . Wherever they get to work fertile fields and charming [small estates] emerge under their hands; the forests are thinned, swamps are drained, roads are built and thriving trades arise, that the lazier Spanish race never achieved."[80] Gerstäcker shared the expansionist convictions of contemporary German liberals and used his own experiences to advance these goals throughout the public sphere. He above all trusted that imperial conquest could alleviate the troubles of workers and the frequently underemployed in society. In addition, he thought that colonialism could assist in their creation of a united German state through the official promotion of emigration.

Ernst von Weber, the contemporary ethnographer who introduced this chapter, also galvanized public interest in colonial affairs with nationalist gestures. After studying at the Bergakademie Freiberg (University of Mining and Technology) and University of Berlin, Weber worked as a farmer near his hometown until his early twenties. In 1851, he embarked on an extensive agriculturist tour of southern Europe, the Middle East, North America, and South America.[81] Weber's travels eventually led him to southern Africa, where he stayed between 1871 and 1875. After returning to Germany, Weber chronicled his experiences overseas in a two-volume memoir entitled *Four Years in Africa*.[82] A self-styled ethnographer, he dedicated considerable space in his volumes to descriptions of local populations. In overt and general terms, for instance, Weber wrote that Africans "are on average a handsome and imposing people, with their energetic, vigorous and expressive heads reminiscent of the portraits of a Rubens, Teniers, Ostade, and Van Eyck." He continued that "nothing is lacking except the opportunity for a good upbringing and accumulation of knowledge, which are so difficult to obtain in their completely isolated places" and that it is unfortunate not "to make something capable of these robust and solid people, and of their good natural dispositions."[83]

The following year, Weber completed a travel account that espoused a staunchly procolonial and nationalist narrative. Entitled *The Expansion of German Economic Districts and the Foundation of Overseas German States*, it questioned whether Germany could continue to maintain a powerful position in the world while its rivals expanded their populations and lands into new regions of the globe. "Should not Germany also be a queen among the nations," Weber mused rhetorically, "like the English, the Americans, [and] the Russians?"[84] He also portrayed opponents of imperialism as selfish narcissists who "only had the prosperity of individuals in mind, but never the position of the German nation as an equal sister among the other nations."[85] A staunch supporter of German expansionism, Weber, three years before the German geographer Friedrich Ratzel coined the term *Lebensraum* in his famous *Anthropogeographie*, maintained that Germany needed to acquire more territory to survive.[86] "The German people in its present-day form," he argued, "are like a young ostrich, which is kept in a chicken cage. Its growth is forcibly suppressed by the cramped cage bars, while its neighbors, the ostriches kept outdoors (i.e., the Russian and English tribes), have the fullest freedom to develop into vigorous giant birds."[87] Weber beseeched political leaders to act on behalf of the collective good. Above all, he desired the creation of a "German master nation overseas [that could] free itself from a miserable and disgraceful erosion of nationality."[88]

Though the Paulskirche did not forge a unified German state in 1849, travel narratives, novels, and protocolonial magazines carried the spirit of liberal expansion into the post-*Vormärz* era with spectacular success. They used a variety of formats, from fanciful accounts of "wild spaces" and tales of hazardous expeditions to scientific studies and nationalist orations on the glory of empire. "In the Steppes of Africa," an article that appeared in *Die Gartenlaube* in 1871, demonstrates this in several notable ways. "Unfortunately, during my travels in Africa," the piece begins, "I have never been able to go hunting, and I must regret it all the more because I am so enthusiastic about all the excitement of those who have had such a good time on African soil."[89] Many *Die Gartenlaube* readers likely shared this long-held desire for adventure. "Even though I cannot report from my own experiences and on my own initiative," the author, Robert Hartmann, continues, "I believe I can compensate the reader with the descriptions of my friend Schweinfurth, the famous African explorer, who has given me his own adventures, of which I will include my own color sketches."[90] Though Hartmann personally had yet to track wild game in Africa, he goes on to describe various expeditions from a position of authority. Schweinfurth provided legitimacy to Hartmann's descriptions and gave him the means to cast his account as absolute truth. *Die Gartenlaube*'s retelling was, therefore, no different from Hartmann's experience, and it thereby enabled its readers to encounter the orient vicariously through Schweinfurth's narration as well.

Hartmann goes on to describe the landscape. "The central country-side forms Africa for antelopes [and] mainland steppes, forests, river and sea areas host numerous numbers of species. On the thin-bushy plains of the African South," he explained, "graze herds in fabulous numbers. It is true that from year to year these monstrous herds are more thinned and pushed inward by the pioneers of civilization, by sportsmen keen on hunting pleasures, but nevertheless the steppes of the Herero, Betschuan, and Kaffirs still afford significant numbers of these creatures."[91] This short paragraph encapsulates the thematic arch of imperial literature after 1848. Hartmann portrays southern Africa as a land of open prairies and herds of animals, while simultaneously chronicling how "pioneers of civilization" are beginning to alter the natural order of the region. He does not immediately offer an opinion on this development, for it provides his audience an opportunity either to visit Africa before its exoticism is gone or to take part in a grand "civilizing mission" on the African continent. Either scenario promoted liberal notions of imperial expansion.

Through its relentless dispersal of information, together with racist and romantic narratives about Africa, Asia, and South America, geographic literature broadcast a proimperial message across German-speaking Europe. Regardless of whether editors like Keil or authors like Gerstäcker did so purposefully, they styled their German readers as natural colonizers and argued that they should embrace their imperial aspirations proudly. This narrative effectively shaped other tropes as well, most notably xenophobic stereotypes that cast the Global South as "backward" and Europe as "advanced." As a result, *Die Gartenlaube* and *Globus*, along with novelists, explorers, and missionaries, prepared their audience for the potential of colonial rule. Liberals and the *Bildungsbürgertum* firmly ensconced imperial expansion in their ideal vision of a unified German state. After official German unification in 1871, these same sources continued to promote empire in ever-expanding socially diverse circles, most especially in Germany's imperial capital: Berlin.

AN IMPERIAL REALITY: GERMANS AND THE BERLIN CONFERENCE, 1884–1885

In a speech before the Reichstag in 1881, German chancellor Otto von Bismarck declared his opposition to overseas expansion in unequivocal terms. "As long as I am chancellor," he declared, "we will not pursue a colonial policy. We have a fleet that cannot sail . . . and we should not possess any vulnerable parts of the world that would fall prey to the French just as soon as it gets going."[92] Later that same year, Bismarck quipped that African colonies are to Germans as "sable furs [are] to Polish families with no shirts."[93] Bismarck's position on the matter seemed clear and resolute. Yet within three years, he reversed his entire position on a German imperial project. Much to the satisfaction of German liberal nationalists and other advocates of colonial expansion, Bismarck's policy of *Realpolitik* now looked upon overseas conquest as a necessary enterprise.

No event marked this transformation more clearly than Bismarck's invitation to host the West Africa Conference in Berlin in November 1884. Today more commonly known as the Berlin Conference or the Congo Conference of 1884/1885, the occasion brought together representatives from all over Europe and the United States to formalize what scholars now call the "scramble for Africa." Germany had entered the scramble three months earlier when the Reichstag officially designated Southwest Africa a *Schutzgebiet* (protectorate) in August 1884. The West Africa Conference provided German leaders their first occasion to show off Germany's newfound great power status as well as a receptive venue to affirm the country's standing as the newest member of Europe's imperial club.[94] After the conference's conclusion in February 1885, German women, men, and children who held dreams of territorial conquest could point to a colonial domain that existed in the real world and not only fantasy. Citizens could now officially construct a global German identity upon an actual African empire.

Historians have long disputed the reasons behind Bismarck's sudden interest in overseas colonies in 1884. Arguments before the late 1980s generally followed a common narrative: imperial conquest served the "Iron Chancellor" as a means either to quell political discontent and divert attention away from national economic crises in Germany or to curb the growing influence of German social democratic forces through foreign policy and overseas distractions. Historian Hans-Ulrich Wehler made this argument most prominently. He maintained that Bismarck adopted a "social imperial" agenda to divert "outwards [the] internal tensions and forces of change in order to preserve the social and political status quo" in the Kaiserreich.[95] In many ways, Bismarck's oft-cited interview with Eugen Wolf, the famous contemporary journalist, seemingly corroborates Wehler's thesis: "Your map of Africa is really quite nice," he told Wolf in December 1888, "but my map of Africa lies in Europe. Here is Russia, and here (pointing to the left) is France, and we are in the middle; that is my map of Africa."[96] Bismarck's insinuation that continental affairs outweighed colonial matters underscored his commitment to domestic policy and his maintenance of a geopolitical status quo in Europe. In his research on German colonial expansion, Pogge von Strandmann also stressed the importance of political affairs, particularly in Bismarck's desire to resurrect the fortunes of the National Liberal Party in the aftermath of the 1881 federal election, which resulted in the expansion of Left and socialist factions in government.[97] Strandmann concluded that Bismarck, aware of the issue's importance to liberal audiences, used the prospect of colonial expansion to reestablish the National Liberals at the expense of the political Left.

Scholars today owe a considerable debt to Wehler and Strandmann, along with Horst Drechsler, Helmut Bley, Helmuth Stoecker, and others, for generating interest in the German overseas empire. At a time when most historians concentrated on the rise of Adolf Hitler and the genocidal violence of the Nazi Party, they expanded the reach of German history beyond the borders of Europe and temporal scope of the Third Reich. But if, as with the historiographical conversations of the 1960s and 1970s, we conclude that imperial conquest served only as a political mechanism, we reduce its place in German history to nothing more than a component in a larger debate on the supposed existence of a German *Sonderweg*. In spite of Bismarck's extensive power and political skill, the machinations of one man alone do not reflect the full nature of the imperial debate in precolonial Germany. What is more important are the agents behind the political stage and how they influenced German nobles and politicians to expand their conception of German nationhood in the first place.

These pressure groups, as we have seen, included proimperial advocates and statesmen both before and after the *Vormärz*, and the press organs that spread their cause to a ready audience. From the gallery of the Paulskirche to the pages of *Globus*, prominent members of society, major political parties, economic interest groups, nationalist associations, social clubs, patriotic leagues, and overseas German enclaves clamored for recognition. Above all, they asserted that the German nation could reach its full potential only if it also acquired territory beyond the geographic scope of Central Europe. These associations did not concern themselves with Bismarck's "map of Africa." They recognized that federal authority rested in Berlin but also that their collective influence on public opinion could sway the fortunes of political power. From newspapers and novels to national rallies and student organizations, the imperial consensus's engagement with society gave its supporters an opportunity to participate in empire at a moment when many aristocratic German officials looked upon colonial expansion with suspicion. After the Berlin Conference began in 1884, therefore, it should come as no surprise that liberal nationalists promoted their cause even more vociferously.

Bismarck's invitation to host the West Africa Conference propelled colonialism to the forefront of German national politics. Though members of royal families and political leaders ultimately made all of their consequential decisions behind closed doors, German citizens generated excitement and served as unofficial participants as well. On the eve of the Berlin Conference, for instance, *Die Gartenlaube* praised the moment as the start of a new era in colonial policy. "There was a time, barely a few years behind us," the editorial claimed, "when zealous patriots raised their voice to warn that a 'living danger to German nationality' was the increasing colonial expansion of the English. [Against the wishes of] politicians of the old school, Germans today herd together all the nations to deliberate on a peaceful solution to pending colonial questions. . . . Most have come as friends, even the traditional Gallic enemy has appeared as an ally[, and] the German community has taken the first steps at the conference."[98] Other publications, meanwhile, took note of the famous celebrities who ventured to Berlin in support of European imperialism. *Over Land and Sea*, a popular Sunday magazine that gossiped about entertainment and world news, celebrated the arrival of U.S. delegate Henry Morton Stanley, the renowned journalist and explorer. "The man whose name is now on the lips of the whole educated world [and regarded as the] intellectual initiator of the conference," the cover story boasted, was in Berlin for "the founding and promotion of a civilizing task that is among the noblest goals of human knowledge and civilization."[99] After the conclusion of the conference the following year, Stanley hailed it as a moment "of unparalleled munificence and grandeur of ideas" in the *Scottish Geographical Magazine*.[100]

For both participants and observers, the Berlin Conference provided a forum in which German patriotism, scientific discovery, and the defense of "civilization" could crystallize into a common national cause. As a result of Germans' interest in its proceedings and the attention popular press organs awarded it, Bismarck and sympathetic politicians used the conference as an opportunity to establish "order and justice in the place of arbitrariness and violence."[101] The newest imperial power in Europe emerged as a central player in global colonial affairs. Enthusiasts of overseas conquest, in particular, did not fail to take advantage of their newfound influence and strove to cast the German African territories as essential components of German nationhood. Interested parties from across the German social spectrum cited the Berlin Conference as a harbinger of future success. They maintained that colonial rivalries were now a thing of the past, that resource-rich trade outposts could now fill German markets with fresh produce and consumer goods, and that missionaries, explorers, and settlers could finally leave for Africa and "civilize disparate communities" in need of so-called enlightened reason.[102]

Commercial enterprises and merchants took special care to posit colonial markets as a solution to periods of stagnation. Carl Peters, the leader of the Gesellschaft für deutsche Kolonisation (Society for German Colonization, GfdK) and eventual founder of the Deutsch-Ostafrikanische Gesellschaft (German East Africa Company), followed in Friedrich List's tradition and described Africa as a potential windfall for the entire nation. Peters first articulated his colonial ambitions publicly in *The Presence* in March 1884. As a means to stoke nationalist attitudes, Peters crafted his arguments with geopolitical overtones, specifically in reference to Great Britain. "English society, with its amazing colonial possessions," he wrote, "is capable of using those forces which it has produced, or to be more precise, of caring for its members in an adequate way."[103] Meanwhile, the young German lacked the same prospects and could not reach his full potential. As a result, Peters concluded, the "English state is like a tree which gets light and air in order to develop its branches freely and luxuriantly in all directions; the German state is like an even more noble trunk which is confined in a gorge among rugged mountains, and is thus hindered on all sides from developing its boundless virality."[104]

Apart from the general public, the Berlin Conference gave political leaders a forum to resolve pressing issues in the name of global peace and cultural morality. At the beginning of the conference in November 1884, delegates moved to draft a set of principles upon which they could determine the international legality of all future imperial projects. In February 1885, representatives authorized the General Act of the Berlin Conference,[105] which bound each of the so-called great powers to conventions related to trade rights, navigation, territorial acquisition, and occupation standards. It also recognized safeguards for the protection of indigenous populations. In mandating a universal standard for colonial conquest, the General Act was one of the first truly international agreements in modern history. For example, in article 35, which set out the principle of effective occupation, signatories mandated that colonial powers had "the obligation to ensure the establishment of authority in the regions occupied by them on the coasts of the African continent sufficient to protect existing rights and, as the case may be, freedom of trade and of transit under the conditions agreed upon."[106] Article 35 stipulated that imperial governments needed to demonstrate genuine control of a colony in order for rival powers to recognize the sovereign legality of the occupation. Treaties with local leaders, local acceptance of a colonial state's national flag, and the presence of an official administration and police force all qualified as acceptable conditions of control.

This standard also extended to the economic domain. If a colonial authority did not regulate or utilize a region's natural resources to their fullest potential, powers could appeal the legality of the occupation to other signatories. Most consequential, however, the "principle of effective occupation" authorized imperial governments to use all means at their disposal to create and maintain regional stability. In other words, if indigenous populations failed to realize the "benefits" of imperial rule, conference delegates deemed it permissible to use systemic violence to show them those benefits. Nineteen years after Europeans drafted the General Act, Nama and Ovaherero polities discovered the genocidal potential of "effective occupation" at the hands of German soldiers in DSWA.

"Great national movements are not the result of single deeds, single years," proclaimed Timothy Fabri in the *Colonialpolitsches Correspondenz*, the official organ of the Deutscher Kolonialverein (German Colonial Association). "They are rather subject to the laws of a slow, unseen growth. . . . The question of the broadening of our overseas military and economic zones . . . is not merely the product of our own day. Since the end of the last century, such pleas have grown louder. . . . These suggestions gained a tangible form in the years after 1848. What the homeland does not offer, foreign lands shall provide."[107] While Fabri's assessment did not represent the views of every German citizen, it certainly spoke for a majority of liberal audiences and groups who constituted the imperial consensus. Though the question of colonial expansion influenced German society long before 1884, the West Africa Conference ushered in a new era of national possibilities.

Above all, the conference signaled that German nationhood had the potential to include regions outside the territorial boundaries of Europe. Influential politicians such as Bismarck certainly expressed their own concerns about the viability of a state-run colonial project. But the formal reality of a German colony overseas, first in Southwest Africa and later in East Africa, strengthened the convictions of those who viewed *Deutschtum* as a force intimately linked with a colonial periphery. "If German politics proudly and decisively employs its means of power in the world in the interests of our nation," Carl Peters exclaimed on the eve of the Berlin Conference, "then we will have found the safest way to maintain all our limbs which are spread across foreign lands."[108] Peters's message gave voice to colonial advocates at a time when the imperial consensus enjoyed significant influence in the public sphere and the German Reichstag. Moreover, it heralded the intertwined evolution of the German question and the colonial question between 1848 and 1884. Regardless of individual benefit or collective purpose, the conference established the legitimacy of Germany's colonial ambitions in the eyes of domestic and international audiences. In the words of *Die Gartenlaube*'s editorial board, it marked Germany's departure "from the old Brandenburg fort" in the direction of "new worlds of vitality."[109]

"LONG LIVE THE NEW ERA!"

"We now stand before the future," *Die Gartenlaube* proclaimed in 1883. "Is it too bold if we imagine this as rosy and propitious if we assume that in the future something still more important awaits under Wilhelm and for our naval foundation in the well-suited Fatherland? In this we believe; long live the new era!"[110] *Die Gartenlaube*, like many other contemporary periodicals, proliferated the colonial aspirations of the imperial consensus with great purpose and success. In doing so, it cultivated an atmosphere that gave rise to influential pressure groups who promoted the cause of German imperialism and nationhood at the highest levels of government and society. Over time, women, men, and children came to picture themselves as natural colonizers, a mental transformation that effectively crafted the notional foundation for colonial conquest. Though this conceptual revolution did not eliminate or transform the mindset of every citizen in Germany, it did influence the delineation and eventual formation of the German state in 1871.

In contrast to their contemporary European neighbors, Germans' colonial and national aspirations evolved concomitantly and in multiple venues between 1848 and 1884—from the benches of the Frankfurt National Assembly and the Hall of Mirrors in the Palace of Versailles to the vivid descriptions of plants and animals in travel narratives and the 1885 General Act of the Berlin Conference. While this progression did not determine Germany's historical advance to a culturally unique or authoritarian "special path," it did press educated and middle-class citizens to entangle their imperial and national fantasies together into one cohesive narrative. The simultaneous absence of a colony and metropole allowed national enthusiasts to champion cultural virtues that later distinguished much of the Kaiserreich's domestic and imperial agenda. "We see in Germany a powerful agitation and hear the loud call for a definitive solution to the colonial question," *Die Gartenlaube* asserted in another article. "Here a great field of action has opened up for all, irrespective of party position, and this high end seems to us attainable without the complications posed by war or the sacrifice of human life."[111] Illusions of territorial seizures and racist articles of Africans proved tangible and inspired supporters to promote a colonial legend that heralded Germany as an instinctive imperial power.[112]

Among supporters of the imperial consensus, Germany's occupation of Southwest Africa in 1884 represented that "great field of action." No longer in the domain of fantasy, a formal colonial empire expanded the geographic perspective of *Deutschtum* and simultaneously gave voice to a diverse range of communities in Germany's national conversation. Ernst von Weber perhaps exemplified this spirit best in his *The Expansion of the German Economic Area*. After a complimentary discussion of Great Britain and its imperial achievements in the eighteenth and nineteenth centuries, Weber expounded upon the colonial potential of the new German Reich. "The Teutonic element is sufficiently equal to the Anglo-Saxons," he boasted, "and it is just as easy to turn German elements into a world empire."[113] Weber followed with an allusion to the national dangers of remaining an ancillary colonial participant. "Instead of the fact that the German nation always sends its children only as serving elements to foreign states, and thereby makes the latter (and among them especially their greatest business competitors) even richer and more powerful," he proclaimed, "would it not instead be better and more reasonable, finally, to find the cause for an overseas German nation-state, which would propagate German glory and honor in the southern hemisphere and which would be freed from the ignominious and shameful de-nationalization which fell helplessly from all hitherto emigrated ethnic Germans?"[114] For Weber, the answer was clear. As his work and that of many others proliferated throughout the nineteenth century, the answer also became clearer for more and more women, men, and children outside of the imperial consensus as well.

Colonial enthusiasts had a profound effect on the development of German nationhood in the nineteenth century. While collective impressions of national identity varied from region to region and town to town, German liberals coalesced around a conviction that they were natural colonizers and thereby entitled to expand the nation-state beyond Central Europe. The practice of imagining colonialism instigated a widespread desire to establish a global empire. Whether in their public proclamations, in deliberations in newspapers and political rallies, or through sojourns to regions on what they considered the world's periphery, members of the imperial consensus generated an atmosphere that made German colonization a reality in 1884. The aspiration to secure the world's forbidden fruits a fantasy no longer, Germans embraced the national ramifications of colonialism and began to consider the possibilities that their new empire offered them.

German missionaries were members of the first institution to dedicate themselves to a life overseas. As the next chapter will elucidate, their experiences in Southwest Africa forged tangible connections between metropolitans in German states and the future colony, and formal encounters in Africa transformed missionaries' own identities as messengers of God.

CHAPTER 2

"Between *Heimat* and Heathens"
Religious Chauvinism in Southwest Africa

"THE SOULS OF MEN"

"We asked Jonker [Afrikaner] who had given him the right to Damaraland, whereupon he asked us if all the places and springs we saw first were not ours. We tried to make it clear to him that land and springs are not the focus of a missionary, but rather the souls of men, that no man, by seeing land, is entitled to take it away from the rightful owners (natives)."[1] Rhenish missionary Carl Hugo Hahn wanted desperately to convince Jonker Afrikaner, leader of the Oorlam (Orlam), of his evangelical intentions. In July 1844, more than two years after his arrival as the first member of the Rheinische Missionsgesellschaft (Rhenish Mission Society, RMG) in Southwest Africa, Hahn was still in search of his first religious conversion among the Ovaherero. While a series of factors frustrated his early efforts, including translation problems, supply shortages, cultural differences, and general collective distrust, Hahn believed deeply in his assignment. In a subsequent exchange with Rev. Richard Haddy of the London Wesleyan Society, the two men agreed "to extend our labors . . . in every direction 'where Christ has not yet been named.'"[2] Hahn also avowed in his diary that he had only one purpose in southern Africa: to save what he considered "heathen populations" with the "word of God."[3]

As more time passed, however, with little to show for their efforts, many other individual missionaries who subsequently followed Hahn to

Southwest Africa started to look upon their prospective congregations with hostility. In a letter to his superiors in Barmen, Westphalia, for instance, missionary Heinrich Schöneberg disparaged the Otjikango Herero (Ovaherero) in explicit language. "Human emotion is still unknown to them," he claimed, and due to "their doglike nature, sharing of wives, their sodomy, their incest and sins with animals . . . God is exterminating the Herero."[4] While undeniably civilizational in thought and prejudicial, Schöneberg's hostile impression did not emanate solely from a deep-seated cultural or racial animus toward all Ovaherero people. His resentment was certainly intolerant and Eurocentric, but it emerged primarily as a response to Ovaherero opposition to Christian dogma. The Ovaherero proved measurably more resistant than other local groups to Rhenish missionaries' worldview. Conversion rates among the Ovaherero only started to rise in the aftermath of Germany's imperial acquisition of Southwest Africa in 1884, forty-two years after the RMG arrived in the future colony.

In an era when a majority of Germans who fantasized about Africa remained in Central Europe, Rhenish missionaries were among a select minority of individuals to dedicate themselves to a life overseas. They aspired above all to spread Protestantism and to deliver educational and medical support to peoples in Southwest Africa who they alleged were in desperate need of Christianity.[5] The RMG grew into a powerful fraternity in southern Africa as a result, affecting the contours of the German question and public debates on imperialism. This chapter traces the influence of Rhenish missionaries as agents of evangelism and German nationalism between 1842 and 1884. It concentrates particularly on how recurrent failure and an inimical environment pressed some missionaries to embrace a new form of evangelism that intertwined contemporary nationalist beliefs with foundational Christian philosophies, a practice this chapter defines as religious chauvinism.

Though the RMG frequently modified its proselytization efforts throughout the nineteenth century, religious chauvinism afforded missionaries a sense of moral conviction and spiritual stability in their charge. On the one hand, it encouraged them to promote an inclusive dogma, similar to the outlook of Hahn and his Rhenish cofounder, Franz Heinrich Kleinschmidt, that viewed all people in the world as equal before God. Missionaries believed that evangelism did not thrive on the exclusion of others, and that man-made boundaries, such as a person's country of origin or even their ethnicity, should not preclude them from the supernatural experience of Christian conversion. Ethnic orientation, gender, or place of birth did not matter, so long as disciples were willing to accept Christianity as the one true religion.[6] On the other hand, Rhenish missionaries almost uniformly agreed that Africans could not achieve salvation through faith alone. This interpretation led some missionaries to assert that a thorough acceptance of the Gospels of Matthew or Mark, for instance, also required African converts to adopt Western-style clothing, a "Protestant work ethic," and patriarchal divisions of women and men in society.

In this manner, Rhenish missionaries infused their otherwise religious worldview with contemporary and racist perceptions of Black Africans. While they claimed to regard "heathens" in strictly spiritual terms, many of them unquestionably looked upon their African congregation through a civilizational prism that over time influenced how they preached in Southwest Africa. Rhenish missionaries, therefore, brought not only "salvation" but also unsolicited political advice, "modern" infrastructure, and stratagems designed to secure peace between the diverse populations in the region. In this way, the Rhenish Mission gradually acquired more authority and prestige over the course of Germany's precolonial age. While they remained first and foremost members of a pietist religious society, Rhenish missionaries strengthened their influence in southern Africa using measures that increasingly reflected those of modern state agents. If Africans failed to see the benefits of Christian civilization voluntarily, clergymen felt justified in bringing it to them in the form of churches, schools, farms, and commercial marketplaces.

In the two decades before Germany formally raised the imperial flag in southern Africa, religious chauvinism acted as a catalyst for the RMG to expand its political and theological presence in Southwest Africa. It allowed church leaders in Barmen to promote their "Godly work" in an otherwise "heathenish land" and simultaneously encouraged priests and Christian converts in Klein-Windhoek, Okahandja, Rehoboth, and Otjimbingwe to profess their intention to exorcise paganism from the continent. At a time when the imperial consensus looked to German unification and overseas expansion as solutions for society's ills, the RMG performed as a formative colonial association for their otherwise fictitious cause. Most Rhenish proselytizers did not intentionally align with protocolonial organizations in Germany. Regardless of their personal intentions, however, missionaries increased public awareness of Africa for women and men throughout the German lands. In doing so, they empowered metropolitans to encounter the future colony on an informal basis in literary commentaries, official accounts, and religious sermons.

Rhenish missionaries' adoption of religious chauvinism also demonstrates how imperial contact altered the delineation of German national identity in the nineteenth century. Though missionaries left Europe to spread Protestantism, most did not fathom that some Africans might not want to accept Jesus Christ as their savior. This misconception was their "colonial fantasy"—that missionaries could shepherd grateful Africans toward salvation with nothing more than faith and the gospel. But it also reveals the extent to which precolonial interactions altered missionaries' worldview. After the veneer of their evangelical aspirations gave way to the realities of life in Africa, Rhenish missionaries looked upon their German identity as both a means and an end to convert Southwest African polities to Christianity. The gulf between *Heimat* and heathens expanded due to these exchanges, widening the cultural delineation of Germandom and conceptually linking colony and metropole together for citizens in Europe.

"THIS IS THE HIGHEST ORDER": THE EVANGELICAL ORIGINS OF THE RHENISH MISSION

On New Year's Eve in 1838, missionary Hahn reflected on "the great blessing of religious togetherness" among his Protestant order in Barmen. "The Lord was in our midst," he wrote in his diary, "with Christmas [having] gone by quietly." He then recorded a few verses that had "proven refreshing" throughout the year:

This is the highest order
Who seeks wisdom
Jesus has become us
Made by the Father himself.
Learned through faith only
And found with pleasure
For what treasures lie
Also in nature.[7]

While these lines serve as a powerful example of Hahn's deeply held Christian beliefs, they also underscore the importance of evangelism to the Rhenish Mission as a whole. "Salvation through wisdom" and "learned faith" acted as foundational principles for all members of the RMG. Those who joined its ranks above all embraced spirituality as an essential element of communal life. In particular, they believed that the transcendent experience of religious conversion created an inherent desire among converts to engage in Christian works of charity. "I would like to help those in need," Hahn professed in November 1837, "not only physically, but especially spiritually. . . . Mainly I do not want to talk much or reason about spiritual things the head only knows, *but instead experiences [that] the heart has not seen.*"[8] This aspiration aroused a palpable need among Rhenish missionaries to spread Christian morality in their local communities and towns. Soon thereafter, the RMG looked to propagate these same works in regions beyond Europe. "The young and old should be [our] central sphere of activity and first point of contact," missionary Heinrich Richter announced in 1828. "Around this [initiative] the first circle of a congregation should be gathered if the Lord gives grace to it. . . . What our missionaries should be are preachers *where there is no church!*"[9] Evangelism was, in other words, the RMG's raison d'être.

While historians today acknowledge the evangelical intentions of Rhenish missionaries, they have traditionally diminished religion as a critical factor in the evolution of a German colonial project in Africa. Most scholars before the *Wende* instead focused on the RMG's role as a formative imperial organization. East German historian Heinrich Loth, for instance, asserted that "Southwest Africa is a classic example of how the activities conducted by a Christian missionary society over several decades [made] it possible to paralyze a country's natural powers of defense and to pave the way for colonial subjugation."[10] The inherently "destructive role" of Rhenish missionaries, he continued, amplified imperialists, capitalists, and other bourgeois organizations' calls for overseas expansion, culminating in Bismarck's colonial policies in the 1880s. Horst Drechsler, meanwhile, claimed that Prussian king Wilhelm I privately guaranteed the Rhenish leadership state protection in Southwest Africa as early as 1868.[11] Loth and Drechsler each crafted teleological narratives that conflated a "colonialism under the habit" and a "German place in the sun" as part of the same general enterprise.[12] Cultural racism also informed many of these conclusions. Former Rhenish missionary Heinrich Vedder, for example, contended that "the role and responsibility of the white race in Namibia as carriers of Christian Western civilization" necessitated a strong European presence in southern Africa.[13] His own private beliefs on the "superiority of the white race" led him to posit colonialism as an intrinsic aspect of Rhenish evangelism and to underscore Germany's obligatory responsibility as an "enlightened power" in the imperial age.

The crucial and even violent role of the RMG in Germany's colonial history is beyond dispute. Neither the limitations of Cold War–generated accounts nor the explicit bigotry of colonial apologists negates that fundamental reality. We should not, however, simply cast Rhenish missionaries as nothing more than German imperial agents in an inevitable settler-colonial story. Such an assumption too easily misconstrues the theological intentions of the RMG, especially in the 1840s and 1850s, and ignores the international collaborations that a variety of religious orders carried out in Europe during the nineteenth century.[14] This is not an attempt to apologize for the RMG's conduct in Africa but rather an effort to denote how missionaries used Christianity to justify their presence overseas. The fact that Nama and Ovaherero women, men, and children did not invite the RMG to their shores requires us to evaluate the Mission's conduct through a critical and protoimperial lens. But any framework that cursorily conflates the formative Rhenish Mission with the subsequent German colonial administration fails to account for the evolutionary nature of the RMG's motivations. More than any other factor, Christian proselytization empowered Rhenish missionaries to distinguish themselves from secular actors who also sought to influence affairs in Africa. While some pastors eventually adopted religious chauvinism as a means to increase their conversion rates among Africans, many did not align with any German imperial or national movement. The fact, therefore, that some missionaries later espoused nationalist discourses as part of their ministration is even more telling about the impact of religious chauvinism on Rhenish dogma, especially during the 1860s and 1870s.

In order to avoid any teleological chronology, we must first account for the theological origins of the Rhenish Mission. The RMG formed in Barmen on 23 September 1828. In its Statutes of the Deputation of the Rhenish Mission Society, its leadership declared that they must take "immediate action for the empowerment of the Kingdom of God among non-Christian peoples by sending and entertaining missionaries, by automatically joining existing ones, or by founding new mission stations."[15] We should not "exclude reaching out to colonies," the statute continued, "for their ancestors descended from Christians, though presently lack preaching evangelists and are in danger of falling into heathenism."[16] As a means to prevent the world from devolving into barbarism, the RMG's leadership considered two objectives paramount: training their own missionaries and sending them to countries in Africa, Asia, and North America. In this spirit, Rhenish missionaries established a *Missionsseminar* to prepare ministers and their families for a future life overseas.

The *Seminar*'s "Deputation" placed a significant obligation on instructors and new members to meet the demands of the RMG's religious charge. It dictated that all participants "must be prepared [to serve] as missionary assistants and schoolteachers, [as well as] fully equipped servants of the ministry so as to educate Gentiles."[17] Heinrich Richter, the *Seminar*'s first head instructor, pushed these requirements further and mandated that entrants also receive extensive artisanal instruction before completion of the program.[18] "The Catechism Seminar is the heart and central point of our mission society," Richter asserted in 1829, "but there must be [some flexibility] in the choice and conditions of teaching. When the Lord gives us a specific field of work, the syllabus must adapt to it."[19] Richter's curriculum, therefore, emphasized a broad theological program, including the introduction of biblical content, history of Christianity, pastoral theology, missionary and natural history, geography, and speech exercises in English and Dutch.[20]

We know the private impulses that inspired missionaries to travel abroad due to their participation in the Rhenish *Seminar*. After entrants completed their training, they were required to write a curriculum vitae before they departed for their assignments. Though formulaic in nature, these documents tell us a great deal about the motivations of Rhenish missionaries. They include descriptions of a missionary's private life, education, choice of profession, as well as an account of their own conversion experience. Nils Ole Oermann's detailed analysis of the central register in Wuppertal has shown that the RMG sent 129 missionaries to southern Africa between 1839 and 1914.[21] A majority were in their early twenties when they joined the Mission.[22] Of those, sixty-four members had at least some experience as artisans, twenty-one as agricultural laborers, seven as fully ordained ministers, five as accountants, three as civil servants, and two as secondary school teachers. Finally, most came from large families in Westphalia, Württemberg, and the area surrounding Barmen. As a result, a majority had no personal knowledge of the world beyond Europe before they enrolled in the seminary.[23] Missionary service in Africa, moreover, did not carry a high level of social prestige before 1884. To the contrary, it usually meant working in solitary conditions and in what many Europeans considered a hostile environment. A missionary could also expect

a low-paid, lifetime job with no guarantee of success.[24] In addition, a majority of evangelists did not possess the skills required to converse with and
proselytize to communities in southern Africa.[25]

These factors are important to emphasize because they affirm the
centrality of Christian morality for those who joined the RMG and why
they desired to spread Protestantism throughout the world. Missionaries
were not initially concerned with "the land and springs," as Hahn expressed
to Jonker Afrikaner at the beginning of this chapter. Instead, they accepted
their role as God's messengers on Earth. Individual quests for glory or
deep-seated imperial ambitions played little or no part in official RMG
evangelical efforts in the 1840s. From personal desires to introduce Africans to God's word to collective impulses rooted in orthodox pietism,
Rhenish missionaries pursued their religious responsibility with an absolute belief in their theological purpose.

Carl Hugo Hahn personifies the RMG's pietist initiative in these early
years. From a German Baltic province in the vicinity of Riga (Lettland),[26]
Hahn initially wanted to work as an engineer and enrolled in the engineering school of the Russian army in his late teens. After one year of schooling,
however, his professional desires began to turn toward the Protestant ministry. As Hahn's future wife Emma Sarah later recalled, he decided to devote
his life to the Lutheran pietist movement in 1837.[27] The following year, Hahn
entered the RMG seminary in Barmen. Immediately following his ordina-
tion ceremony in 1841, his superiors assigned him to establish the first
Rhenish mission station in Southwest Africa.[28] Over the course of his thirty-
year career, Hahn returned to Europe only twice. At the time of his death
in 1895, no other German missionary had served longer in southern Africa
than "old father Hahn."[29]

While Hahn's childhood afforded him knowledge of regions outside
of Central Europe, his background generally exemplified the experiences
of many Germans in the nineteenth century. Hahn grew up speaking multiple languages and did not attach any special significance to that ability
along national lines. When he eventually relocated to Westphalia, he did
so for professional reasons, not out of any inherent desire to live in a
German homeland.[30] After he departed for southern Africa in 1841, Hahn
focused exclusively on his theological mission as a representative of the
RMG. He wrote in an official deputation that "as far as God has commanded
people to preach and live the gospel to others, he has also given the possibility that they will accept and live it. [My charge] is to integrate natives"
into the Christian fold.[31] At no time during his formative years in Southwest

Africa did Hahn align himself with colonial or national movements in the German states. Instead, he took steps to proselytize his theological beliefs to those who he felt needed it most without any *explicit* racial animus or national determination. Admittedly, he did embrace civilizational conceptions of the world, which later compelled him to adopt more centralized methods of religious conversion.

Franz Heinrich Kleinschmidt's profile also exemplifies the theological intentions of Rhenish missionaries during the 1840s. Kleinschmidt grew up in the small village of Blasheim (near Lübbecke) and trained as a carpenter and blacksmith.[32] After the formation of the RMG, his religious impulses pressed him to enroll in the *Seminar* in Barmen. Before he could complete his studies, however, Kleinschmidt's superiors sent him to the Cape Colony to join Jonker Afrikaner's Oorlam community in Damaraland.[33] Upon his arrival in the Northern Cape in May 1838, Kleinschmidt started to learn Nama (Khoekhoegowab). He struggled considerably with the language and regularly prayed for "help, diligence and gift."[34] While still in the Northern Cape, Kleinschmidt met Zara and Johann Heinrich Schmelen's second daughter, Hanna, whom he married later that same year.[35] The Schmelens were both members of the London Missionary Society (LMS) who had lived in southern Africa since 1811. Though it was a marriage of love first and foremost, Hanna proved an indispensable partner for Kleinschmidt. She not only helped him perfect his language skills but also shared the same theological convictions as other Protestant missionaries in the region. Eventually, in May 1842, Franz Heinrich and Hanna, together with missionaries Hahn and Hans-Christian Knudsen, traveled north of the Orange River into Southwest Africa.[36] After founding several mission stations in southern Namaland, Hanna and Franz Heinrich translated the Bible into Nama and also prepared a Dutch-Nama dictionary in 1855.[37]

Kleinschmidt's expedition to southern Africa was his first experience outside of Central Europe. Though his reflections demonstrate a sense of curiosity and excitement, Kleinschmidt departed Barmen with a desire to spread Protestantism exclusively.[38] He never regarded himself as a representative of Germandom, but instead as a "devoted brother" to his fellow man.[39] Franz Heinrich's marriage to Hanna, moreover, denotes both his general character and his theological ambitions. Hanna's "mixed-race" ancestry ("Cape Coloured") neither diminished Franz Heinrich's devotion to her nor caused concern among his superiors in Barmen. While Franz Heinrich shared contemporary European views on patriarchy and familial life, he never regarded Hanna as his racial unequal. In fact, Kleinschmidt relied on her to communicate with Nama and Oorlam, especially in the early years after his arrival. Nevertheless, in September 1842 he expressed frustration at his inability to connect with potential converts. "A woman, who was very lively and happy when she saw us," Kleinschmidt wrote, "spoke to me, but I understood nothing. I pointed up and said: Tsuékwap (God), and she understood and laughed nicely. . . . Oh, what a pity and obstacle, not to understand the language of the country. Oh Lord, give the gift of pleasure!"[40] Franz Heinrich realized his own limitations and learned how to overcome them with the essential aid of Hanna. His Rhenish superiors regarded such relationships positively and believed that proper "Christian marriages" between pastors and African women could advance their pietist goals more quickly.

In the immediate years before their departure for southern Africa, Rhenish missionaries desired an opportunity to defend Christianity against what they regarded as new and dangerous manifestations in the world, including heathenism, collective idleness, and enlightened secularism. Though their personal views regarding Africans' theological practices reflected many of the cultural and racial prejudices of future German colonists, the first Rhenish missionaries in Africa justified their presence primarily along religious lines. "All troubles are spared the missionary," Hahn wrote in March 1842, "for when the Lord sends such hunger for his word into the land, people [will] do everything by themselves only to hear God's word!"[41] The RMG championed a theology that strove to introduce Christianity to new communities around the globe. As Hahn later remarked to the leadership in Barmen, the greatest threat to evangelism was not necessarily the lack of a German element in Southwest Africa but rather the abundance of "non-Christian temptations" that perverted the souls of Africans.[42] He and his initial cohort, therefore, strove to work with anyone, regardless of nationality or race, to cultivate a new Christian flock on the African continent.

In spite of its early intentions, however, the RMG soon evolved into a crucial institution for imperial groups in German-speaking lands. At the same time that the German question commanded the attention of bourgeois liberals and other members of the imperial consensus, Rhenish missionaries started to embrace their national heritage as a means to further their pietist assignment overseas. While an essential factor in the eventual materialization of a colonial project in 1884, the RMG's acceptance of German nationalism was far from inevitable. Rhenish evangelists adopted religious chauvinism only after they confronted the fallacies that underlay their precontact views. In the face of linguistic challenges, limited resources, a hostile environment, and "non-Christian elements," individual pastors appealed to "civilization"—as well as to God—for answers. An alliance of "kitchen and altar," as Hahn later reasoned, provided missionaries an occasion to achieve more success with Africans, as well as an opportunity to assist in what they saw as the social and economic "development" of Southwest Africa.[43]

Though they remained true to their religious enterprise, Rhenish missionaries increasingly called for centralized methods of conversion that were beholden to German social practices and traditions. Nama, Oorlam, Ovaherero, and others saw their means of expression and traditional freedoms wane considerably as a result. As the next section will demonstrate, where the RMG's Christian dreams failed, its espousal of cultural nationalism fostered the growth of a robust German presence in Southwest Africa. Rhenish missionaries expanded the territorial contours of Germandom and actively influenced German discourses on imperialism in the decades leading up to 1884.

FROM "ALTAR" TO "KITCHEN": EVANGELISM AND RELIGIOUS CHAUVINISM IN SOUTHWEST AFRICA

In May 1842, missionaries Hahn, Kleinschmidt, and Knudsen crossed the Orange River into Namaland. While the RMG's first expedition into Southwest Africa received little fanfare in Europe, Hahn described the experience with a clear expectation of success. "I rode in the afternoon after four o'clock with a boy named Daniel, a Kookfonteiner [Steinkopfer] who had brought Brother Knudsen home," he wrote. "The said boy Daniel is my best student from the school in Komaggas, in whose heart are the unmistakable traces of the Holy Spirit. I took [him] as an assistant because being alone is difficult and it is also my intention to train him as a national agent for Damaraland."[44] Though casual in tone, Hahn's diary excerpt depicts how he planned to spread Christianity in Southwest Africa. He and his Rhenish colleagues believed God's grace knew no boundaries. Africans simply needed to hear the gospel for themselves. Hahn's observation of the "unmistakable traces of the Holy Spirit" in his student Daniel confirms this conviction in clear terms. Rhenish missionaries consequently trusted that Africans could serve as effective evangelists on behalf of the RMG. Regardless of the voice who was preaching, they presumed that the Word of God alone was enough to shepherd "lost souls" on a path toward salvation. Only after their arrival in Namaland did Hahn and his fellow travelers learn the fallacies behind such absolute and civilizational assertions.

Scholars have generally viewed the frustrations that arose among missionaries as motivated by racial hostility and with an eye toward the formal colonial period. George Steinmetz, for instance, has argued that contemporary German "representations of the Ovaherero were overwhelmingly hateful, even exterminationist," and cites the Rhenish Mission as one of the most fervent institutions in promoting racist stereotypes.[45] Among the sources Steinmetz references is a lengthy report Hahn sent to the Barmen leadership in 1873. "It is entirely absurd and ridiculous," Hahn wrote, "when you encounter a carriage and are greeted by twenty or more Black beauties dripping with butter and red dye. Among the . . . Christianized natives, however, carriages, and many other things which are a caricature among the others are perfectly justified. These [individuals] are clean, wear European clothing, pursue orderly lives, cultivate the earth . . . and do not ramble on foot through the countryside."[46] Hahn's account is absolutely infused with racist language and overtones. But what Steinmetz construes as an "overwhelmingly hateful, even exterminationist" attitude does not account for Hahn's tremendous irritation at his own failure to convert Ovaherero communities to Christianity. This does not excuse the role of racism and its place within the RMG but instead underscores the impact of precolonial encounters on Rhenish orthodoxy. In the face of institutional failure, Hahn and many of his followers learned to look upon Ovaherero as negative elements who threatened their pietist mission. While contemporary racial views were never absent in Rhenish missionaries' decision process, they did not dictate every measure the missionaries devised in southern Africa. Extermination, moreover, was the antithesis of evangelism, and if the RMG adopted such a program, they in no way could style their mission in a Christian framework.

What we need to consider, therefore, are the other reasons behind the Rhenish Mission's transformation from Christian shepherd into religious chauvinist. As we have seen, the RMG aimed to spread Protestantism to groups that its members viewed as lost souls. Their pious zeal inspired an internal confidence that they, as God's messengers on Earth, knew what was best for Africa's diverse populations. Rhenish ministers relied upon their devout faith, as well as their brethren in the LMS, for guidance and encouragement. "Individuals should never want to go out as missionaries," Hahn professed in his diary, "who do not have much love for children and who do not want to make them a special subject of their care and concern."[47] He also thought his own background offered some potential advantages: "One cannot overvalue the benefit of a practical knowledge of the German school system. Mere theory is not enough. . . . The wanderings [*Umherziehen*] of the people [could present a problem], but schools are necessary to accomplish anything decent and lasting in this community."[48] The RMG leadership decided to follow this example and focus on religious education as the basis of its evangelical charge in Southwest Africa.

Hahn wrote at length about their initial efforts to foster a Christian following in Namaland. In June 1842, less than one month after his company's departure from Steinkopf, he praised the establishment of a mission school in Bethanie. "It draws more and more hungry souls. Our school, which we hold every day in the open air, has about seventy students."[49] Three months later, Hahn celebrated the triumphal expansion of the school system in emphatic terms. "Our schools, namely the men's school directed by Kleinschmidt, the women's school directed by Sister Kleinschmidt [Hanna] and the children's school directed by me and [Brother Jan] Bam, include 280 to 300 students, of which about 170 are children between four and ten years old. The zeal [*Eifer*] for the school is extraordinarily great."[50] His only regret was "the severe lack of supplies, especially books and paper tablets." Though these material shortages presented limitations, Hahn regarded the RMG's achievements as significant. Before the end of 1842, the Rhenish mission school in Bethanie reached its maximum capacity.[51]

The RMG expanded its efforts to other areas as well. Franz Heinrich and Hanna Kleinschmidt enjoyed particular success away from Bethanie during this early period. In 1845, Heinrich, Hanna, and Johann Heinrich Schmelen traveled to Glenelg Bath, a small settlement in central Namaland, to found a new mission station. The missionaries renamed the encampment Rehoboth and started to baptize the local population. Before the conclusion of the year, Franz Heinrich and Hanna converted eleven adults and six children, among them Willem Swartbooi, chief of the Red Nation (Khoekhoe/Khaiǁkhaun), as well as his father and brother.[52] These numbers grew steadily over the remainder of the decade. Swartbooi aided the RMG's evangelical mission in Rehoboth considerably. In 1846, he granted Franz Heinrich permission to construct a "spacious new church" with the capacity "to hold several hundred people."[53] After its completion, the Jungfrauverein in Cape Town donated a large bell for the church's steeple.

Rehoboth's new school system also flourished as a result of the high conversion rate. Before the conclusion of 1849, the Rhenish mission school catered to over 150 students. Subjects included language training, religious history, and various artisanal courses. In addition, over forty girls enrolled in an affiliated program that taught weaving and household and domestic practices.[54] In both schools, spiritual study made up a sizable component of the daily curriculum. Franz Heinrich believed deeply that Nama and Oorlam should assume central leadership roles in the church. In order to meet this goal, he arranged for Swartbooi's son to enroll in a mission school in Cape Town that specialized in missionary training. After his graduation, Swartbooi's son worked as a teacher and religious instructor in Rehoboth.[55] Franz Heinrich also prepared materials for individuals who were unable to attend school and Sunday service regularly. The Rhenish station in Rehoboth quickly emerged as an exemplar for all other Rhenish mission centers in Namaland. The RMG leadership regarded it as a major triumph and as a positive sign that Rhenish missionaries could realize their evangelical charge throughout the entirety of Southwest Africa.[56]

Though enrollment numbers in this period indicated growth, Rhenish missionaries looked to religious conversions as the most accurate measure of their impact in the region. In general, the RMG enjoyed nominal success with Nama before the end of the 1840s. Hahn and Kleinschmidt understood, however, that the few conversions they did secure were largely the result of Nama's familiarity with the LMS in the Northern Cape. The two Rhenish missionaries, therefore, wanted to increase their influence into new areas, particularly farther north in Damaraland. They initially had reason for hope. On 24 December 1842, Jonker Afrikaner brokered an agreement that ended an extended period of conflict between Oorlam, Nama, and Ovaherero over regional political influence.[57] Rhenish missionaries could now venture north into Damaraland for the first time. Hahn wrote at length about what he called "the Christmas peace" in his diary. "Never in my life have I experienced such a Christmas evening. The peace is the greatest gift that could be given to us."[58] Hahn left for Damaraland the following year, going as far north as Windhoek and its surrounding areas.[59] After failing to construct a mission station at the court of Jonker Afrikaner near the site of Windhoek, he trekked to nearby Otjikango (Otjiherero) and founded Neubarmen (Groß Barmen) in 1844. "The people here," Hahn wrote effusively, "are exceptionally friendly and accommodate

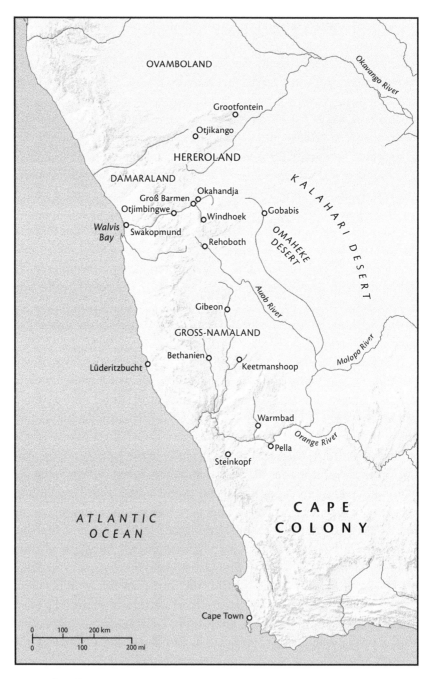

FIG. 4 Rhenish Mission stations in Southwest Africa and the Cape Colony, ca. 1870. Image: Erin Cartography.

[Brother Kleinschmidt and me] with wild onions [*uintjies*] and sour milk. The name of the local captain is Kasupi."[60]

Hahn moved quickly to establish a physical presence in Groß Barmen, building a large church and school before the conclusion of the year. His diary indicates that he dedicated most days to language instruction, evangelism, and writing about "the fantastic beasts," including lions, hyenas, hogs, zebras, and kudus, that lived among them.[61] Before the conclusion of 1850, the Rhenish school in Groß Barmen enrolled nearly 280 students.[62] Due to this progress, Hahn invited Hanna Kleinschmidt to open a school for girls based on the model she established in Rehoboth. "The zeal at our schools is great," he often reported to the Rhenish leadership.[63] After considerable effort, Hahn drafted a German-Otjiherero grammar book based on the lesson plans he and his fellow missionaries developed in Groß Barmen. Johanna Uerita Gertze, Carl Hugo's first Ovaherero convert, and his wife, Emma Sarah Hahn, were essential figures in the completion of this manuscript.[64] They supported Hahn's linguistic work and also won the trust of several Ovaherero during this vital period in Damaraland. Hahn eventually published the entire collection during a brief sojourn in Westphalia in 1857.[65] Finally, the station in Groß Barmen also gave Hahn and subsequent Rhenish evangelists the means to shift the local economy in an agriculturalist, centralized, and more market-based direction. Though this effort did not immediately transform Ovaherero socioeconomic practices, Rhenish missionaries soon looked upon their creation of a market-based economy as an extension of the RMG's Christian mission in Southwest Africa.

These noteworthy triumphs, however, proved token victories in an otherwise difficult environment. While Rhenish missionaries continued to found religious settlements in Namaland, their efforts in Damaraland failed to attract the same level of interest with Ovaherero. Among the RMG's most significant setbacks occurred in 1851, when Jonker Afrikaner suspended the "Christmas Peace" with the Nama.[66] The threat of renewed hostilities placed the RMG in a precarious position. Hahn's situation worsened the following year when Afrikaner withdrew his invitation for the Mission to proselytize in Damaraland.[67] Though missionaries themselves faced little physical danger as a result of this new decree, Afrikaner's decision paralyzed the RMG's entire evangelical operation in all areas north of Namaland. At the same time, Ovaherero women and men started to develop a collective distrust of Rhenish missionaries the longer they stayed in Damaraland. Even before Afrikaner stymied their evangelical efforts, relatively few Oorlam, Damara, and Tjimba (Ovaherero) viewed the RMG favorably. The only Africans who gathered in Groß Barmen, Otjimbingwe, and Windhoek permanently before 1852 were poor and disaffected individuals in search of shelter.[68] In these cases, "acceptance" of Christianity provided them reliable access to food, medicine, and safety. After realizing the true nature of this situation, Rhenish authorities called into question the legitimacy behind every Ovaherero conversion in Southwest Africa.

Such factors had a profound effect on the entire Rhenish mission. They forced missionaries to grapple with their prior contention that faith alone was enough to guarantee a permanent Christian stronghold in southern Africa. Faced with a challenge to their worldview for the first time, many missionaries started to develop a general dislike for all Ovaherero peoples. Hahn, most notably, went through a rapid transformation. In both his diary and dispatches to his superiors, he increasingly focused on what he considered the Ovaherero's negative cultural and social qualities: thievery, sloth, apathy, and laziness. "The natives steal one thing after another," began one such entry. "Today, for example, an iron rod and a large round metal bowl, the latter belonging to the Kaspupis people. Katjari [unknown] sent messengers after the thief, which meant that we later received the bowl. The piece of iron was found buried in the sand."[69] Hahn recorded stories of this nature on a regular basis, repeatedly castigating Ovaherero in strongly pejorative and racist terms.

Among the clearest instances appears in a two-page report entitled "The Character of the Ovaherero." In it, he takes aim at their communal behavior, comparing them with French citizens using contemporary stereotypes. "The Ovaherero," Hahn alleged, "appear to have more in common with the French than any other nation in Europe: garrulous, trifling, laughing, quarrelsome, boastful, crawling at a moment in the highest rage and anger in others; brave where there is no resistance. All want to learn, but are especially lacking in stamina. If the Ovaherero had journalists, then their newspapers would surely bear the character of the French, full of lies, bragging, and false rumors. They fornicate more than almost all other African people, as the French over all other Europeans. In vanity they are second to none."[70] Hahn's disdain for the Ovaherero was intense. He condemned them for conduct that he associated with heathenistic excesses, comparing it to the "dangerous extremes" of French society. In his own words, race did not prevent them from achieving salvation, only their so-called heathenism. Hahn therefore claimed that the Ovaherero, like the French, needed to open their hearts to God's grace so that "he could purify and sanctify" their character.[71] This argument does not vindicate or romanticize Rhenish missionaries' Eurocentrism but instead reveals the evolution of their theological identity in Southwest Africa.

The RMG's underlying source of agitation in the 1850s was that few Ovaherero were interested in Christian "purification." This reality took an especially hard toll on Hahn and Kleinschmidt. An entry from Hahn's diary in March 1854 captures the intense shift in his personal demeanor: "This whole period from [March] 15th I have been physically and mentally ill, but more the latter. My mind is depressed and broken and in constant battle, with only a few lucid moments. Although I have felt advances by the devil, I cannot say that I feel abandoned by the Lord. My path, my obligation, however, is dark."[72] Hahn exhibited clear signs of depression and fatigue. The constant setbacks alarmed him deeply, challenging his pietism and compelling him to consider new methods for spreading Christian salvation. In spite of his melancholy, however, Hahn remained loyal to his religious duties. After he returned from his five-month sojourn in Westphalia, he renewed efforts to improve the RMG's relationship with Jonker Afrikaner. In addition, he also founded a new mission station in Ovamboland (north-central Namibia) that same year.[73] Nevertheless, his desire to achieve a major breakthrough in Damaraland forced him to reconceptualize his approach vis-à-vis Ovaherero. Before the conclusion of the decade, Hahn developed a new method, which he later called *christliche Kolonisation* (Christian colonization), that drew upon his own biblical and personal background.[74]

Hahn envisaged a small group of Christian artisans and merchants at the center of a mission station. They would act as religious agents who strove to introduce civilized cultural practices and trade to so-called African heathens. "This is the only way to make a difference," Hahn said in his diary. "Some crafts can be organized here with certain advantages. . . . There should also be a shop at each station, which would not only be useful, but would also make it possible for missionaries to stay away from barter. That would be the greatest blessing."[75] Pietism was no longer Hahn's exclusive concern. Fourteen years after his arrival in southern Africa, he wanted to cultivate an autonomous Christian society that centered on trade, capitalism, and European civilization. He elaborated further on these ideas in a report to Barmen in February 1863. "To civilize the wild barbarians," Hahn wrote, "cannot be achieved by preaching the gospel; the exemplary life of the *individual* is not adequate either. Through it [Ovaherero] still do not learn to build houses, sew dresses, cultivate gardens, etc. It is here that Christian morality, trade, and enterprise are needed."[76] Hahn determined that settlements along European models of civilization could facilitate the spread of Christianity in Southwest Africa. If Nama, Oorlam, and Ova-herero polities needed to rely upon mission stations for food and supplies, he reasoned, African leaders could no longer control local affairs without facing immediate consequences.

A robust commercial economy, in addition, had the potential to encour-age more Christians from German-speaking regions in Europe to proselytize overseas. "The natives understand and value culture, [even] before they are capable of grasping the gospel and use of education," Hahn told the Barmen leadership. "A national orientation will assist in combating the anar-chic conditions that they face, [and] make it in their interest to respect our position."[77] If the RMG could establish a permanent presence in Damaraland, Hahn concluded, missionaries could transform the religious dynamics of the region more easily. *Christliche Kolonisation* as official policy eventually gained traction among other Rhenish missionaries as well. At the annual Hereroland Missionary conference (Otjimbingwe) in 1867, participants established two primary goals of missionary activity: "spreading the gospel" in combination with "Christian culture."[78] These twin objectives permitted advocates of religious chauvinism to claim that Africans were not inher-ently evil but merely "culturally ignorant" as a result of their "spiritual darkness."[79]

Christliche Kolonisation also encouraged Rhenish missionaries to chal-lenge what they considered the negative influence of other Europeans in Southwest Africa, namely Catholic missions, independent investors, and secular societies in search of economic fortune.[80] Hahn and his colleagues regarded poor and unaffiliated merchants in unsavory terms, most espe-cially the English ones. "I must say from previous experience," Hahn wrote in 1859, "that the so-called educated English, being beyond the reach of law, are an extremely rude people and treat the natives like animals. They direct their lust toward women and girls, and rudeness toward men."[81] Missionary Johannes Rath also shared Hahn's assessment of English trad-ers. As the founder of the Rhenish station in Otjimbingwe, Rath was distressed about their presence in Damaraland.[82] "The other whites, who [are] mostly British and have a shorter time in Otjimbingwe," he explained in the 1857 *Rheinische Stationschronik*, "deprave the natives, and not only set a bad example, but also, being already corrupt, [are] tempted by forni-cation and drunkenness."[83] This white scum, as Hahn called them, motivated the RMG to seek more centralized control over affairs in Southwest Africa as an aspect of *christliche Kolonisation*.[84]

In 1870, the RMG founded the Missions-Handelsgesellschaft (Mission Trade Society, MHG) in Otjimbingwe as the first step in enhancing its own economic influence in Damaraland.[85] To domesticate their African congregations, Rhenish missionaries also inaugurated agricultural and horticultural programs.[86] Finally, Hahn and his supporters encouraged local communities to plant gardens, wear cloth clothing, and vacate their traditional homes in favor of European-style housing. Through these initiatives, the RMG wanted to exhibit "positive behavioral models" to Ovaherero women, men, and children.[87] Missionaries believed that they could instill capitalism and Christianity in Damaraland systematically over the long term. At the same Hereroland Missionary conference in Otjimbingwe, Hahn argued that "an alliance of kitchen and altar" had the potential to secure the Rhenish Mission's existence for the foreseeable future and to emancipate Ovaherero from the financial and sexual desires of white European speculators.[88]

The MHG also stimulated the growth of a collective German spirit among Rhenish missionaries for the first time publicly. Through its adoption of protocapitalistic measures, the RMG helped transition Southwest Africa gradually "into a thoroughly German settlement."[89] An incipient national discourse started to pervade Rhenish evangelical practice, from conversions and attitudes toward Ovaherero to language training and trade with other European powers. Missionary Carl Gotthilf Büttner, who first landed in Walvis Bay in January 1873, personifies this development in overt terms.[90] Büttner initially harbored sentiments toward Africans similar to those of his predecessors in the 1840s. "I have to admit," he wrote to the leadership in Barmen in April 1873, "that I have the same favorable impression of the Herero that the other brothers had when they came here."[91] He also remarked that his few Ovaherero students "were not much more difficult to approach and communicate with" than his former students in Germany.[92] "For a race that was supposed to stand nearest to the apes," Büttner continued, Ovaherero had considerable "interest in politics and self-governance."[93] He also encouraged social interactions between the white and Black races and championed the positive impact of "mixed-race marriages." On a visit to the Western Cape in 1873, he reported that "it was especially good to see that while in many other places the difference between whites and coloreds seems almost like a caste difference, in Saron [north of Cape Town] everything is a jumble."[94]

The longer Büttner stayed in Southwest Africa, however, the more negative his assessments of Black Africans and non-German Europeans grew. In December 1873, he portrayed both the land and the people as "empty" and "leached" of spirit.[95] The following year, Büttner asserted that "in Europe, you really cannot imagine what it means to have a whole people made up of whores, thieves, liars, and misers, in which even the most honest men deserve to be put in jail at least once each weekend."[96] Less than one year after his arrival in Damaraland, Büttner had lost his optimistic worldview and labeled the Ovaherero a lost people. His attitude on the topic of German colonialism also started to change as he acclimated to the region. Büttner believed that only a strong national presence could steer the country toward the path of salvation. His general pessimism toward Ovaherero notwithstanding, Büttner resolved that a centralized German occupation was the only hope for both the people and the local economy. Such an endeavor additionally promised to undermine England's influence in Southwest Africa, which Büttner in his writings regularly condemned. "Of course it was [our] aim to import first and foremost German merchandise into Damaraland," he asserted in his 1884 book *The Hinterland of Walvis Bay and Angra Pequena.* Such an effort "would make it possible to supplant the English trademarks" throughout much of southern Africa.[97] Büttner's procolonial views eventually compelled him to leave the RMG and return to Germany in 1886, where he joined Carl Peters's vehemently procolonial Evangelische Missions-Gesellschaft für Deutsch-Ostafrika (Evangelical Mission Society for German East Africa).

Friedrich Fabri, the chief inspector of the RMG between 1857 and 1884, also embodied the growth of religious chauvinism among Rhenish missionaries during this period. Though scholars frequently identify Fabri as the author of the well-known procolonial book *Does Germany Need Colonies?*, he also played a significant role in the RMG during the precolonial era. Fabri began his career as a Lutheran pastor in Bavaria before he joined the Rhenish Mission. Though he never completed any formal seminary training, Fabri's pietist sentiments and knowledge of the British Protestant missionary system elevated his stature among the Rhenish leadership. After he assumed the inspectorship in 1857, Fabri advocated for the RMG to mirror the British model in Southwest Africa. He envisaged a centralized program, one that would condition missionaries to serve as representatives of Germandom overseas on the one hand, and link evangelism and national prosperity together on the other.[98] In order to advance these causes, Fabri founded the Missions-Handels-Aktien-Gesellschaft (Mission Trade Stock Company, MHAG) in 1869.[99] While formally unaffiliated with the Mission Trade Society, the MHAG evolved into a powerful extension of the Rhenish Mission in southern Africa. It eventually established branches in Otjimbingwe, Walvis Bay, Okahandja, Rehoboth, and elsewhere through-out the colony.[100]

The MHAG, like its competitors, imported arms, alcohol, and other supplies, and exported foodstuffs, predominantly cattle, to Germany. Fabri believed that the Rhenish Trade Stock Company had the potential to strengthen German interests at the expense of the British. He famously elaborated on this idea in *Does Germany Need Colonies?* "It would be advis-able for us Germans," he instructed, "to learn from the colonial skill of our Anglo-Saxon cousins and begin to emulate them in peaceful competition. When, centuries ago, the German Reich stood at the head of the states of Europe, it was the foremost trading and seagoing power. If the new German Reich wishes to entrench and preserve its regained power for long years to come, then it must regard that power as a cultural mission and must no longer hesitate to also resume its *colonizing vocation*."[101] Shortly after founding the MHAG, Fabri declared that all Rhenish missionaries serving overseas were official agents of the German state.[102] This decision enabled him to establish the RMG as a political authority in Southwest Africa and to demonstrate Germany's colonial potential to other European powers.

Fabri's efforts went a long way toward nationalizing the work of Rhen-ish missionaries overseas. While it continued to operate as an independent society, the RMG under his leadership fostered strong ties with the newly unified German government after 1871. The same year he published *Does Germany Need Colonies?*, Fabri also helped found the Westdeutscher Verein für Kolonisation und Export (West German Association for Colonization and Export), which represented Rhenish and Westphalian industrialists and promoted their business interests through colonial conquest.[103] In 1883, Fabri accepted a position as vice president of the Deutscher Kolonialverein (German Colonial Society), and two years later he received an honorary membership in Carl Peters's Gesellschaft für deutsche Kolonisten (Society for German Colonies).[104] Few figures championed imperialism more than Fabri in the precolonial era. His official role as director of the RMG, however, signifies the evolution of Rhenish pietism in the two decades before 1884. Fabri integrated Christianity and German identity as elements of the same national philosophy. In his mind, the success of one also elevated the other, leading him to conflate Rhenish evangelism and German colonial ambition into one common national cause.

Members of the RMG and imperial enthusiasts in Germany were not the only ones to acknowledge the new and important role of German nationalism in Southwest Africa. Thure Johan Gustav Een, a Swedish

merchant who landed in Walvis Bay in 1866, enjoyed an extensive relationship with European and African clients in Damaraland. Two years after his
arrival, Thure partnered with the famous Swedish ornithologist Axel
Wilhelm Eriksson in an effort to improve his business prospects.[105] In 1870,
after a period of financial strain and general frustration, he made a series
of observations of Rhenish missionaries while traveling in Ovamboland:

> Already before I had undertaken the journey to Ovamboland, I
> had learnt through the newspapers from the Cape of the great war
> between France and Germany. All whites who were not of German
> nationality wished the French army to be victorious and we awaited
> news from the front with intense interest. When the victories of
> the German forces became known, the Germans, in their usual
> manner of course, started bragging and blustering and behaving
> arrogantly. Of course these wonderful victories with all their
> bloody deeds, which have taken European civilization a step back-
> ward, also had to be observed and celebrated with German
> thoroughness here in the wilderness.[106]

Een's assessment, though disparaging and likely infused with personal bias,
indicates that Rhenish missionaries openly celebrated the military outcome
in the Franco-Prussian war as a German victory. Later in the same commentary, he cited Hahn as a central proponent of these nationalist displays. "To
begin with, Mr. Hahn, the High Priest of the missionaries," Een wrote, "took
down the mission flag, a red cross with a white background, and raised the
flag of the North German Confederation instead. The holy sign of the cross
had to be replaced by the standard of '*das grosse Vaterland*.'"[107] Een concluded
with a sharp summation of the whole affair: "The common symbol of peace
of the Celestial Empire *for all peoples* had to give way to the German nation's
flag of victory."[108] Rhenish missionaries' adoption of religious chauvinism,
as Een's conclusions illuminate, did not occur inside a vacuum.

While members of the RMG received a steady flow of news and information that guided their actions in Southwest Africa, so, too, did citizens
in Europe from Africa. As we have seen, missionaries like Hahn and Fabri
communicated frequently with the leadership in Barmen during their
tenures overseas or as representatives of the RMG. Excerpts from these
accounts often found their way into official Rhenish reports and newspapers, where interested parties could read about the fate of Christianity
overseas and receive first-hand portrayals of African polities, mysterious

beasts, and resource-rich landscapes. The *Barmer Missionsblatt*, the Rhenish Mission's official journal, for example, had over twenty-one thousand subscribers before the end of the nineteenth century.[109] The *Missionsblatt*, much like *Globus* and *Gartenlaube*, regaled readers with detailed stories of life in southern Africa.

One such story from August 1857, infused with the precolonial fantasies that defined the RMG's efforts at that time, both exoticized and glorified Southwest Africans as potential Christian converts. "Behind the red people, deeper into the interior of the country," the author described, "lies Amraal's tribe, who has been urgently requesting a missionary for a year, and then, after long many deserts in the country, comes the fertile area of Lake Ngami and the beautiful Linokanoka Country with its rich population, towards which our missionaries are already looking with the longing of Christian exiles."[110] Two decades later, the same journal championed the right of Germans to spread the gospel through collective strength and imperial conquest. Newspapers, nationalist clubs, anthropologic and ethnographic societies, and Pan-German leagues also participated in this practice. Together, they acquainted broad segments of German society with southern Africa, furthering the motivations of colonial enthusiasts who sought an overseas empire.[111] Thus, Rhenish missionaries both actively and implicitly participated in metropolitan constructions of a global German identity through their adoption of religious chauvinism.

As future German colonists discovered after 1884, however, religious chauvinism did not change one fundamental truth in Southwest Africa: Rhenish missionaries were reliant on Africans for their own survival. This power dynamic certainly vexed members of the Rhenish leadership in the immediate years after their arrival in southern Africa, but only as it related to their pietist mission. When the RMG adopted *christliche Kolonisation* in the 1860s, Nama, Oorlam, and Ovaherero influence over regional matters emerged as a more significant problem.[112] It is important to note that Africans had their own affairs and interactions that were entirely unrelated to the interests of Rhenish missionaries. While many people engaged Rhenish missionaries for trade, schooling, and theological purposes, the RMG did not consume every aspect of Nama, Oorlam, and Ovaherero daily life. This fact is significant because it illustrates why the RMG adopted religious chauvinism in the first place. If they really wanted to have permanent success in southern Africa, Rhenish missionaries needed to build a base of support that commanded local and eventually regional attention. To do so, however, required more than a handful of Protestant missionaries thinly

spread over a large area. The RMG thus increasingly relied on nationalist rhetoric and contemporary imperial aspirations to attract more attention
in Germany and among Nama, Oorlam, and Ovaherero in Southwest
Africa.

Jonker Afrikaner's death in 1861 and its immediate consequences exemplify the RMG's limited authority over local events. Jan Jonker, Afrikaner's
second-oldest son, assumed the leadership of the Oorlam, but this change
in control did not resolve the hostile relations between Ovaherero and
Oorlam in Damaraland.[113] Jan Jonker, moreover, regarded the RMG as a
highly suspicious institution. He often raided Rhenish mission stations,
churches, and schools, further alienating Rhenish priests and converts in
the region.[114] Hahn responded harshly, accusing Jan Jonker of "disgusting
hypocrisy" and suffering from "inner and exterior decay."[115] While Jan
Jonker was aware of Hahn's feelings, the RMG was not his principal concern.
His goal, to rule Damaraland as the paramount authority, did not require
him to receive either the blessing or the support of the RMG. Unsurprisingly, it put him in direct conflict with Ovaherero and Nama groups, further
destabilizing the territory, from the point of view of the Rhenish missionaries. At the same time, Ovaherero leaders desired more sovereignty in
the areas surrounding Windhoek and Okahandja, as well as an end to the
Oorlam raids on their cattle.[116]

Since this atmosphere was not conducive to evangelism, Rhenish leaders moved to facilitate another peace agreement between the warring
parties. After a period of strenuous negotiation, Jan Jonker and Maharero,
leader of the Okahandja Ovaherero, signed an accord with Hahn and four
other missionaries who served as mediators.[117] The "Okahandja agreement"
of 1870 recognized Jan Jonker as paramount chief of Southwest Africa and
also awarded Ovaherero control over specific territories in Damaraland.
Rhenish missionaries officially adopted a neutral position at the meeting
but played an active role as advisors. While Hahn and his colleagues tried
to present themselves as apolitical figures, in reality they were seeking to
strengthen the RMG's role as a centralized authority.[118] All parties viewed
the peace as a victory. For Rhenish missionaries, it not only brought an end
to the violent instability in the region but also enabled them to once again
expand their reach further into Damaraland and Namaland. In the immediate aftermath of the accord, the RMG focused its efforts in present-day
south-central Namibia, particularly in the area surrounding Gibeon.

In 1869, the RMG officially recognized 150 Ovaherero converts in
Damaraland.[119] Eight years later the number grew to 983, and in 1883

Rhenish missionaries documented 1448 Ovaherero Christians in Southwest Africa.[120] Though these numbers represented only a small percentage of the overall population, officials in Barmen regarded any metric of progress as a positive sign. Given the notable difficulties and collective failures Rhenish missionaries endured after their first appearance in Damaraland, Hahn, Kleinschmidt, and subsequent evangelists had reason to celebrate. In addition, some polities also started to produce crops and rely upon the RMG for more than just theological guidance.

These advances were decisive for two reasons. First, the spread of Christianity in Southwest Africa enhanced the RMG's recognition among both Germans and Africans. The Okahandja agreement allowed Rhenish missionaries to expand their presence throughout the country and also gave citizens in Germany greater access to and information about southern Africa. Second, Rhenish efforts to centralize their control in Southwest Africa coincided with Germany's unification in 1871. As a result, apolitical spectators, merchants, Black Africans, and other non-German Europeans in the region increasingly looked upon the RMG as an extension of the German state. Rhenish missionaries in turn used this development for their own political and theological purposes, extending the reach of their original evangelical charge to include both "kitchen and altar" as well as the imperial aspirations of citizens and national enthusiasts in the German metropole. Religious chauvinism unified these two contrasting spectrums of ideas, making the RMG an essential force in the eventual founding and occupation of Germany's only settler colony on the African continent.

"REPRESENTATIONS OF EUROPEAN CIVILIZATION"

In the *Yearbook of the Rhenish Mission Society (1846–1847)*, Hugo Hahn described Ovaherero as "handsome and strong . . . but more deeply submerged in pagan horror than just about any other southern people."[121] He alleged that their "entire character [consisted of] robbery and murder, theft and whoring, [and] hypocrisy and lies."[122] These highly racist sentiments reflect Hahn's deeply conflicted personal history with Ovaherero, as well as the institutional challenges the RMG faced in southern Africa. Importantly, however, they also demonstrate the significant transformation Protestant evangelists underwent after their arrival in Southwest Africa. From their own religious convictions and notions of spirituality to their impressions about nationalism and the potential virtues of imperial expansion, Rhenish missionaries exemplify the impact of colonial encounters on German identity in the preimperial era.

As God's supposed shepherds on earth, Rhenish missionaries justified their actions in divine terms. Evangelism knew no ethnic or physical boundaries, and the missionaries shared a desire to expel heathenism from the African continent. Humanity, they argued, was equal in the eyes of God. The success of their mission, therefore, was essential. Failure would ensure eternal damnation for the souls of Africans, a fate that the RMG pledged to prevent at all costs. As women and men, however, missionaries used racist language and embraced prejudicial stereotypes for their African congregation. When faith alone proved inadequate to spread Christianity, the RMG adopted capitalist and nationalist measures to enhance its authority in Southwest Africa. Churches, mission stations, schools, and permanent farms, Hahn and his colleagues believed, could act as "representations of European civilization" and create the necessary preconditions for Nama, Oorlam, and Ovaherero to eventually reach salvation.[123] In this manner, religious chauvinism created an intense drive among missionaries to forge a Christian stronghold in southern Africa, as well as a strong conviction that German civilization was the only instrument that could guarantee the success of their pietist charge.

From church registers and mission reports to detailed publications and maps in magazines, Rhenish missionaries influenced the public discourse on imperialism. In doing so, they established the RMG as an essential outpost of Germandom overseas in the minds of hopeful imperialists and nationalists between 1842 and 1884. Germany's formal colonial era thus began with significant public understanding of the overseas world. Even if their perceptions followed highly subjective and racist imaginings, German citizens were familiar with the potential of empire and what an African colony might afford them in the metropole. Whether through romanticized accounts and public exhibitions or in board games and human performances, colonial encounters in DSWA fused colony and metropole together into one national empire during the precolonial and formative colonial eras.

PART 2

Colonial Encounters, 1884–1904

Anyone who thought this system was wrong usually attacked indigenous people and only received lenient treatment. But this was not enough to break the system itself. In other words, the change in our system had to be preceded by a significant increase in our means of power, both materially and in personnel. To answer the question "how much," all one needs to do is look over at Southwest Africa today.

—Theodor Leutwein, 1907

CHAPTER 3

"A Blessing to Itself and the Motherland"

Extolling Empire in the Age of Imperial Conquest

"WHOEVER HAS SEEN THE COUNTRY KNOWS"

In January 1909, twenty-five years after authorities designated Southwest
Africa a German protectorate, *Reichskommissar für Südwestafrika* (Reich
Commissar for Southwest Africa) Wilhelm Külz extolled the virtues of
empire. "Whoever has seen the country knows that a new German land
can be created here with an active population; they also know that the way
is still open to give Germans [in Südwest] opportunities that would make
it a pleasure to live in this country. May German Southwest Africa blossom into such a land that is a blessing to itself and the motherland in the
not too distant future."[1] Külz felt optimistic about the colony's future. In
his estimation, much had changed since 1884, when "the whole administration was like a body without a backbone, without flesh and blood."[2] Now,
thanks to the "significant population and economic expansion of recent
years" and wholesale "local participation in state administration, [our]
municipal and colonial wishes go hand in hand" into posterity.[3]

Külz was hardly the first to celebrate the potential of a German colonial project in Africa. As we have seen, intellectuals, missionaries, merchants,
and other members of the imperial consensus fashioned positive imageries of conquest long before the existence of a formal empire. After the
Bremen tobacco merchant Adolf Eduard Lüderitz purchased stretches of
Angra Pequena (Lüderitz Bay, in present-day Namibia) in 1882, popular

features on colonialism grew even more vociferous in their proclamations.[4] "Angra Pequena, the largest of the German possessions just acquired," wrote the travel writer Karl Emil Jung in 1884, "stands in sharp contrast to Cameroon and not only in the configuration of her soil and her ability for European trade, but importantly also: German settlement, and her social and economic conditions."[5] Shortly after, Chancellor Otto von Bismarck extended security rights over Lüderitz's territory, making Southwest Africa Germany's first overseas protectorate. While DSWA started as nothing more than a prospective enterprise for Lüderitz and his monied investors, supporters of colonial expansion focused only on one fact— empire was no longer a national aspiration. It was finally a reality that provided them a stage upon which to manifest their imperial desires.

Africa captivated German citizens throughout the late nineteenth century. Though individuals shared wildly disparate motivations for imperial conquest, as well as numerous opinions about the necessity of colonial occupation, DSWA pressed both supporters and detractors to scrutinize their identity in global terms. Even those who did not agree with the supposed merits behind an overseas empire still had to reconcile with its existence. Whether in the correspondence of imperial administrators within the Auswärtiges Amt—Kolonialabteilung (Foreign Office—Colonial Division, AAKA) or through exposés in sympathetic newspapers, traveling fairs, and ethnographic performances, Germans encountered DSWA on a regular basis. They read, for instance, how "extensive colonization can now begin [thanks to] the fading away of the ignorance of Southwest Africa's true value" and that "the scoffers and their dubious friends are starting to lose heart."[6] Administrators and travelers proclaimed that "the place is completely uninhabited [except for] thousands of guinea fowl, partridges, steppe chickens, laughing pigeons, lovebirds, which are very colorful, [and] kudu antelopes that become visible in the bush when the jackals bark at night."[7] Young Germans assumed the role of "intrepid explorers" in *Die Kolonisten*, a board game that taught players about the principles of empire in the safety of their apartments and homes, absent the biological, economic, and "indigenous hardships" of real-life colonialism.[8] Official and unofficial organizations saturated audiences with amusements that celebrated the benefits of overseas conquest in real time, helping link colony and metropole together in the minds of women, men, and children over the course of the imperial era.

This chapter exposes the entangled relationship between Germany and DSWA through the lens of colonial propaganda and testimonials, public displays, ethnographic spectacles, and general recreations. These forces most notably affected individual interpretations of the *Heimat* ideal in Germany. As we saw in chapter 1, *Heimat* played an essential role in the imperial consensus's efforts to link national unification and overseas conquest into one common narrative. As a subject intimately related to German nationalism and its origins, it has attracted considerable attention in the historiography. Celia Applegate and Alon Confino, for example, have shown how impressions of *Heimat* cultivated a national conversation among German-speaking polities in the nineteenth century that otherwise had little in common.[9] They argue that nationhood afforded citizens a "striking potential [to] integrate diverse and frequently hostile groups" in accordance with their shared heritage.[10] Though their assessments have pushed scholars to look beyond monolithic or simplistic causalities for the origins of nationalism, Applegate and Confino still rely upon geographic familiarity as *the* chief inspiration behind contemporary uses of *Heimat* in the nineteenth century. While places of birth, everyday experiences, linguistic colloquialisms, and histories played crucial roles in Germany's national development, we must also recognize that German identity did not evolve inside a cultural or spatial vacuum. If factors such as print media and mass transit made it possible for subjects in Württemberg and Prussia, over time, to identify as members of the same national community, it was also possible for peoples and romanticized descriptions from the "exotic unknown" to shape how citizens constructed their identities. In this manner, an emphasis on Germany's imperial domain provides occasion to consider how a faraway colony with dissimilar ecologies and social dynamics grew into an extension of German memory and tradition.

Colonial conquest, of course, did not lead every person to interpret their identity through the prism of imperialism. To the contrary, this chapter means to demonstrate the fluidity of German identity, emphasizing how public engagement with DSWA prompted individuals to revise their conceptions of *Heimat* in a more spatially inclusive manner. Though Germans from all backgrounds, political parties, and regions participated in this process, those identified in chapter 1 as adherents to the imperial consensus were especially open to expanding their impressions of *Heimat*. If only due to their more favorable financial status and greater access to bookstores, cafés, and newsstands, university professors, capitalists and corporatists, members of the middle class, and urban socialites were the principal consumers of media from DSWA. Constant exposure to information about the colonial world helped these women, men, and children normalize the conceptual idea of a national overseas imperium. As more and more individuals participated in empire during the routine parts of their daily lives, *Heimat* developed into a malleable idea that encouraged German citizens to recognize familiarity in not only the local and regional but also the global. Advocates also increasingly integrated civilizational outlooks of the world into their delineation of *Heimat*, thereby raising the potential for mass violence and racial segregation in the colonial domain, as did metropolitans' tacit acceptance of such measures in German society.

The evolution of the *Heimat* ideal was principally the result of colonial encounters, which were occasions when Germans and Africans interacted with one another, such as through treaty negotiations, trade networks, correspondence, and military conflict. Encounters also included informal points of contact, particularly those that newspapers, missionary reports, and travel literature generated in southern Africa and the metropole. Though colonialism was a controversial issue in German society, political speeches and tabloid headlines about Africa elevated empire into a national story before the turn of the twentieth century. As the following two chapters will show, formal encounters between Africans and German settler colonists altered the evolution of the imperial government in structurally violent ways. From warfare and African displacement to child separation and white settlers' embrace of hypermasculine notions of national belonging, German colonial occupation transformed DSWA into an overseas embodiment of the national state.

This chapter, however, calls attention to the exhibitions, proclamations, and vivid descriptions from southern Africa that informally enmeshed colony and metropole, colonizer and colonized, together in sustained contact. Germans did not have to travel overseas to encounter the empire; instead, they could personally engage first-hand accounts and exposés in museums, or sample foreign products and commodities, all from the comfort of their own homes and neighborhoods. Whether in isolated towns, rural communities, or urban cities, pictures of untamed landscapes, tales of exploration, and self-congratulatory testimonials of discovery inundated political debates and public discussions in Germany. Over time, these informal encounters emboldened citizens to perceive Germany and DSWA as one joined unit—a global *Heimat* that extended past the spatial confines of Central Europe.

"Extolling empire" gave voice to aspiring imperialists and hesitant moderates who initially looked upon southern Africa as an abject region unfit for the cultivation of *Deutschtum*. While not every citizen considered the Orange River as integral to their national sovereignty as the Rhine, or the harbor at Swakopmund as economically important as those in Kiel, after 1884 they nevertheless still regarded them as German.[11] In an age that many viewed as one of boundless opportunity, informal colonial encounters elevated the status of imperialism throughout the *Kaiserreich*. A fantasy no more, Germany's *Heimat* abroad expanded the boundaries of German identity, linking newsstands in Windhoek with cafés, parades, and general amusements in Berlin, as well as making the existence of empire tangible in metropolitans' lives.

"GARDENS OF ABUNDANCE": POLITICAL FANTASIES AND REALITIES AFTER 1884

"If something is ever to become our colony," Adolf Lüderitz wrote in May 1883, "Germans must be able to live there."[12] In the same article praising the initiatives of "Bremen's famous son," the editors of the *Deutsche Kolonialzeitung* (*DKZ*) also published a romantic portrayal of Southwest Africa from Lüderitz's personal correspondence. "One mountain of sand came after another; ostriches, antelopes, and zebras crossed the path and disappeared in the distance or in the dark of night. On the way [into the interior], one gets on the extended ox wagons of the German [Rhenish] missionary Bam from Bethanien, who was just brewing his evening coffee and hospitably serving his riders."[13] Lüderitz evokes a forlorn landscape devoid of urban poverty and industrial development, purposely casting the region in desolate terms so as to generate interest in its limitless potential, most especially among affluent German investors and politicians.

In addition to *Die Gartenlaube* and *Globus*, readers had access to a myriad of publications that covered Germany's imperial domain. Among the most influential was the *DKZ*, which served as the main press organ of the Deutsche Kolonialgesellschaft (German Colonial Society, DKG). As the editors acknowledged in the first issue, the *DKZ* "would seek to arouse interest and understanding of Germany's colonial-political tasks in all circles."[14] The DKG's large membership gave considerable voice to this effort, allowing the weekly periodical to stimulate the imaginations of imperial adherents throughout the entire country. Though Lüderitz championed colonialism as a worthy enterprise in the pages of the *DKZ*, a personal search for riches initially guided his own colonial ambitions. In the aftermath of

FIG. 5 Adolf Lüderitz, ca. 1885, from Hans Schinz, *Deutsch-Südwest-Afrika* (Leipzig: Oldenburg, 1891). After Bismarck forced him to sell all of his overseas territory to the German Colonial Society for Southwest Africa (DKGfSWA), Lüderitz organized another gold expedition in 1886. While sailing near the conjunction of the Fish and Orange Rivers in 1886, Lüderitz's boat capsized and he drowned in the rough waters. Photo: Wikimedia Commons / Seeteufel.

his purchase of Angra Pequena in 1882, Lüderitz looked to augment his regional holdings further, primarily along the southwestern coast. The following year, he concluded an agreement with Captain Josef Frederiks of the Bethanien Oorlam for all of the land south of Angra Pequena to the Orange River, stretching inland for twenty miles.[15] He envisaged these acquisitions as the start of a much larger expansionist project in southern Africa. After Bismarck extended "German protection" over his territory in 1884, Lüderitz obtained additional territory from Kamaherero, supreme chief of the Ovaherero, and Jan Jonker Afrikaner, Jonker Afrikaner's second-eldest son. He sought to establish a commercial empire based on mineral extraction and regional trade, as well as a protective outpost from which Germany could expand into Central Africa.

At the same time, in the new metropole, sympathetic groups and organizations moved to underscore the importance of Southwest Africa to the German state. Carl Gotthilf Büttner, the former Rhenish missionary introduced in the previous chapter, for instance, celebrated Lüderitz's land deals as a national victory. "The significance of the newly acquired territory," he wrote in July 1884, "will only become fully manifest if one does not take a narrow view of the situation, but looks upon it as a way of gaining access to Africa's interior."[16] The famous German geographer Alfred Kirchhoff, meanwhile, noted that "suddenly everyone is talking about Angra Pequena. . . . It appears that we Germans are finally beginning to take a serious and practical interest in overseas countries in order to use them for our colonial endeavors."[17] In the same issue of the *DKZ*, an unnamed contributor proclaimed sharply that "it should and must be colonized. There is agreement in extensive circles in Germany."[18] The Deutscher Kolonialverein (German Colonial Association) unsurprisingly agreed, subsequently adding that "a vigorous and purposeful colonial policy sharply drawn by Prince Bismarck . . . offers a rich field of activity that is fruitful for Germany."[19] Though German overseas settlement did not begin in earnest for several more years, these stories indicate how quickly enthusiasts acted to galvanize support for the imperial cause. Even before the German government extended protection rights over Lüderitz's territorial holdings, newspapers worked to portray Southwest Africa as a German land of abundance that could improve economic and social opportunities for everyone.

While jubilant headlines roused audiences in Europe, they could not diminish Lüderitz's personal financial problems. He staked a majority of his fortune on land procurement in Africa in the early 1880s, and when that venture did not yield the immediate financial returns that he envisaged, he funded several speculative gold expeditions along the coast of Southwest Africa. After these plans too failed to generate any success, he went bankrupt in November 1884. In response to this crisis, Bismarck ordered Lüderitz to sell all of his assets and territorial claims to several prominent investors in Germany.[20] The railroad entrepreneur Adolph von Hansemann, investment banker Gerson von Bleichröder, and industrialist Count Guido Henckel von Donnersmarck were among the most prominent figures to capitalize on Lüderitz's misfortunes.[21] In concert with representatives from Deutsche Bank and other conspicuous German financial institutions, these men founded the Deutsche Kolonialgesellschaft für Südwestafrika (German Colonial Society for Southwest Africa, DKGfSWA) on 30 April 1885.[22] The company's board styled the DKGfSWA as both a private trading organization and a "nonprofit patriotic society acting in the national interest."[23] The DKGfSWA effectively embodied Bismarck's long-held assessment of the ideal imperial project: monied stakeholders assumed all of the financial risk and reward, while the German government claimed ownership with only a minimal presence in the colony.

German colonial rule and its corporatist beginnings are important to acknowledge because they do not easily convey why DSWA evolved into such an important factor in public conceptions of national identity. The colony's origins as a private enterprise notwithstanding, imperial testimonials, political propaganda, and a general curiosity for the unknown propelled imperialism into the national spotlight. DSWA's status as Germany's first overseas protectorate, moreover, pressed women and men to familiarize themselves with a foreign and exotic world.[24] Images of landscapes and of animals and farmhouses, rich descriptions of starlit skies and sandy savannahs, and harrowing portrayals of occupation acquainted Germans with the reality of imperial domination. What many once considered strange and alien suddenly became common and memorable. Individuals did not have to visit Windhoek personally or wade in the frigid waters off Swakopmund's coast to experience a shared closeness with *their* empire. Even the designation "German Southwest Africa" contributed to this collective mindset. It simultaneously announced Germany's claim to the territory and invited citizens to perceive the colony as a rightful constituent of the metropole itself. Informal encounters thus provided individuals the emotional capacity to receive a foreign state as an equal part of the nation.[25] When Germans referenced the colony as "our Südwest" after 1884, they did so because these interactions made it possible for them to deem DSWA a cultural and geographical extension of Germandom, thereby expanding the *Heimat* ideal on a global scale.[26]

Imperial officers were among the most visible figures to propagate news from and about southern Africa. In May 1885, Bismarck appointed Dr. Heinrich Ernst Göring as the colony's first *Reichskommissar*.[27] Though he was only one of a literal handful of administrators in the new protectorate, Göring possessed considerable control over imperial affairs. Bismarck assigned him as the head German negotiator in the region, the commissioner of justice, and also granted him broad authority over all political and social matters of state. In the formative period of German rule, Africans ignored Göring's presence entirely and paid little attention to his early attempts to establish protection treaties with the colonial administration.[28] Nevertheless, Göring and his associates increased public awareness about imperial activities among metropolitan associations and individuals. In reports, newspaper articles, and official correspondence, these officials informed audiences with stories about DSWA's farming potential, open horizons, and abundance of wildlife, as well as stirring encounters with local groups and ecosystems.

Göring wanted above all to create an agricultural, classist, and self-reliant economy that would not require extensive financial support from the German government.[29] He promoted such narratives about DSWA as a means to entice rich and aristocratic families to emigrate overseas. Soon after his arrival in the colony, for example, Göring drafted a statement on the probable success of large-scale farming in south-central Namaland. "Hoachanas and areas around Lietfontein, Kalkfontein, and other places are water-rich and are areas with fertile soil that would be most suitable for settlement by white people. The local missionaries grow wheat, corn, potatoes, and all garden fruits in abundance, cultivate large-scale beekeeping, and have very impressive herds of cattle."[30] Göring was dubious that mining exports alone could sustain the colony economically.[31] Shortly after assuming his position as *Reichskommissar*, he wrote that there was "very little prospect of mining interests ever asserting themselves again in the first German colony. If a corporation such as the German Colonial Society for Southwest Africa can only operate at a financial loss, then it will be hard to find any German capitalists who will invest purely for the enthusiasm of doing so."[32] Instead, Göring publicized agricultural endeavors.[33] He believed that cattle farming, in particular, might appeal to wider circles and also increase DSWA's economic prospects for the entire German Empire.

In addition to Göring, many other, less prominent figures also considered agriculture the colony's economic future. Adolph von Hansemann of the DKGfSWA, for example, drafted a report for the AAKA in 1890 and contended that "thirty-four water stations, which once belonged to chiefs Piet Haibib [Topnaars] and Jan Jonker Afrikaner, are suitable for settling immediately."[34] Franz Weller, a self-described "simple farmer in Lietzow," meanwhile, seized the "occasion to present [his] thoughts on how thousands of Germans could forge a home in German South-West Africa." He explained that "due to time constraints, poverty, and poor circumstances, thousands of unfortunate families will be more productive [in the protectorate]."[35] In a follow-up report, entitled "Something Social and Colonial," Weller celebrated both the challenges and the opportunities that such an enterprise would offer his fellow countrymen. "It is not a paradise that opens its doors, it is not a country in which milk and honey now flows, but the outcomes that we wish to see in our new territory will only happen with one magic word: effort!"[36] He continued, "In German South West

Africa, due to the life-giving natural water deposits and small oases, we can create sustainable and productive arable farming plots."[37] Testimonies like these fueled speculation among a diverse range of citizens about Africa's importance to the German nation. While administrators often wrote about topics that inspired only a small number of women and men to consider emigration themselves, they nevertheless informed how Germans could envisage their colony. Berlinerin and Berliner, for instance, might not relate to the physical toil of rural farm life, but descriptions of potato fields and water stations allowed them conceptually to associate landscapes in Namaland with those in rural Brandenburg and the Rhine River valley. Citizens in Essen, meanwhile, could fantasize about the fertile soil and prairies in Bethanien as they negotiated the industrial squalor and pollution that shrouded manufacturing neighborhoods in the Ruhrgebiet. Imperial officers used these missives to capture what they perceived as the natural order of their surroundings in the colony. Germans in Central Europe thus enjoyed the chance to concentrate on either the qualities that they found comforting and recognizable or those that they deemed fresh, enticing, and mysterious.

Along with German administrators, private citizens, captains of industry, and soldiers commented on their experiences in DSWA. Dr. Max Buchner, a German physician and self-proclaimed ethnologist, for example, drafted editorials for Die Gartenlaube and other popular journals during the early colonial period. In an effort to compel officials to establish a segregated society in DSWA, he regularly filled his commentaries with racist caricatures and generalizations about the supposed "evil will of the Blacks."[38] Buchner's racism, of course, was not unique to Germany and its imperial domain. Racism underlay the cultural and structural fabric of all European colonialisms in the nineteenth and twentieth centuries. But importantly— and in stark contrast to white German settler colonists after 1904—his perceptions did not yet shape *every* aspect of the colonial state. That is not to say that racism did not influence Germany's formative imperial ambitions; rather, it is to assert that it was one of many violent factors that sculpted German colonial policy between 1884 and the so-called Herero Aufstand (Herero Uprising). Civilizational demonstrations of power certainly attracted attention and roused public interest, but ideas of racial supremacy as such were not exclusively what inspired enthusiasts to support imperial conquest overseas, most especially among women and men in the metropole.

In 1885, for instance, he scripted a brief on DSWA's ecology, proximity to other European colonies, and prospects for industrial development.[39]

"The West African coastal country," he wrote, "rises to a 1000-meter-high plateau, which extends east almost to the Indian Ocean. Green savannas, composed of long-stemmed grasses, shrubbery, and gnarled tree cover, dominate its surface, lush forests thrive in the valleys, which are bursting with vitality."[40] Buchner purposely used rich portrayals of abundance to entrance urban and rural, rich and poor, aristocratic and peasant readers in order to craft shared expectations about the realities of empire. In doing so, he also seemingly authenticated Göring's promises about the opportunities that awaited those courageous enough to make the long journey overseas. "The highlands of South Africa," Buchner affirmed, "are more suitable for the breeding of cattle than almost any other part of the world, and a good part of the cultural future of its inhabitants will be tied to this almost completely free line of business."[41] Beautiful descriptions and the prospect of an easy fortune alerted Germans to the expansive character of their African *Heimat*, helping to alleviate the unease of anti-imperial and apathetic voices in the metropole.

Members of Germany's imperial "protection force" (*Schutztruppe*) also made pronouncements concerning the prospects that awaited their fellow countrymen in southern Africa. Major Curt von François, among the first soldiers to arrive in DSWA, completed a comprehensive survey for German chancellor Leonardo von Caprivi in August 1890 on central Damaraland's soil quality, terrain, average climate, cattle prices, rainfall, and general quality of life. "The ground is white and covered with a thick bush," François asserted, "which increases in thickness further to the east. There are also beautiful sections of trees—likely acacia—that adorn the sandy beds of the large water veins."[42] He continued that "the rains run from October to March, and usually occur in the afternoon. Powerful thunderstorms and strong gusts of wind produce large amounts of water."[43] François supplemented these findings with information from a Herr Heidmann, a Rhenish missionary who collected statistical data on the region's annual rainfall following his own arrival in 1886. He even included a drawing of his personal garden in the report, which showed a diverse array of produce, such as plots for tobacco, cabbage, peas, melon, and grapes.[44] François was so confident about these prospects that he went on to found the city of Windhoek in the same location in October 1890.[45] Remarkable imageries like these offered Germans a way to grasp the genuineness of the imperial age. In addition, they provided overwhelming evidence of colonial fortune. One merely needed to seize the moment and participate in Germany's grand adventure in Südwest.

Though imperial officials aspired to capture what they saw as DSWA's natural order, they also continued to propagate colonial fantasies to the German public. Perhaps the most egregious was the myth of German imperial domination. In the years between 1884 and 1894, Kaisers Wilhelm and Wilhelm II's colonial authority existed almost entirely on paper. Africans, not Germans, controlled land rights and access to cattle and regional trade markets and enjoyed numerical superiority. Only upon their arrival did settlers discover that that "their" African homeland was far from the oasis they read about in colonial missives and newspapers. Among the most powerful polities were the Witbooi Namaqua in southern Namaland and the Ovaherero in north and central Damaraland. African resistance forced the German administration to rely heavily on the metropole for its regulatory and military needs. As the next chapter will reveal, when calls to suppress their regional dominance grew louder in the imperial and national press, the German government expanded its presence considerably, culminating in Chancellor Caprivi's declaration of DSWA as a settlement colony in March 1893.[46]

Two additional instances also helped transform the protectorate from a decentralized, private boondoggle into a German settlement colony. The first was Göring's adoption of the Statute of the German Colonial Society for German Southwest Africa in April 1885, which granted the DKGfSWA monopoly control over all corporate enterprises in the protectorate.[47] It also established legal codes and various methods for how the Company could allocate its preliminary investment of 800,000 marks.[48] Most significantly, the Statute represented Germany's first attempt to displace Africans from their traditional homelands.[49] Though Göring and his fellow commissioners lacked the physical means to enforce the Statute, it signaled that the colonial administration wanted absolute hegemony over all activities in DSWA. Thanks in large part to the rampant proliferation of imperial propaganda in the metropole, however, imperial enthusiasts and international observers were at odds about the long-term future of Germany's colonial project in southern Africa.

Among the most pressing dilemmas for imperial officials was the dearth of white German families in the colony. Due in large part to accounts of instability and regional unrest, very few citizens before the turn of the twentieth century yearned to forge a new life overseas. In order to assuage their fears, Kaiser Wilhelm II appointed Dr. Paul Rohrbach as the first *Ansiedlungskommissar* (Commissioner for Settlement) for DSWA. As a private citizen, Rohrbach had traveled extensively throughout much of Asia and

Africa during the 1890s.[50] He was also a prolific writer and enjoyed considerable recognition among citizens throughout the metropole. The German government charged him with finding the most efficient way to increase white settlement in Namaland and Damaraland. Soon after his arrival, Rohrbach drafted numerous agricultural and ethnographic studies on DSWA. He was careful to style his discoveries for a public audience, often emphasizing conditions and scenarios that might attract people whom he viewed as ideal colonists, namely young and married couples who were financially stable and harbored nationalist sympathies.

In October 1903, Rohrbach visited thirteen settlements between Nosob and Valgras over an eight-day period. After his return to Windhoek, he exalted the "hardworking and patriotic farmers" he had encountered during his expedition. "Hoffnung, Ondekaremba, Acyembamera, Ommjereke, Thalheim, Wiese, Seeis, Nendamm, Franenstein, Soigtland, Haris, Valgras, [and] Lichtenstein," Rohrbach exclaimed, "can all be categorized as successes. . . . Self-sufficiency and a genuine willingness to work among settlers were on full display."[51] Rohrbach regarded a diligent work ethic, independence, and sobriety as markers of "whiteness," as well as virtues that distinguished desirable from undesirable settlers.[52] He also advocated a rigid "segregation of the races" so as to maintain a cultural order in the colony. "The native element," Rohrbach claimed that same year, "will maintain its place next to the white one . . . because the Africans are adaptable to a European-style economy."[53] Rohrbach's racism was not any more pernicious than Buchner's civilizational worldview, but it produced significantly more tragic outcomes for African polities due to his proximity to the colonial government.

Even for Rohrbach, however, racial hierarchy was not the solution for everything during this formative period. In particular, Rohrbach also harbored serious anxieties about social class, fearing that German citizens without financial means or a stable family life might seek opportunities overseas, only to fail and become a burden on the colonial government. A blind desire to sculpt a self-sufficient, and thereby successful, colony spurred Rohrbach's policy proposals and public characterizations more than any other factor during this period. Racism and class consciousness played important roles in determining his colonial experience as well, of course, but not to the same degree as after the so-called *Herero Aufstand*. As a result of these positions, Rohrbach considered poor single men the worst potential colonists. Not only did they require greater support from the German state, but they were also, he maintained, more likely to take African wives or sexual partners.[54] "If the colony is to keep its German character," Rohr-bach wrote in the German newspaper *Der Tag*, "it will be necessary to push the settlement of German families most zealously."[55]

Though he represented only one voice among many others in DSWA, Rohrbach's opinions carried considerable influence within nationalist circles in Germany. Societies such as the Alldeutscher Verband (Pan-German League) viewed the scarcity of white German families as the single great-est threat to the colonial project in Südwest. While Göring's passage of the Statute of the German Colonial Society for German Southwest Africa did not in itself represent a significant moment for German nationalists, the colonial administration's inability to enforce its authority provoked atten-tion among the most devout imperial enthusiasts in the metropole. In the face of these challenges, more and more citizens supported measures that encouraged the political growth of their African *Heimat* in tangible ways, such as increased settlement, a stable political and social landscape, and greater economic and structural "development."

The second instance that helped transform DSWA into a settlement colony was the outpouring of commentary from and about southern Africa. The convergence of imperial euphoria and high-profile setbacks pressed more people to contemplate the extent of German imperial power. As repre-sentatives of Germany's small presence in the colony, imperial administrators regularly complained about their lack of supremacy. The combination of official anxiety and stubborn confidence led to mixed views about the longevity of the imperial project. Heinrich Vogelsang, a merchant from Bremen and original partner of Adolf Lüderitz, for instance, described the situation in March 1885. "During my stay in Damaraland, Jan Jonker [Afri-kaner], who is currently nothing more than a robber chief[,] . . . shot a local shepherd, which has spread general turmoil and fear in the country. The fear of the natives is so great that I could hardly get people for my wagon to travel from Otjimbingue to Rehoboth. I tried to get Jan Jonker to meet me, but my attempts were in vain."[56] Newspapers all over the world printed similar stories about DSWA. In London, readers learned in April 1888 that Germany's "shadowy patronage of Angra Pequena [will] disappear over time sooner or later."[57] The *Cape Argus* scolded that "the anarchy [in the colony] contrasts curiously with the tenacity with which the authorities in Berlin hold to their position."[58] Many German publications followed suit. The *Koloniales Jahrbuch* wrote in 1889 that in "the eyes of Germans this 'protectorate' meant little more than the intention to keep other nations away from the country. . . . There is no reason why South West Africans should either love or fear the Reich."[59] Even the *DKZ* blistered leaders for their lack of action and transparency. "Either the German Reich does something to maintain its reputation," the paper argued, "or it must abandon the territories it has gained. The current situation is shameful for Germany."[60]

In spite of the pessimistic tone of these reports, German and international press agencies generated awareness about life in southern Africa in the metropole. Stories about so-called rebellious Africans endeavored to make German women and men believe that national apathy threatened the entire imperial experiment. If financial and imperial security was vulnerable, so, too, was their national pride. Instability abroad threatened the legitimacy of colonial rule at home.[61] Even if they did not personally subscribe to patriotic narratives or expect to profit from empire, German citizens advocated for more centralized programs to reinforce the colonial state. "It is quite gratifying to hear such a cheerful voice from the Southwest African 'desert,'" a German settler remarked in 1891 after learning about the growing support for colonial rule in the metropole. "As bad as the opinion of German Southwest Africa was in Germany recently, [I am pleased] that another view has now taken hold."[62] Thanks in large part to these warnings, the Reichstag passed a number of measures to enhance the size and scope of the imperial administration during the 1890s.[63]

Though they possessed only a small amount of real power in the colony, Göring and his associates educated Germans about the fantastic possibilities that awaited them in Südwest. "The excellent climate," Curt von François wrote in 1893, "the extensive pasture land on which Europeans can make a living as cattle breeders, the weak indigenous population, which only inhabits a small part of the land, and finally its geographical location all determine that with time the shortest transport route from Europe to the areas of the upper Zambezi will pass through *our* Protectorate."[64] Observations such as these offered a politically and socially heterogeneous audience answers to a host of issues, from concerns over the so-called social question and lack of clean living environments, to daydreams about DSWA's open prairies and unquestioned beauty.

Colonial advocates, in addition, found opportunities to celebrate the challenges that awaited them overseas. For some, their unrelenting belief in "white Germandom" promised to bridge the deep divisions in German society. "The view of a country where the white race faces the natives," explained one such account, "strengthens the feeling of solidarity and contrasts the dividing social influences with a strong moment of unification. The prospect of new living conditions revives the lower strata of people

that hope for an improvement in living standards and independent existence; [colonialism] arouses initiative and a thirst for knowledge. The
national feeling is strengthened in connection with all of these aspects.
Instead of being consumed by idealistic and communist dreams, the spirit
rejuvenates."[65] So-called inferior races were thus not hostile forces deserv-
ing of annihilation but worthy adversaries who added to the "rejuvenating"
experience of conquest. Racism, again, pervaded this collective mindset
but did not explicitly justify mass imprisonment or murder. It did, however,
intensify the *potential* for systematic brutality, a circumstance that only
grew more and more pronounced the longer Germans occupied DSWA.
Racial violence, as a result, steadily evolved into an indispensable measure
of the colonial state and its supporters.

In their capacity as imperial policy-makers, administrators, investors,
and members of the protection force all provided their fellow countrymen
occasions to encounter Südwest informally. Thanks to their meticulous
and sensationalized missives, DSWA played an active role in conversations
about German identity and the demarcations of nationhood over the course
of the formative colonial era. Imperial representatives also informed enthusiasts and detractors alike about the authenticity of empire. Whether in
official testimonials or popular accounts in the *DKZ* and *Deutsches Kolonialblatt*, citizens learned to look upon the territory as more than a colony.
Over time, many did so in highly irredentist terms. "Southwest Africa" no
longer represented a two-dimensional delineation on a map for people to
ignore casually; "German Southwest Africa" instead demanded attention
from all citizens who espoused a spiritual connection with the nation-state.
While their utopian visions for the colony never materialized into a lived
reality, imperial officers during the formative era afforded Germans the
ability to encounter southern Africa as a part of their daily lives. In doing
so, they helped establish DSWA as a "garden of abundance" for citizens to
contemplate, defend, and enjoy in familiar spaces on their own terms.

"BRINGING COLONIALISM TO EVER WIDER CIRCLES"

"For years, we have advocated for the Reich government to awaken from
its deafness toward the national press and our urgent requests to support
German colonization in our colonies so as to make the territories really
German. We can now affirm," the *Rheinisch-Westfälische Zeitung*, an influential newspaper among middle-class and nationalist-oriented Westphalians,

stated proudly in September 1902, "that the government has at last opened its ears!"[66] The paper applauded the colonial administration's decision to provide settlers with free land and financial support in DSWA. Such a directive, its editors believed, marked the moment when "national settlement of the country [could] begin earnestly."[67] In Swakopmund, meanwhile, the *Deutsch-Südwestafrikanische Zeitung* advertised an impressive array of fine luxuries and merchandise to its readers. The Woermann Line promoted its steamships' "regular departures from Hamburg on the 25th of each month [with] connections in Port Nolleth [Nolloth] and Cape Town," while the Gustav Damm Company offered "homeland and tropical uniforms, as well as riding jackets and riding pants, cut clean and precise," for affordable prices.[68] In the same section, Bayerische Staatsbrauerei offered Weihenstephan beer for sale "either for solo use or bulk distribution."[69]

Beyond the pages of colonial and national newspapers, large public spectacles conveyed graphic evidence of the imperial world to metropolitans. Berlin's 1896 Deutsche Kolonial-Ausstellung (German Colonial Exhibition) in Treptow Park, for instance, invited visitors to peruse a vast assortment of commercial goods and ethnographic displays. "The middle hall of the ground floor in the Tropical House," the *DKZ* advised its readers, "is dedicated to the exports from our colonies."[70] The exhibition included a variety of sensational curiosities and products for visual consumption, such as "rice and maize, assorted beans, sugar cane . . . Usambara coffee, Cameroon and Togo coffee, cocoa beans and powder, cola nuts, vanilla, red pepper, ginger, cloves, tobacco, hippopotamus and rhinoceros hides . . . wild Southwest African ostrich feathers, guano, trepang, Polynesian ivory nuts, and shark fins."[71] Exotic commodities, agricultural yields, and an abundance of merchandise hinted at the incredible value of Germany's imperial domain. German sightseers also watched African performers give musical pageants, dance recitals, and work demonstrations in both European dress and traditional clothing. These presentations afforded observers a chance either to confirm or to revise their precolonial impressions about the overseas world, as well as an opportunity for Africans to demonstrate their so-called enlightened transformation. As members of the Ovaherero delegation admitted to Dr. August Schreiber during the Berlin Exhibition, they wanted to impress upon the German public what "heathens looked like" back in DSWA.[72] From dinner tables and public parks in Cologne and Berlin to newsstands in Swakopmund and Windhoek, citizens and settlers consumed information that unveiled the normalcy of empire.

In many respects, Germany's conquest of Southwest Africa and its perception in the metropole was a mass-media creation. This observation is not meant to dismiss the brutal realities of Germany's occupation of DSWA, which was an inherently violent project that resulted in the detention, subjugation, and mass murder of countless people between 1884 and 1914. Rather, it seeks to recognize the important role that media and public spectacles played in colonialism's transmission to Germans audiences in Europe. Imperialism and the "colonial Other" constituted a substantial element of metropolitan advertising, visual culture, and commercial opportunity for both rich and poor throughout the Kaiserreich. These outlets enabled bankers, industrial workers, farmers, schoolteachers, politicians, and many others to establish familiarity with the colonial world. Their lack of personal connections or experiences overseas notwithstanding, citizens gradually incorporated southern Africa's ecology and diversity as constituent features of Germany's national future. "Empire" was both a hierarchical, physical orchestration of state power and an organic construction anchored in popular culture, official media, novels, and photographs. The global expansion of the *Heimat* ideal emerged from this same process. While administrators created the juridical demarcations of the colonial state, journalists, travel writers, ethnographers, and museums scripted histories and crafted anthropological displays that together forged one national-imperial storyline. In the minds of citizens both abroad and in the metropole, therefore, Germandom naturally extended beyond the spatial confines of Central Europe. Not only was it a necessity to "spread *Deutschtum* across the Earth," as the *DKZ* argued in October 1902, but the idea required little or no justification among many women, men, and children in Germany by the turn of the twentieth century.[73]

Newspapers and popular magazines functioned as the primary media to carry information between colony and metropole. All major German publications printed stories from and about DSWA frequently after 1884. These accounts included flattering testimony on the progress of colonization and reports on settler relations with Africans, the imperial government's diplomatic rapport with neighboring powers, the availability of new commercial products, and an array of other subjects both lighthearted and serious. Three dailies from the colony also imparted rich information about life and general conditions in southern Africa: the *Deutsch-Südwestafrikanische Zeitung* (formerly the *Windhoeker Anzeiger*), *Der Südwestbote* (formerly the *Windhuker Nachrichten*), and the *Allgemeine Deutsche Zeitung*. These papers featured articles on festivals and on Christian celebrations and services, statistics on harvests and crop yields, and jingoistic rationales for the defense of Germany's overseas territories.[74] Publications and emotive headlines created a palpable closeness between citizens in each different locale. When markets in Europe disseminated periodicals from DSWA, a wide cross-section of Germans could engage the imperial domain and draw a cultural meaning from the experience. A transnational flow of gossip, news, adverts, flyers, illustrations, and pictures thus fashioned a "national community" that linked colony and metropole together through informal and aesthetic discourse.

While colonial and domestic newspapers covered a wide number of subjects, the most important aspect is that they published stories about DSWA regularly. Reliable access to information about life overseas allowed Germans to connect emotionally with the colony and their settler-colonial brethren. Regardless of social class or education, metropolitan Germans particularly sought out articles that concentrated on the human element of imperialism. In May 1902, for instance, the *Norddeutsche Allgemeine Zeitung (NAZ)*, a leading newspaper among German conservatives, endorsed a plan for the Reichstag to build more language schools in DSWA after learning about the experiences of a German lecturer who had visited the colony earlier that same year. "He described in a moody and haunting way," the piece began, "how Germans immigrating to the protectorate from the first moment fall prey to the dishonorable denial of the mother tongue. As soon as he got ashore in Swakopmund, happy to step on German soil again after the long journey, [he recounted] all sorts of strange, barbaric words that drowned him out while he was in the middle of a conversation."[75] This "deeply flawed and shameful" situation, the *NAZ* determined, necessitated action, most especially from spectators in the metropole.

Thanks in part to the piece's dire and foreboding prose, DSWA's "language crisis" quickly earned the attention of the Allgemeiner Deutscher Sprachverein (German Language Club, ADSV), founded in Braunschweig in September 1885 by Hermann Dunger, a German nationalist and language teacher from Dresden. Together with Herman Riegel, an art historian and museum director from Potsdam, the ADSV advocated "the expulsion of foreign words (most notably French) from the German language."[76] Dunger and Riegel believed that the state of affairs in Europe and the colonies demonstrated a "lack of sensitivity to the purity and beauty of the language" and called for "all nationally minded Germans to appear publicly against word abuse."[77] If colony and metropole were indeed equal constituents of Germandom, then these criticisms extended to German-speaking populations everywhere in the world. The *NAZ*'s account of DSWA's so-called language crisis eventually incited members of the Sprachverein to confront "the native influences" that they condemned in imperial society.[78] In order for Southwest Africa "to become German," they concluded, "German must be the only language spoken between colonists and the native servants!"[79] Linguistic purity, in other words, was a worthy cause that also had the potential to enmesh colonial and metropolitan affairs even more closely.

That same year, the *Deutsche Warte*, a Berlin daily newspaper focusing on politics and society, cast Germany's occupation of Southwest Africa as a national success. "The German Colonial Congress has sufficiently proven that the alleged colonial fatigue, which should affect even the most active and optimistic [people] in Germany, in truth does not exist. An open exchange of ideas and thoughts," the editors asserted, "reveals that one has to make sacrifices for colonial purposes. Not only does Germany's great power necessitate it, but so does [our] hope for an economic boom in the protected areas."[80] The colony's financial promise, readers learned, was no longer a distant oasis but an actual reality. In addition to political stabilization, the article continued, "trade has also seen a significant increase. Domestic trade [in DSWA] is therefore livelier, especially since the government, in anticipation of the ever-increasing demand, has reduced export duties on ewes and cows from 10 and 100 marks to 2 and 20 marks."[81] In a similar fashion, the *Kölnische Zeitung*, a prominent paper among bourgeois and classical-liberal Germans, boasted "that the railway to Windhoek is now open and the pier in Swakopmund looks very solid. The one improves the other's value, and both make for substantial improvements and transportation facilitation in the colony."[82] Editors of the *DKZ* agreed, proclaiming in June 1903 that metropolitan citizens could expect sizable agricultural yields from DSWA. "We have there, apart from the coastal belt, a plateau that is excellent for livestock. . . . We also have small livestock, such as wool sheep and Angora goats, and have good prospects. . . . If the area were really not as promising, the merchants there would be the first to withdraw their assets they had won and not invest them there again."[83] Descriptions of open plateaus, Angora goats, and prosperous farmland alerted citizens to the striking features and value of their African protectorate. Germans were certainly not of one mind regarding the necessity for imperial conquest, but a relentless flow of news pressed even the most adamant detractors to accept the authenticity of imperialism. Individuals might personally object to "the substance of all policies of colonization [and the] exploitation of a foreign population," as August Bebel, chairman of the Social Democratic Party (SPD), maintained in January 1889, but they still embraced a concept of "cultural occupation" that they believed could benefit the German nation.[84] German rule in DSWA, in other words, had evolved into a collective debate about conduct and practice, not existence. After 1884, Bebel and the SPD, together with working-class workers, pacifist organizations, religious societies, and rights activists, advocated for a *humane* colonialism, but not necessarily an alternative to colonialism.[85]

This stream of information from DSWA galvanized enthusiasts both to demand more public attention for their hard-won victories and to urge Germany's leadership to support it. "Prince Bismarck is at the helm," the *DKZ* editors boasted in July 1889, "and steers the vehicle of Germany's foreign policy with a master's hand. But the sails must also be swelled with a national enthusiasm and fresh determination when it comes to advancing our colonial enterprises. . . . [We must] stand together on colonial issues that affect the entire nation."[86] A critic of overseas imperialism for much of his political career, Bismarck agreed in the late 1880s that an influx of German settlers in southern Africa "would benefit the national interests of everyone." In February 1889, for instance, he told Göring that "the settlement of the protectorate through German immigrants is of the greatest importance for the colony's future. A speedy settlement of the areas suitable for farming would contribute to a faster development of the country. . . . We cannot overlook that there currently exists a dangerous influence and prevalence of non-Germans in the protectorate."[87] The *DKZ* celebrated Bismarck's new perspective on colonialism. "We have the great honor and pleasure of having a leader, 'our prince,' at our head, who, thanks to his purposeful, skillful and extremely gracious leadership and his tireless interest and work for our ideas, is an excellent representative of colonialism."[88] Bismarck's change of heart on the German imperial project is perhaps the clearest example of the effect of informal colonial encounters in the 1880s.

Along with the explosion of books, periodicals, and international newspapers, museums, clubs, scientific societies, and school curricula acquainted Germans with the imperial domain. Perhaps even more importantly, public spectacles, dioramas, and ethnographic performances encouraged individuals to see and understand Germany's empire on their own terms. In 1890, for instance, the City of Bremen hosted the Northwest German Trade and Industry Exhibition in a trade hall that planners built specially for the occasion. While representatives from a host of commercial enterprises stressed the financial opportunities of overseas expansion, the DKG, Protestant and Catholic mission societies, and imperial enthusiasts organized several large displays to showcase "the exotic wonders of Africa and the Orient," including impressive collections of pictures, trophies, and artifacts from German, British, French, and other European colonial territories. A tower of elephant tusks drew the awe of patrons, Burmese artisans attracted praise for their precision and skill, and facsimiles of a Sumatran "Battak-Haus" with accompanying wax figures of people and animals presented colonial life in clear detail.[89] A rich assortment of ebony carvings from Cameroon sat between vast quantities of weapons and trophies, and a large painting of a "Mexico group" showed a scene of village life.[90] Even before visitors entered the trade hall, a decorative Chinese pagoda floating at the center of a lake mesmerized onlookers.[91]

These displays amused and titillated almost everyone who visited the trade hall. As *Daheim*, a politically conservative family magazine, wrote after the start of the exhibition, the "luxurious display of Indian and East-Asian products is particularly noteworthy. The Orient tempts the eyes with its all-encompassing splendor. . . . [The African section showcases] representations of murals and ethnographic collections that make this trade hall so interesting to the visitor."[92] Diverse arrays of artifacts and advertisements for commercial-industrial merchandise invited a broad cross-section of society to take part in the festivities. Visual evidence from Germany's colonies, while not the exclusive focus of Bremen's trade fair, also reminded patrons of Africa and Asia's imperial ties to the metropole. They particularly attracted a flurry of attention from many leading domestic press organs. "The highly controversial German colonies in Africa," wrote the prominent *Leipziger Illustrirte Zeitung*, "are represented in an extremely far-reaching display, which offers to every spectator a didactic comparison of the relative worth of the individual possessions." Though not everyone appreciated the economic potential of empire, the article continued, "the ethnological collections out of the personal possessions of our African explorers . . . lend us a view of the personal relationships, the household life, the customs and habits of the natives."[93] Gustav Meinecke, the editor of the *DKZ*, proclaimed that Bremen's exhibition will "carry the colonial idea into ever wider circles."[94] While one might expect such a declaration from the German Colonial Society, the fact that so many individuals visited the trade hall suggests that Meinecke's views were not far from the truth. Indeed, official estimates place the number of visitors in 1890 as high as 1.2 million.[95] In many cases, the Bremen exhibition was the first venue where

FIG. 6 Opening of German Colonial Exhibition, Berlin, 1896, postcard. Various proimperial societies and organizations printed and sold cards like these to promote colonialism to large audiences. This one exoticizes the flora and fauna of Germany's overseas imperial domain and the extent to which exhibition organizers went to transform Treptow Park into an imperial setting. Berlin, Deutsche Kolonial-Ausstellung. Photo: akg-images.

passive spectators informally experienced German Africa and Asia. For those in attendance, visibility fabricated a national connection with the imperial world. The more citizens saw of their colonies, the more they wanted them to succeed.

Berlin's 1896 German Colonial Exhibition, among the so-called contemporary wonders featured at the beginning of this section, was perhaps the grandest public forum to showcase Germany's colonial project. The AAKA, along with several private financiers and notable captains of industry, sponsored the exhibition, which took place in the capital city's spacious Treptow Park between 1 May and 15 October. In the words of Paul Kayser, president of the AAKA, the purpose of "the exhibition was to use the objects on display to give a picture of the cultural work carried out in the German colonies over the course of twelve years and to mark the current level of development of the individual protectorates."[96] In order to accomplish this ambitious task, organizers built colorful façades and a reading pavilion with decorative paintings, presented a series of lantern-slide lectures, and handed out thirty thousand free colonial atlases.[97] Event planners invested in these lavish exhibits in order to promote colonialism to as many people as possible. One did not need to board a Woermann Line steamship and disembark in Swakopmund to experience the marvels of empire. Instead, one merely needed to stroll through Treptow and have one's fellow countrymen bring the colony to one in the form of scientific presentations and anthropological displays.

The exhibition also operated as a transnational *Völkerschau* (human display), where Germans and Africans both performed for and observed each other simultaneously. While *Völkerschauen* were not unique to Germany in the nineteenth century, this one surpassed all others in its aggressive effort to showcase colonialism in a beneficial light. Executives wanted to manufacture two outcomes: first, for so-called natives to demonstrate the "oriental splendor" of Africa, and second, for "performers" to portray Berlin as a modern wonderland to their countrymen upon their return to the colony. "The Exhibition Committee was careful to make life as agreeable as possible for the natives and to impress upon them the highest possible conception of European culture," Eugen Neisser wrote in the AAKA's official report on the exhibition. "When they later returned to their homes, they would recount impressions of Berlin to their tribal comrades and thus spread respect and servility before the 'clever white man.' The Blacks were thus not only shown the exhibition, they were also driven around and taken to the sights of the imperial city."[98] Neisser went on to describe some of the spectacles that the AAKA prepared for the African commissions, which included walks through German history museums, a tour of the Zoologischer Garten, various theaters and plays, and military events. "After the natives visited with troops [at one particular ceremony]," Neisser related, "Emperor [Wilhelm II] took the opportunity to speak cheerfully, especially about the Maasai and their slim body shape and dexterity."[99] Racial perversions and stereotypes functioned as the conceptual frames for this meeting between Wilhelm II and the African delegation. Neisser purposely sought to contrast "enlightened" and "benighted" so as to inspire other Germans to witness the *Völkerschau* in Treptow.

On another occasion, the German Kaiser met with Ovaherero representatives from DSWA. Friedrich Maharero, Paramount Chief Samuel Maharero's eldest son, was among those in the delegation, and he took the opportunity to confirm to Wilhelm the Ovaherero's loyalty to Germany and the imperial government.[100] All reports indicate that the Ovaherero representatives wore Western-style clothing for a majority of their time in Berlin. Thus, colonialism in its "enlightened" and "savage" forms was on full display for everyone to see and participate in for themselves. Germany's

FIG. 7 So-called Human Display, German Colonial Exhibition, Berlin, 1896, postcard. The organizers strove to portray African polities in orientalist and racist terms. Like other similar promotions, this postcard depicted Black Africans the way many metropolitan audiences imagined them before they visited Treptow. Human displays (*Völkerschauen*), in particular, played upon these collective voyeuristic sentiments in especially explicit ways. Note how the artist chose to give the figure in the foreground a threatening facial expression and pose, together with what he believed were "traditional" articles of clothing and weapons. Photo: akg-images.

overseas *Heimat* seemingly encompassed elements of normalcy and strangeness, two dynamics that enticed those who wandered through Treptow to inquire about and marvel at their national reach in the world. The 1896 Deutsche Kolonial-Ausstellung alone attracted over 1 million visitors during its six months of operation.[101] Pleased with the exhibition's success, organizers encouraged other imperial societies to sponsor similar showcases throughout Germany in subsequent years. Some of those that followed included the 1897 Deutsch-Ostafrikanische Ausstellung in Leipzig and the inauguration of the Deutsches Kolonialmuseum in Berlin, as well as more modest displays in Regensburg, Nuremberg, Hamburg, Aachen, and other smaller towns throughout Germany.[102]

While these exhibitions indicate the relative ease with which individuals could incorporate imperial narratives, imagery, and merchandise into their daily lives, they also denote the popularity of ethnographic studies among wide segments of the metropolitan population. Public discourses on ethnology and race, of course, were neither new in 1896 nor inherently exclusive to Germany's colonial project in Africa. Independent merchants and Rhenish missionaries, as the previous chapter discussed, were perhaps the most notable figures to circulate ethnographic texts and racist characterizations of Black Africans for German readers in the preimperial era. Thanks in large part to widely circulated periodicals like *Globus* and various other publications, many citizens harbored strong views about the purported behavioral and physical manifestations of Africans long before the 1896 Berlin Exhibition. Scientific texts and ethnographies also continued to generate interest among the general public after 1884. Not only did *Völkerschauen* and museums promote sustained curiosity in the non-European world, but the reality of a German settler colony instigated a collective desire among citizens to learn more about indigenous populations in DSWA.

As individuals informally encountered their African subjects through mainstream channels in Europe, metropolitans wanted more avenues to understand, inform, and shape colonial policy in Africa. From proimperial bureaucrats and their Tuskegee allies in the United States who sought to transform Togolese into sharecroppers to Rohrbach's desire to enforce a rigid "segregation of the races," colonialism influenced German views on ethnography and race in profound ways.[103] Pageants, parades, musical performances, and sensational exhibits expanded the reach of empire to segments of society who never considered how the cultural demeanor of Nama or social practices of Ovaherero might impact their daily lives in Germany. While many women and men continued, in spite of the prevalence of information in the metropole, to look upon the colonial world as foreign, they nevertheless accepted DSWA as an example of Germany's global reach.

Along with pamphlets, maps, and *Völkerschauen*, citizens also gleaned information about their overseas empire from games and school curricula. Toys, in particular, allowed young Germans to participate in civilizational dialogues about imperialism and acts of colonial violence.[104] Like their colonial-enthusiast parents, children pushed the boundaries of their imaginations. Tin miniatures and military figurines, for instance, permitted them to raise Germany's flag in a foreign country, or to join a campaign and defeat a colonial uprising, such as the so-called Boxer Rebellion or Herero Uprising. Regardless of socioeconomic status or a family's allegiance to the nation-imperial project, young Germans wanted to "play empire" in all its forms, and toymakers were active participants in this imaginative process. Children and young adults not only learned about empire in museums or from their parents but also brought it to life on playgrounds and kitchen floors throughout the Kaiserreich. Whether staging Henry Morgan Stanley's famous meeting with David Livingstone or historic battles in the Opium and Anglo-Boer Wars, figurines, miniatures, and toys afforded young Germans a means to fashion close national ties with the overseas world.[105]

Similarly, board games imparted lessons and strategies to their primarily adolescent users, introducing real-life characters and scenarios into a regulated course of play. Games featuring imperial conquest, in particular, allowed children to perform as courageous "bearers of civilization" from the comforts of their own homes, further injecting the normalcy of empire into German national discourses in the late nineteenth century. *Deutschlands Kolonien-Spiel: Eine Reise durch Deutschlands Kolonien* (Germany's colonies game: a trip through Germany's colonies), for example, afforded players a chance to travel to the various German territories abroad, from Europe to Africa to Asia, in a single afternoon. "This game, in which we take a great journey through the colonies," the rules began, "will be greeted joyfully by all."[106] The instructions explained that anyone over eight years old could participate capably, and that each game was played by two to six players.[107] A playing track numbered one to fifty-three sat on top of a map of the world, with a large *Reichsadler* (imperial eagle) perched in the center. All players started with an equal sum of money, which they used to advance forward or to perform various missions on respective stops, and rolled dice on their turn. Competitors began in the port of Hamburg (number 1), and the first to reach Kiautschou, China (number 53), won the game. In each location, one either gained or lost money based on the scenario presented there. If a player landed on number 2, "Im Kanal," for instance, text on the board game announced that "a favorable trip through the canal immediately brings the traveler to no. 8 [one space away from Togo]." An unlucky voyager, meanwhile, might stop on number 5 and discover that "nasty seasickness occurs and will force them to miss one turn."[108] While the dice almost always determined the fate of travelers in *Deutschlands Kolonien-Spiel*, young children—as well as a handful of adults—nevertheless learned that colonialism required bravery, fortitude, financial security, and luck to succeed. They also discovered that both riches and dangers awaited them in Germany's vast overseas domain. If a player landed in Cameroon (number 12), for example, "natives carrying out exercises in a war canoe" forced the traveler to yield two marks to

FIG. 8 *Deutschlands Kolonien-Spiel*, original game board and stations. Creators intended for setup and game play to follow a simple pattern so as to entice a primarily young audience to experience Germany's colonial realms in fun and safe environments. The original instructions went so far as to state that the "colorful illustrations" should make "the world more vivid and tangible." Image: Das Reichskolonialamt, Deutschlands Kolonien-Spiel, http://www.reichskolonialamt.de/inhalt/kolonienspiel/kolonienspiel.htm.

the central till. An even worse fate befell any participant who arrived in New Guinea (Finschhafen, number 29). "A hostile gang of natives," the space read, "wounds the traveler and forces [them] to return to number 19 [Angra-Pequena]." More fortunate players instead disembarked in Damaraland (number 15), where they earned three marks because "the local chief bestows on them a diplomatic gift." Those who arrived in Groß-Namaland (number 18), meanwhile, paid the till two marks, but for a worthy prize: "the hide of a freshly slain antelope killed by the natives."[109]

Deutschlands Kolonien-Spiel aimed to "familiarize German youth with the German colonies and thereby awaken their interest" in the form of artistic maps, dynamic game play, and chance occasions with "friendly and dangerous natives."[110] Similar contemporary board games, such as *Die Kolonisten, Das Kamerun-Spiel oder King Bell und seine Leute*, and *Neues*

China-Spiel, followed a similar pattern. The reality of Germany's imperial project extended not only to colonial enthusiasts in Hamburg and settlers in Windhoek but also to children in times of leisure. Games offered parents and teachers fun ways to instruct young Germans about the national value of empire. Along with museum tours, public exhibitions, picture books, and their own observations of the colonial Other in *Völkerschauen*, toys, and amusements encouraged children to experience the overseas world in the safe confines of their homes and neighborhoods. Over time, they believed that the *Heimat* abroad belonged just as much to them.

Educational curricula advanced a similar agenda. From their earliest days in school, children learned about the overseas world and Germany's rightful place as one of Europe's "great powers."[111] Most especially in the disciplines of geography, history, and anthropology, primary, secondary, and university students all gathered information on Germany's newly acquired flora and fauna, ecologies and environments, and African and Asian populations in considerable detail. Dr. H. A. Daniel's 1891 edition of *Guide to Geography Instruction*, for instance, asserted that physiological characteristics were closely intertwined with sociocultural habits and environment.[112] After a comprehensive review of this assertion, Daniel instructed readers to name all of the races that lived in Africa. Many other educational resources advanced similar ideas on race, ethnicity, and social hierarchy. What united them was a general acceptance of the so-called superiority of "Caucasians" and "whites" over their "Black and sedentary" fellow human beings. While the contemporary interest in geography and history courses does not mean that every teacher prepared lessons according to a uniform patriotic-imperial narrative, such curricula nevertheless brought students informally face to face with the colonial domain.[113] Even if lectures or textbooks presented material unbiasedly, societal pressures often shaped how students received and contemplated the tutorials. In an atmosphere that consistently presented the non-European world in imperial terms, young Germans integrated their own perspectives with an instructor's pedagogy that often mirrored the views of their parents, political officials, and the characters in their games.

As media outlets, trade shows, and exhibitions linked colony and metropole together in one central narrative, all citizens, regardless of age, felt compelled to view Africa and Asia through an imperial lens. Mass media, public spectacles, childhood amusements, and educational programs ushered metropolitan citizens into Germany's imperial age. From kitchens and exhibition halls in Berlin and Bremen to toy stores and schools in Regensburg and Dorf Dussel (Wülfrath), Germans consumed information about the normalcy and promise of the colonial age. The wide availability of resources from and about DSWA empowered industrial and middle-class workers, imperial enthusiasts and antagonists, and women, men, and children of all ages to connect with the colonial world. Their collective lack of experience overseas or personal connections with a specific settler family notwithstanding, Germans steadily incorporated southern Africa's ecology and social makeup into their daily lives after 1884. While official policy-makers continued to influence and shape critical events in the colony, informal encounters informed Germans about the realities of life, both triumphant and tragic, in DSWA. The Kaiserreich's imperial project in southern Africa, therefore, was both a physical orchestration of state power and an organic product of popular histories, travel accounts, ethnographic showcases, and childhood games of chance. Citizens in the metropole came to accept that Germandom not only did, but also should, extend beyond the geographical demarcations of Europe. Such a position, in the words of Carl Gotthilf Büttner, "rested on a solid foundation, even if the new home [*Heim*] still requires more work."[114]

"WHERE ONCE ONLY DRY SAND GREETED THE FIRST GERMAN LANDINGS"

In May 1908, the *DKZ* extolled the successes of Germany's empire in Southwest Africa to its large metropolitan readership. "A quarter of a century has passed since our arrival, and much joy and suffering has occurred in South West Africa; but we have already achieved many things in this short span of time. Where once only dry sand greeted the first German landings, today a flourishing community . . . has emerged, and between Kunene and the Orange River there are currently more than 10,000 white people, most of whom are German sons, who have found a new home here, as Lüderitz once foresaw."[115] Though he did not live to see Southwest Africa emerge as "a flourishing community," as the *DKZ* claimed, Lüderitz passionately championed colonial conquest as a worthy enterprise. His influence on the evolution of Southwest Africa, first as a protectorate and later as a German settlement colony, is clearly evident, most especially in official accounts, periodicals, and memorabilia that proliferated between colony and metropole in the years following his untimely death in 1886.[116]

At the same time in Germany, sympathetic news outlets and proimperial organizations, together with anthropologists, missionaries, museum curators, teachers, and toymakers, underscored the national value of empire in their respective disciplines, fields, and occupations. Dr. Erwin Rupp's contemporary vision for DSWA was typical of the era. "So far, good work has been done in German Southwest Africa by establishing and maintaining order. . . . We have a protectorate which distinguishes itself more than the other German protectorates as a vast land with healthy air under a temperate sky, as a land which allows the white man to carry out his work, which can be a home to German women and which grants their children great prosperity."[117] While not every citizen wanted to emigrate overseas and settle Southwest Africa's open terrains, the more women, men, and children informally experienced colonial life, the more they embraced the colony as a rightful extension of the German nation. DSWA may have started as nothing more than a potential lucrative enterprise for a small, monied cadre of investors, but, thanks in large part to colonial administrators and mass media, it gradually evolved into something much more significant to a national German audience. An overseas empire, these outlets and personalities made apparent, no longer existed exclusively in the hearts and minds of imperial enthusiasts but rather in the cultural spirit of the German nation.

Individuals unquestionably possessed disparate motivations for imperial conquest, as well as numerous opinions about its necessity. Colonial Southwest Africa, nevertheless, pressed Germans to scrutinize their identity in global terms. One might not have agreed with the supposed merits of a colonial empire, but they still had to reconcile themselves with its existence. Imperial propaganda, political testimonials, public displays, and ethnographic showcases all forged an entangled relationship between Germany and DSWA during the formative colonial era. Civilizational perspectives and contemporary racism influenced these informal encounters as well. While relatively few metropolitans explicitly cited racial dominance as a cause for overseas conquest before 1904, collective prejudices provided the foundation for Germany's imperial project in Southwest Africa. These outcomes—informal entanglement and structural racism— simultaneously elevated the status of imperial conquest among all citizens and sculpted *German* Southwest Africa as "a blessing to itself and to the Motherland."

While informal encounters exposed large numbers of metropolitans to the colonial world, Africans did more to transform the lived realities of

Germany's imperial project than any other agents or factors. Hendrik Witbooi and Samuel Maharero, in particular, challenged the colonial government in ways that even the most pessimistic, anti-imperial citizens could not believe were possible. This fact not only led to an expansion of Germany's modus operandi overseas but also progressively moved settlers to rely upon systemic violence to maintain their imperial station in DSWA.

CHAPTER 4

"I Have Done All I Can"

African Resistance and the Evolution of German Colonial Violence

"I CONSIDER IT ILL-JUDGED OF YOUR EXCELLENCY"

In March 1889, Captain Hendrik Witbooi of the Witbooi Nama sent a letter to *Reichskommissar* Göring. "I appeal to you," he wrote, "be so good as to distance yourself from chiefs who engage in treachery [against me]. I consider it ill-judged of Your Excellency to cooperate with those who cannot make peace and are therefore envious of me. Stay neutral . . . so [Captain Jan Afrikaner and I] can fight it out between ourselves."[1] Though the origins of Witbooi and Afrikaner's conflict preceded the arrival of German officials in Southwest Africa, Witbooi's requests were part of a targeted response against the colonial government. He wanted German administrators, in particular, to vacate the "protection treaties" they had negotiated with Afrikaner following their seizure of DSWA in 1884. On the surface, those treaties offered both sides acceptable outcomes at what the popular German periodical *Koloniales Jahrbuch* regarded as "minimum cost."[2] Africans could maintain a degree of sovereignty in their traditional spheres of control, while white settlers could exploit the colony without fear of rebellion. Many Khoikhoi and Bantu leaders also believed that German soldiers could help safeguard their cattle herds from local rivals.[3]

German promises of independence and security, however, never swayed Witbooi. From the very start of the colonial era, he contested imperial hegemony with all means at his disposal. Witbooi's anticolonial program principally centered on his conviction that Nama were masters of their own fate and had a natural right to live outside the bounds of foreign control.[4] After the colonial administration raised the imperial flag in Southwest Africa, he tested the limits of German power using a variety of methods. Witbooi attacked rival groups aligned with the colonial state, rendered trade routes that ran through his territory impassable, forbade white settlers from prospecting on his land, and refused to sell cattle, supplies, and property to imperial forces.[5] He also wrote letters to colonial officers in which he mused on religious matters, his relationship with other regional groups, and the inherent contradictions behind "protection" treaties. Though the signatory powers of the Berlin Conference officially regarded Southwest Africa as a German protectorate in February 1885, colonial authorities could effect very little policy without the support of local populations.[6] In practical terms, Germany's marginal foothold in DSWA before 1894 was largely a result of the aid of Rhenish missionaries and the mercy of Africans—not the other way around.[7]

Along with the Witbooi Nama, the Ovaherero (Herero) were among the strongest polities to challenge German supremacy in DSWA. While the Ovaherero were a diverse and multifaceted Bantu society, Maharero Tjamuaha, and subsequently his son, Samuel Maharero, led one of the biggest factions (Okahandja) of Ovaherero at the start of German colonization.[8] In the formative colonial period, many Bantu populations cooperated waveringly with imperial administrators, mostly for their own political and strategic reasons. Maharero Tjamuaha, for instance, signed a protection treaty in October 1885 in an effort to defend his substantial cattle herds against Witbooi Nama raids in central Damaraland.[9] He soon discovered, however, that the German administration was too weak to provide any real security and eventually rejected the entire government as a false power.[10] After the *Schutztruppe* defeated Witbooi in September 1894, Ovaherero evolved into Germany's primary African antagonists, most especially in the eyes of white settlers. As authorities, merchants, and traders moved to seize more land and cattle in DSWA, Samuel Maharero faced calls from his fellow countrymen to resist German demands forcefully, first in the imperial court system and through political appeals, and finally on the battlefield. During the so-called *Herero Aufstand*, German officers, military recruits, and imperial administrators responded to Samuel Maharero's opposition with sweeping genocidal measures under the command of Lieutenant General Lothar von Trotha.

Scholarship on German colonialism has developed considerably over the past twenty-five years. Much of the recent literature has focused on colonial-era violence and its impact on the emergence of exclusionary political movements in Germany before and after World War I.[11] Jürgen Zimmerer, among the foremost researchers in this field, cites the Herero-Nama genocide as a "significant [moment] in the pre-history of the Holocaust."[12] He writes that it "stands at a decisive interface" between ad hoc massacres on the Australian and American frontiers and "the highly bureaucratized crimes of the Nazis."[13] While he is cautious to avoid crafting a new and uncritical "special path" in German history, Zimmerer identifies structural continuities in the Kaiserreich and Third Reich, such as specific individuals, personnel, national ideologies, and expansionist fantasies, that he sees as links between "Windhoek and Auschwitz."[14] These factors lead Zimmerer to conclude that the Herero-Nama genocide provided the necessary experiential impetus and social conditions for the Nazis' "war of annihilation" in Eastern Europe several decades later. The Herero-Nama genocide, by breaking what Zimmerer refers to as the "ultimate taboo," unquestionably made future genocides possible after 1908.[15] But preconditions alone do not mean that events in DSWA inevitably fashioned an atmosphere that made the Holocaust a likely outcome in post–World War I Germany.

In stark contrast to the Wehrmacht and *Einsatzgruppen* in 1941, most white German settlers did not embark overseas in 1884 or even 1904 with the explicit intention of committing systemic mass murder. This argument does not absolve colonial Germans of their brutal and inhumane history in Africa. Rather, it seeks to trace how Germany's imperial government evolved into a practitioner of genocide in the early twentieth century. If we recognize the *Vernichtungsbefehl* and its annihilatory consequences as genocide—which this study certainly does—we must also scrutinize the dangerous potential of the formative colonial era that helped make it possible in the first place. The same underlying capacities for mass killing existed in other colonial projects in Africa, as well, including those under British, French, Belgian, and Portuguese occupation.[16] Eliminatory continuities, moreover, are not the sole rationale for examining Germany's imperial occupation of DSWA. Searches for a fixed point of exterminatory violence overseas and its potential Nazi inspiration ultimately shift attention away from the very communities that suffered at the hands of German imperial agents, rendering them nothing more than historical annotations to Kaiser Wilhelm II's genocidal atrocities in 1904.[17] The significance of the

Herero-Nama genocide's possible Nazi connection and present-day legacy aside, we must acknowledge that Africans played a more decisive role in Southwest Africa's colonial history than simply being martyrs in imperial Germany's "genocidal moment."[18]

This chapter, therefore, seeks to reorient our understanding of the relationship between colony and metropole, with a focus on how the Witbooi Nama and Ovaherero influenced the evolution of German imperial rule *before* the Herero-Nama genocide. An emphasis on the prominent role of Africans in Germany's early colonial history reveals how peoples in places like Windhoek and Okahandja manipulated the imperial government's efforts to control and exploit Southwest Africa through formal colonial encounters. As calls to suppress Nama and Ovaherero grew louder in the imperial and national press, the German government moved to expand its role in southern Africa, culminating in its declaration of DSWA as a settlement colony in March 1893. In a span of less than ten years, what started as a minor commercial enterprise in a faraway African territory had grown into a juridical constituent of the German nation. As Witbooi and Samuel Maharero revealed the truths of colonial life to settlers, officials grew more determined to neutralize noncompliant African populations. After more soldiers and military equipment arrived in the colony, the size and scope of the imperial regime grew. The financial commitment these efforts necessitated far surpassed what imperial enthusiasts had promised politicians and other delegations in Germany at the start of the colonial era. This fact, in addition to DSWA's dismal economic situation, prompted colonial leaders to rely on the metropole for most of their regulatory and military needs.

Africans played a significant role in this transformation. Their refusal to accept German authority compelled colonial officers to confront their administrative limitations and to question the purpose behind imperial rule in southern Africa. This is not to say that Africans made their own conditions worse through acts of resistance. Colonialism was an inherently violent enterprise, one that pressed entire societies into slavery, economic dependence, and cultural ruin.[19] The conduct, practice, and rationale for imperialism may have differed from empire to empire, but all imperial powers pursued their goals without the consent of colonized populations. Rather, the concentration here on Africans and their successful resistance movements seeks to counter the persistent narrative that misrepresents Nama and Ovaherero as nothing more than passive victims of German domination. More than any other factor, African resistance shattered the

illusion of German cultural superiority, a belief upon which colonial enthusiasts had formulated and justified their imperial-national convictions since
the "liberal revolutions" of 1848. When the veneer of imperial fantasy gave
way to colonial reality, imperial officers increasingly relied on the military
to subdue Nama and Ovaherero populations. In spite of their controversial reception in the metropole, armed aggression and racial malice emerged
as the principal instruments colonial authorities utilized to conquer, defend,
and stabilize *Heimat* Südwest after the turn of the twentieth century.

"I AM A FREE AND AUTONOMOUS MAN"

In August 1894, the popular Berlin newspaper *Berliner Neueste Nachrichten*
wrote that "Witbooi is a character that makes history . . . much like Napoleon Bonaparte."[20] By that time Witbooi had long been a central figure in
Southwest Africa. He was born in the Cape Colony near Pella on the Orange
River in 1830. At the time of his birth, (Kido) David Witbooi, Hendrik's
grandfather, served as chief of the Nama.[21] David Witbooi was the first
leader to establish a permanent Nama settlement north of the Orange River
in Southwest Africa, beginning in the mid-1840s. He eventually led his
people to Gibeon (south-central Namibia) in 1863 and developed a commu-
nalist society centered on cattle, trade, and Christianity.[22] After his death
in 1875, (Kido) Moses Witbooi, Hendrik's father, assumed the chieftaincy
and remained in that position until 1883. Like his father David, Moses
Witbooi followed Christian practices and worked closely with Johannes
Olpp, a popular Rhenish missionary who arrived in Gibeon in 1868.[23] Moses
Witbooi supported Olpp's efforts to build a church and mission station and
also helped found an RMG school in the settlement.

Hendrik Witbooi came of age in this culturally and socially diverse
environment. The third of five children, he devoted himself to Christianity in his adolescence. Missionary Olpp baptized Witbooi and his wife in
1868, an experience that Hendrik later described as the most important
moment in his life.[24] Olpp also celebrated Witbooi's embrace of Christianity, noting in a report to his superiors that the Nama were identical to
Europeans spiritually.[25] After his baptism, Witbooi enrolled in Gibeon's
mission school, where he learned Dutch and German and acquired knowledge in a variety of trades, including carpentry.[26] He became a church elder
in 1875 and used his position to serve the Protestant community in the
region. At the same time, he vowed to act according to divine revelation and

FIG. 9 Captain Hendrik Witbooi with rifle, ca. 1900. In the formative years of colonial occupation, no figures did more to disrupt German imperial fantasies and settlement plans than Witbooi and his Nama followers. Present-day Namibians regard him as one of the forefathers of their country. Photo: Wikimedia Commons / MagentaGreen.

to abjure all non-Christian principles that he feared might undermine his political and religious destiny.[27] Though Witbooi vacated his position as a church elder in 1883, he remained a deeply devout man throughout his life.[28]

In June 1884, Witbooi began the first of several treks north into central Damaraland in search of a new settlement for the Nama. He styled himself a biblical prophet and gained the support of the foremost families in Gibeon. That same year, Witbooi established a settlement at Hoornkrans, an important stronghold in territory under the control of Maharero Tjamuaha and the Okahandja Ovaherero.[29] Witbooi's decision to expand his influence into Hoornkrans initiated a protracted military conflict between both peoples. Several months before this struggle began, however, Maharero Tjamuaha had finalized a protection agreement with officials from the newly arrived German colonial administration. Though he was aware of Maharero's treaty with Germany, Witbooi never wavered in his decision to confront the Ovaherero in Damaraland. Witbooi's campaign against Maharero Tjamuaha in many respects serves as the first example of his total disregard for German authority.[30] At no time did the supposed threat of German political intervention dissuade him from seizing land, cattle, and trade rights from the Ovaherero in the vicinity of Hoornkrans. Witbooi also clashed with other African polities who were under the auspices of German protection, which gradually weakened the colonial administration's political mandate in the colony. The violent encounters between the Witbooi Nama and rival African communities in the mid-1880s were a significant problem for the German imperial government. Above all, instability threatened German economic interests: if colonial administrators could not guarantee stakeholders a return on their investments, commercial and industrial firms had little incentive to "modernize" the protectorate. A period of prolonged warfare, moreover, discouraged potential German settlers from making the long voyage to southern Africa and also ran afoul of the "principle of effectivity," discussed in chapter 1. German leaders, therefore, sought to bring an immediate end to the conflicts between Witbooi and his African rivals.

The fact that imperial officials needed to sign treaties with African leaders indicated that they could not control events in the colony and provoked harsh reactions among prominent enthusiasts in the metropole. It also indicated to the imperial government that displays of national unity or warnings of military force alone were not enough to compel Africans to accept imperial rule voluntarily. Even the language in Germany's initial protection agreements showcased the tilted dynamics of imperial rule during this formative era. Article II of the 1886 "Protection and Friendship Treaty between the German Empire and Manasse of Hoachanas," for example, granted considerable political sovereignty to the so-called Red Nation (Khaiǀkhaun) of Hoachanas under the leadership of Captain Manasse !Noreseb. "His Majesty the German Emperor," the treaty began, "obligates himself to leave in force those treaties which other nations or their citizens have concluded with the Captain of the Red Nation, and at the same time not to interfere in the collection of income in accordance with the laws and customs of his land, nor in the exercise of jurisdiction over his subjects."[31] Though the Red Nation agreed to German protection, Manasse !Noreseb negotiated his right to maintain trade agreements with other foreign countries and also guaranteed his people's legal capacity to follow their own customs and laws without imperial interference. In most criminal cases, moreover, the "Protection and Friendship Treaty" mandated that German

officials first consult with Manasse !Noreseb before issuing a verdict against
any member of the Red Nation. "All civil and criminal disputes between
white people," the agreement declared, "will be tried by those deemed
appropriate by His Majesty the German emperor. The means to determine
disputes between German nationals and other white people and natives,
as well as how the guilty should be punished, will be defined *between the
German government and the Captain of the Red Nation*."[32] Though masters
of the colonial state on paper, Germans could not legally decide juridical
matters without first consulting with their hypothetical subjects. Foreign
governments may have recognized German authority at an international
level, but events on the ground suggested an altogether different reality.

Maharero Tjamuaha's protection treaty of October 1885 granted the
Ovaherero even more independence from the imperial government. Article III accepted their political sovereignty in all civil cases. "The Paramount
Chief [Maharero] assures all German nationals and protected companions
in the entirety of the territory he controls total protection of person and
property. . . . The German nationals and protected companions in Maharero's territory are to be respectful of existing customs and practices and will
not do anything that would violate their penal laws. [They must also] pay
all taxes and fees required of them."[33] Article IV, meanwhile, provided
Maharero Tjamuaha "complete jurisdiction over all misdemeanor and
felony cases" in his areas of control, temporarily extending to European
merchants and traders.[34] While these and other agreements enabled imperial officers to emphasize their hope for greater regional stability and to
declare victory, their nature created several far-reaching consequences.
First, they did nothing except codify what was already a reality on the
ground. Africans controlled the dynamics of the colonial state—from trade
and supply to land rights and cattle—in every way but name. Second, they
publicized the extent of Germany's imperial weakness for the world to see
and contemplate. Once news of the actual power structure in DSWA
reached a metropolitan audience, enthusiasts, politicians, travel writers,
and others lost their ability to frame Germany's colonial narrative informally. Africans assumed an active role in the evolution of Germany's
imperial project and only grew more influential over the course of the
imperial era.

Thus, the fact that Witbooi refused to sign a protection treaty with
German representatives proved even more newsworthy than reports of
successful negotiations with other polities. It served as an open act of defi-
ance, pressing women and men in the metropole to consider the actual

extent of German power in Southwest Africa. It also forced officials like *Reichskommissar* Göring to reach out to Witbooi diplomatically, something that probably few imagined possible or necessary before 1884. In June 1886, for instance, Göring encouraged Witbooi to end his "hostile actions" in the colony. "Act reasonably," he implored him, "realize that the best course is to return home and live in peace with your old father and your tribe. The German government cannot permit chieftains, who have placed themselves under German protection, to support your enterprise of plunging a protected chiefdom into war. . . . I trust you will attend to my words."[35] Witbooi simply ignored Göring's message and continued his campaign for supremacy against the Ovaherero.

Later that same year, Witbooi received a letter from Louis Nels, a deputy officer in the service of Göring, inviting him to participate in a conciliatory meeting between the various warring communities in Walvis Bay, where imperial authorities hoped to facilitate a peace treaty.[36] In response, Witbooi instead chose to remind Nels of the political power dynamic in the colony. "I understand that you want to negotiate peace," he wrote, "you who call yourself a 'deputy.' How shall I respond? You are someone else's representative and I am a free and autonomous man who only answers to God. I have nothing further to say to you. A deputy is less powerful, so I have decided not to comply with your request."[37] Neither Göring nor Nels responded to Witbooi's diplomatic reproach. With the limits of German power on full display, imperial officials were at a loss on how to end the violence in DSWA. Göring understood this reality perhaps better than anyone. In June 1888, he wrote to Chancellor Otto von Bismarck describing the overall situation as "not very encouraging."[38]

Colonial leaders initially had few options for enforcing imperial policy in DSWA. With no sizable German settler community or *Schutztruppe* to enforce their declarations, administrators could do little on the ground to stabilize the military state of affairs. In spite of these limitations, colonial officers responded to Witbooi with blanket threats and open challenges to his authority. Göring most especially never concealed his disdain for the so-called Hottentot chief.[39] He chastised Witbooi in private letters to superiors, colleagues, and journalists, as well as in his personal diplomatic exchanges. On one such occasion, for example, he described Witbooi as "a rebel" and warned that "in civilized countries, he would be dealt with accordingly."[40] In April 1889, Göring went so far as to threaten open war if Witbooi did not halt his attacks against groups allied with Germany. "The German government," he warned, "can no longer tolerate your constant threats—again and again—against territories and peoples that are under German protection. We shall endeavor to prevent [your attacks] with every means at our disposal."[41] For his part, Witbooi adopted a strict diplomatic approach with German officials. In addition, he reached out to other European powers and tried to emphasize the inherent contradictions underlying German imperial directives.

Witbooi's prior relationships with Protestant missionaries and European traders helped him gain access to foreign embassies and international media outlets. In a letter to the British magistrate in Walvis Bay in August 1892, for instance, Witbooi accused the German government of the very crime that protection treaties would supposedly avert. "After what I have heard and seen since the arrival of the Germans," he asserted, "it seems to me that the German himself is that powerful man who wants to invade our country. . . . He rules autocratically, enforcing his own laws. Right and truth do not interest him."[42] Witbooi was well aware of contemporary European geopolitical rivalries. He reasoned that if he could gain diplomatic support from Great Britain, Germany's most prominent European competitor in southern Africa, colonial authorities could no longer pursue their imperial goals without risking a larger war with the British Empire. Through these means Witbooi manipulated "great power" politics to benefit his own pursuit of independence and supremacy in Southwest Africa.

In an effort to broaden his appeal even further, Witbooi emphasized his knowledge of the Bible and regularly cited Christian teachings when engaging German leaders and European diplomats. After Samuel Maharero had negotiated a new treaty with the colonial administration in 1890, for example, Witbooi compared his situation to Christ's after Herod and Pontius Pilate had forged an alliance to "get the Lord Jesus out of the way."[43] When the colonial administration published his correspondence, European audiences gained greater familiarity with Witbooi and the convictions behind his resistance to colonial authority. Witbooi was careful to amend his style and tone in his correspondence with Europeans. In May 1890, for instance, he castigated Göring for his refusal to treat the Nama as a free and independent people. "How you raise such great, weighty, and grave topics in your letter astonishes me," Witbooi wrote. "You have not left me room and scope to ponder all in my heart, so that I might answer you from my own good judgment and free choice. Moreover, you have not approached me as an impartial peacemaker, but uttered abrupt orders as to what I should do."[44] Though forceful throughout his letter, Witbooi pleaded for tolerance and mutual respect. He spoke of Göring as "his friend" and expressed a desire "to live in mutual understanding" with one another. "I say all of this not in arrogance or as a challenge," Witbooi closed, "but only because I cannot put the matter in any other way."[45]

While Witbooi hoped that the inflection and validity of his words might convince German authorities to extend him a free hand in Southwest Africa, his successful resistance only enticed policy-makers to seek immediate solutions to the instability in DSWA. Germany's civil and military presence in the colony began to grow exponentially after 1889, directly reflecting Witbooi's decisive role in Germany's formative colonial history. His diplomatic and military skills obliged imperial leaders to search for new ways to stabilize DSWA politically. Witbooi's engagement with foreign diplomats and Protestant missionaries, moreover, often allowed him to express his motives in terms that European audiences understood—namely, religious freedom, national determination, and foreign intrusion. A variety of factors informed German imperial strategy in the 1880s, including financial constraints, regional and international trade agreements, European colonial rivalries, German domestic politics, and the growth of anticolonial movements after the turn of the twentieth century. Witbooi, however, pressed German leaders to recognize the preeminent status of African peoples in the colony. In this manner, he not only exposed the inaccuracies of European precolonial beliefs but also pressured German administrators to centralize and expand their occupation of DSWA.

The appearance of a small contingent of the colonial *Schutztruppe* under the command of Captain Curt von François in 1889 was the first sign of this expansion.[46] Though the military situation in DSWA remained a significant problem after their arrival, the presence of German soldiers revealed that Witbooi had provoked German authorities to act decisively with force of arms. As imperial and foreign media outlets focused more attention on events in the colony, the suppression of Witbooi evolved into a national story in all corners of the German metropole.

FROM "RELENTLESS SEVERITY" TO THE "LEUTWEIN SYSTEM"

The same year Witbooi began his treks north into central Damaraland, Adolf Lüderitz arrived on the shores of Southwest Africa. After Bismarck proclaimed Lüderitz's territorial possessions a *Schutzgebiet* in 1884, Germany's political leadership wanted to limit their imperial commitment to Southwest Africa and keep state costs at a minimum.[47] As noted in chapter 3, the DKGfSWA emerged out of this collective desire. While the German government retained control over political affairs in the new protectorate, the DKGfSWA assumed a majority of the financial obligations.[48] In return, the Reichstag granted corporate investors monopoly control over all private enterprise in Southwest Africa.[49] Colonial expansion, even into a region "whose economic value was debatable," raised greater social awareness about the protectorate and its potential for the German nation.[50] Though the vast majority of citizens had nothing to gain personally or financially from the DKGfSWA and its operations overseas, colonial supporters believed that the future of Germany's entire imperial project was at stake in the deserts of Southwest Africa.

For advocates of imperial expansion after 1884, however, the most significant problem was Göring's inability to control events on the ground. Instead of stories that glorified African subjugation or accounts of economic development and growth, Witbooi's campaign of resistance enticed journalists to portray the Nama as the true masters of the colony. "Up until now," one editorial argued in September 1887, "the German protectorate of Southwest Africa has existed only in name. People are being told so many things about the might of the German Empire, but no one ever sees it applied. Either the German Empire makes a move to maintain its prestige, or it will have to abandon the territory it has gained. The current situation is one of which Germany must feel ashamed."[51] Though German society was anything but monolithic in its support of colonial expansion, Witbooi's provocations against his African rivals, his diplomatic outreach to foreign embassies, and his total disregard for German authority galvanized enthusiasts on both sides of the issue. Detractors of imperial conquest cited the financial obligations of perpetual war against a determined enemy, whereas proponents argued that Witbooi was a significant threat to imperial rule and thus required a greater commitment from the German state. In turn, public perception of colonialism increasingly grew into a national debate as reports on DSWA proliferated throughout the metropole.[52]

The culmination of this national debate occurred when Chancellor von Caprivi proclaimed DSWA a German settlement colony in March 1893. "We do not intend to make war," he announced before the Reichstag, "but wish to become masters of the country and to consolidate our sovereignty without bloodshed. We possess Southwest Africa once and for all; it is *German territory* and we must preserve it as such."[53] Though Caprivi still aspired to keep the state's financial obligations to a minimum, his decision affirmed the significance of the colony for the German nation-state in definitive terms. The Witbooi Nama alone did not entice Caprivi to declare DSWA a settlement colony. Their persistent opposition to imperial rule, however, compelled German officials to confront the consequences of imperialism. In addition, Witbooi's constant attacks on African rivals demonstrated to colonial leaders that the metropole needed to provide more financial and military support to guarantee success.

Kaiser Wilhelm II's decision to promote Curt von François, the officer who founded Windhoek, to *Landeshauptmann* was the first demonstration of Germany's newfound commitment to colonial governance. François had served both as a paid mercenary for King Leopold II in the Belgian Congo and as a commanding officer in the colonial *Schutztruppe*.[54] As someone who espoused civilizational views of African polities, François saw Witbooi as a mere "tribesman" whom he could defeat with relative ease. "The Europeans have failed to give the Black man the right kind of treatment," he wrote after his arrival.[55] "They made too many concessions, granting all his wishes without bearing in mind that this is only interpreted as a sign of weakness. Nothing but relentless severity will lead to success."[56] François soon discovered, however, that the Witbooi Nama controlled vast herds of cattle and rich expanses of territory, had reliable access to vital resources such as water and foodstuffs, and possessed state-of-the-art weaponry and an abundant supply of ammunition. Moreover, his responsibility as *Landeshauptmann* required him to consider the totality of governance and not just military affairs. On the one hand, he believed that the colony's potential was tied to cattle farming, agricultural exports, and local commercial development. If DSWA was ever to become a rich and marketable colony, future German settlers needed Black African laborers to work on their behalf. François feared that any war with Witbooi could endanger the postwar economic stability of the region.[57] On the other hand, François assumed that if the power dynamic in DSWA did not soon change, Germany's presence in southern Africa might disappear altogether.

François eventually pursued the only course of action that he understood. "Only serious, strong-minded, and forceful actions against foreign nations, as well as quick diplomacy and success in battle," he later wrote, "could excite the support of the German people."[58] On multiple occasions, he submitted requests for military reinforcements and weaponry from Berlin. "I consider it a matter of urgent necessity," he contended, "to bring the force to a strength of fifty men, to equip it with the latest small-bore repeating rifles, and to make available a cannon, complete with one hundred shells and fifty shrapnel shells."[59] While he waited for his soldiers, François arranged to meet with Witbooi at headquarters in Hoornkrans in 1892. François offered to pay him an annual stipend of 5,000 marks if Witbooi promised to cease his attacks against other African populations.[60] He also warned Witbooi that his campaign for supremacy stood no real chance of success. "Large numbers of Europeans will soon arrive by ship, and they must be protected," François informed the Nama leader. "The German government is obliged to protect all who place themselves under German protection."[61] Witbooi responded with an affirmation of his sovereignty. "An independent and autonomous chief is leader of his people and land," he asserted. "Every ruler is chief over his people and country. When one stands under the protection of another, the subordinate one is no longer independent [or] master of his people or country. . . . We are different nations and live by different laws and customs, and come from different countries. Each chief lives with his people according to his own laws and the conditions in which they find themselves."[62] Witbooi justified his resistance campaign in patriotic terms, which not even François could refute. After the meeting, François acknowledged privately to Witbooi that he also "could not bear to be bossed [around]."[63]

The conference at Hoornkrans was a watershed moment in German colonial history. It corroborated François's prior belief that military action was the only reliable solution to what he called the *Eingeborenenfrage* (native question).[64] He again requested more reinforcements and heavy artillery from Berlin. François also inundated German and foreign newspapers with negative accounts of the Witbooi Nama.[65] In spite of his preparation and colonial propaganda, François's war against Witbooi shocked even the most enthusiastic supporters of German imperial domination. In March 1893, 214 soldiers departed for Windhoek from Walvis Bay. François's orders to his troops were clear: "The object of this mission is to destroy the tribe of the Witbooi."[66] In the early morning hours of 13 April 1893, the *Schutztruppe* surrounded Hoornkrans and unleashed an artillery barrage against Witbooi's encampment. Though Witbooi and a majority of his male soldiers escaped the encirclement, German troops killed nearly one hundred Nama women and children as they slept in their homes.[67]

While François hailed Hoornkrans as an immense victory, domestic and international press agencies' depiction of the "battle" had a chilling effect in the metropole. As the South African *Diamond Fields Advertiser* explained in May 1893, a majority of women and men in Germany did not support an imperial occupation that required a "colonization by bullets" to succeed.[68] Accounts such as the one the *Cape Times* first published on

16 May were at the center of François's problem: "Intelligence has been received from Damaraland that on April 12 a German force of 200 men, with Captain François in command, stormed the stronghold of Witbooi and killed upwards of 70 women, ten men and boys, and some infants. The object of the expedition was to punish Witbooi for harrying the Herero tribes, who are under German protection. The official report expresses regret for the death of the women, but, it is urged, a sudden attack and indiscriminate firing were the only means of capturing the stronghold."[69] Two days later, the *Norddeutsche Allgemeine Zeitung* questioned why "some bullets found their way to women and children."[70] Such an atrocity, the editors maintained, "would not further the imperial cause" in a righteous direction.[71] Even the *Frankfurter Zeitung*, whose readership tended to champion imperial-national causes passionately, reminded its subscribers that Hoornkrans was not the first time François had targeted women and children in battle.[72] "Witbooi has carried out his raids in Damaraland for years under the eyes of the *Schutztruppe*, and as a result," the article scolded, "the latter has retaliated where an opportunity arose. Thus, in October 1891, 37 Witbooi women and children were murdered in Damaraland."[73] As late as January 1894, nearly a full year after the attack, the *Hamburger Nachrichten* described how "women and children fled to outposts seeking cover, only to be met by soldiers who shot them down."[74]

Instead of a land of freedom and national promise, Hoornkrans made DSWA look like a place where German authorities sanctioned mass murder indiscriminately. Metropolitans already skeptical about the colony's economic potential were quick to cite the human cost and financial burdens of warfare overseas.[75] Those nervous about Germany's reputation after the massacre, meanwhile, pointed out that Witbooi had evaded capture and now posed a greater threat to German imperial ambitions than at any time since 1884. Many factions also expressed fear that François could no longer confine the war to German colonial soil. The *Vossische Zeitung*, a popular newspaper among Berlin's liberal establishment, cited the arrival of the British warship *Magpie* in Walvis Bay in August 1893 as a cause for great national concern. François's actions, the paper alleged, have done nothing but "attract more circles to the troubles in DSWA."[76] His failure to apprehend Witbooi and the torrent of negative press in the aftermath of Hoornkrans eventually pressed Kaiser Wilhelm II to appoint Theodor Leutwein as governor of the colony in April 1894.

Leutwein's emergence stands as a powerful example of the impact of colonial encounters on public sentiment in Germany. Mass media exposed the imperial world—both its triumphs and tragedies—in vivid detail. Though DSWA was far away geographically, editors and travel writers, together with African women, men, and political leaders, made the colonial project a tangible reality for citizens in Europe. From stories on vast mountain ranges and herds of cattle to stories on "rebellious natives" and acts of military brutality, metropolitans confronted DSWA from the confines of their homes and towns. After Leutwein assumed political control, he used his newfound authority to reshape the entire social structure of the colony. He favored an economy that supported plantation-style estates and affluent German settlers, analogous to the socioeconomic system in contemporary Prussia.[77] Leutwein claimed that well-propertied Germans stood a better chance overseas than "the lonely white farmer who can easily enter into concubinage with a native woman."[78] He also sought to expand the power of the German colonial administration. Though he always maintained that the "personal needs of settlers [should] be taken into account," Leutwein privately doubted that a large-scale settlement program could succeed without the support of a powerful colonial government.[79]

Before his plans could come to fruition, Leutwein recognized that he first needed to reconcile Germany's relationship with Witbooi. In stark contrast to his predecessor, Leutwein favored diplomacy and negotiation over military action. In February 1894, Leutwein wrote Witbooi about François's pending dismissal and expressed his desire to establish a lasting peace between Germany and the Nama. "In consideration of the gallantry shown by yourself and your men," he wrote, "I hope to work out favorable conditions, if you will cooperate in this final chance to put an end to the bloodshed."[80] Three months later, Leutwein explained that "Germans do not intend to wage war against your people, [but instead] wish to work together in peace with you. I therefore hope that your people will accept my pledge that they may return to their homes with my permission."[81] In his reply, Witbooi congratulated Leutwein on his promotion and acknowledged that renewed discussions offered a greater prospect for peace. But he also reprimanded Leutwein for what he called an "unwarranted assault against his people" and warned him that any peace "will require more than a few minutes or a single day to arrange."[82] Witbooi understood that the political dynamics in DSWA had changed after François's attack on Hoornkrans, but his convictions remained resolute. He wanted to impress upon Leutwein that the Nama were a proud nation who simply wanted to retain their cultural and political sovereignty. If Witbooi could frame his resistance campaign in national terms, he thought, Leutwein might respond as a geopolitical rival and not as an imperial master.

The exchanges between Leutwein and Witbooi over the next five months consisted of courteous diplomatic outreach, blunt conversation on protection treaties, and fierce disagreement over the merits of European colonialism in Africa. Though both men never lost sight of their own respective goals, they eventually developed a strong personal bond, as Leutwein later acknowledged in his memoirs.[83] We should not, however, forget the inherently violent circumstances that brought them into contact in the first place. Leutwein, after all, was unapologetic in his belief that Germans were justified in ruling DSWA regardless of Witbooi's personal sentiments or pledges of friendship. He may have approached Nama polities differently than François, but Leutwein still harbored civilizational conceptions of the world and its peoples. Diplomatic overtures and negotiation were perhaps his preferred method of seizing control, but Leutwein retained a sizable military presence in the colony and pledged to forge a decisive outcome one way or another.

In late August 1894, he wrote Witbooi one final time and informed him that he could no longer accept the "unstable peace" between their respective forces. "The fact that you do not want to submit to the German Empire is not a sin, nor does it make you guilty. But it is extremely dangerous for the stability of the territories currently under German protection. Therefore, my dear Captain, all further letters in which you do not offer your surrender are in vain. I hope we shall agree to conduct this campaign, which has become inevitable thanks to your truculence, humanely. I also hope it may be brief."[84] In spite of his desperate situation, Witbooi still refused to give in to Leutwein's demands. He reminded Leutwein of the "massacre at Hoornkrans" and asked him to consider Germany's international reputation and the consequences that might follow another act of colonial aggression.[85] Ignoring Witbooi's counsel, Leutwein encircled his military encampment in August 1894. Low on supplies and surrounded, Witbooi surrendered to Leutwein on 8 September 1894. Witbooi's campaign against German colonial rule—at least for the present—was over.

The Treaty of Protection and Friendship Between the German Empire and Hendrik Witbooi ushered in a new era of colonial rule in DSWA. Though it was only five pages long, Leutwein hailed it as a sign of Witbooi's "wholehearted devotion to the German cause," a belief that he maintained for the remainder of his tenure as governor.[86] News outlets like the *Kölnische*

Zeitung praised the agreement as a positive indication of permanent stability in the colony: "The differences between settlers' letters from 1893 and 1894 are clear!"[87] Most especially, peace with Germany transformed life for Witbooi Nama in profound ways. Article I of the treaty, for instance, established that they no longer dictated affairs in Southwest Africa: "Captain Witbooi wishes for his people and his successor to come under the protection of His Majesty the German emperor. Captain Witbooi promises the German government to support loyally its efforts to keep and ensure the general welfare of Namaland and Southwest Africa forever."[88] The accord also created a special demarcated zone for Witbooi and his followers to inhabit. Leutwein additionally forced Nama to comply with all German civil and penal codes, regardless of where they lived in the colony. Colonial authorities permitted Nama to resolve only "conflicts between natives exclusively" without German supervision.[89] At the behest of Leutwein, however, the imperial government did allow Witbooi and his countrymen to keep possession of their weapons and ample supplies of ammunition. He justified this decision based on his "belief that Captain Witbooi [is] a man of his word."[90]

Witbooi did more to expose the limits of German power than any other person in southern Africa between 1884 and 1894.[91] His devotion to Protestantism, his skillful leadership, and his persuasive diplomacy obliged German officials to question the nature and purpose of colonial rule in Africa: was a peace wrought by bullets an acceptable form of domination, and, if so, who stood to benefit from it? The public response to the "massacre at Hoornkrans" provided a clear answer to both of these questions. Kaiser Wilhelm II's decision to embrace the so-called Leutwein system meant that the German state was financially and politically committed to DSWA. The protectorate's evolution from a private boondoggle into a settlement colony, however, was not inevitable. Though private firms remained essential agents for the creation of a market-based economy in the colony, profit margins were no longer the sole measure of success. As a settler colony, DSWA served as an extension of the imperial state, thus inextricably tying German national interests to southern Africa. The preservation of that reality necessitated regional stability, economic promise, and peaceful relations with African communities—which were only possible after Witbooi's defeat.

Life for Witbooi Nama transformed markedly as well. Despite the restrictive terms in the Treaty of Protection and Friendship, Witbooi committed his people to the agreement unconditionally. Nevertheless, he feared greatly for the Nama's future, as he clarified to his friend Rhenish missionary Tobias Fenchel in Keetmanshoop (southern Namaland) several days before the 1894 Christmas holiday. Witbooi was "very grateful" for the newfound harmony in the region and pledged that "everything on my side would be done to preserve the peace." He also confirmed his trust of Leutwein and said that he considered him a "dear friend." Fenchel also reported, however, that Witbooi had doubts about the long-term prospects for his people. Witbooi explained that he saw insoluble problems ahead, "both for my tribe, for I have nothing, absolutely nothing, on which they can live, and also for my relationship with the German government. There are understanding men among the Germans [referring to Leutwein], who can make allowances for our character as Nama and treat us accordingly: but there are also ruthless men who can only give orders, and they frighten me. They will take their revenge on us, and will seduce our women, despising us."[92] The callous behavior of settlers, traders, and soldiers in Hoornkrans and elsewhere throughout his ten-year resistance campaign convinced Witbooi of the evils behind foreign encroachment. He also rightly assumed that the imperial government's raison d'être was the fulfillment of white German settler interests and property demands, not an equitable peace that guaranteed prosperity for both colonizer and colonized. Though Witbooi kept his pledge to remain subject to imperial law, he accurately described the nature of the colonial state to Fenchel. As he contemplated the seriousness of what awaited the Nama and his allies in defeat, Samuel Maharero moved to take advantage of the new political situation in the colony. So, too, did the German government.

"IN DIRECT CONFLICT WITH OUR COLONIAL AMBITIONS"

In December 1894, the same month that Witbooi discussed the perils of his subjugation with missionary Fenchel, Samuel Maharero welcomed Leutwein and his imperial vanguard in Okahandja. As troops walked along the streets, they saw German flags hanging in windows, throughout market squares, and from rooftops. Members of the *Schutztruppe* recounted that residents proudly displayed the metropole's colors throughout the town, reserving the largest flags for elders and other prominent individuals' homes. When Leutwein arrived in front of Samuel Maharero's house, the Ovaherero leader ordered his fighters to fire a volley into the air in honor of Germany's recent victory over the Witbooi Nama.[93] Though Leutwein traveled to Okahandja in order to negotiate a southern boundary for all

Ovaherero territory in Damaraland, a festive mood prevailed throughout Samuel Maharero's capital. German soldiers and imperial officials, without question, had not experienced such a celebration in their entire ten-year occupation of Southwest Africa.[94]

Politically, Samuel Maharero owed much to Leutwein. Earlier that same year, the German leader had supported his claim as the rightful "paramount chief" over his principal Ovaherero rivals, most notably Nicodemus Kavikunua (Gobabis), with force of arms.[95] Leutwein did so, as he noted in a report to the *Reichskolonialamt* (German Colonial Office) in June 1894, to foment unrest among Ovaherero leaders and subgroups. While the *Schutztruppe* focused its attention on the Witbooi Nama that summer, Leutwein took a long-term view of Germany's situation in southern Africa. In candid terms, he professed that "it is obviously more convenient for us to deal with a politically divided Herero nation than with a closed and unified one."[96] Leutwein later added in his memoirs that "such a beneficial opportunity to influence Herero affairs was not soon again to be expected," leading him to intervene on behalf of a possible German ally.[97] Samuel Maharero, meanwhile, was not aware of Leutwein's hidden agenda. In exchange for German imperial protection and the paramount chieftainship, he agreed to entertain future conversations about the delineation of Ovaherero and white settlers' territory. Their informal alliance thus seemingly promised favorable outcomes for both individuals: stability and evidence of his governorship's potential for Leutwein, and political supremacy and social hegemony for Samuel Maharero.

From the metropolitan perspective, the German victory over Witbooi ushered in a period of relative amity throughout Damaraland for the first time since 1884. Leutwein, however, wanted to use the newly won peace to enhance the colonial government's power regardless of the wishes of Samuel Maharero. He reasoned that he could manipulate the paramount chief's personal ambition to Germany's strategic advantage. In a report to Chancellor Chlodwig zu Hohenlohe-Schillingsfürst, Leutwein explained that the Ovaherero's friendly welcome in Okahandja "was not based on an outpouring of love for us, but rather on love for power, which up until now I have made available to [Samuel Maharero] liberally in order to strengthen his authority."[98] Leutwein assumed that in spite of their military aid, German officials could not count on Samuel Maharero's cooperation reflexively. He aimed, therefore, to govern DSWA using two principal methods: diplomatic outreach and military prowess. Leutwein viewed treaty negotiations as the most effective demonstration of Germany's political supremacy. If

FIG. 10 Samuel Maharero in uniform, ca. 1900. After imperial forces defeated Witbooi in 1894, Maharero and the Ovaherero emerged as the principal threat to German colonial goals in DSWA. In the immediate wake of Lothar von Trotha's "annihilation order" in October 1904, Maharero and approximately twelve hundred Ovaherero escaped across the border into British Bechuanaland (present-day Botswana). Namibians also regard him as one of the original heroes in the country's history. Photo: Wikimedia Commonos / Vysotsky.

colonial authorities could prevent Africans from forming a united front against the German regime, they could divide and conquer the country more easily.

Leutwein's formal encounters with Nama the previous two years had convinced him that any successful occupation of DSWA required a strong state to broker agreements between the various parties throughout the colony. The meeting in Okahandja also afforded him an occasion to organize Southwest Africa into demarcated settlement zones. Leutwein reasoned that if he could force Africans to live in specified districts, German colonists could then settle in resource-rich areas without fear of physical confrontation. A southern border in Damaraland represented the first step toward that goal. Before both leaders gathered to negotiate the delineation of a boundary, however, Leutwein announced his intention to pay Samuel Maharero an annual stipend of 2,000 marks for "maintaining peace and order in the territory."[99] While some officials regarded the offer as nothing more than a bribe, to Samuel Maharero the imperial governor's proposition was a sign that their fluid alliance could continue without a common enemy to bind them together. Therefore, he agreed in principle to a southern border for the first time in Southwest Africa's history.[100]

Samuel Maharero was not naïve; he knew that this contract privileged the colonial administration and also potentially weakened his relationship with other Ovaherero polities, most notably those in the eastern provinces.[101] He believed, however, that the current state of affairs did not favor the Ovaherero in the event of a hostile and prolonged confrontation with German troops and settlers. In his estimation, all factions needed to unite under his leadership first before they could hope to counter Leutwein's overreach with any serious chance of success. Thus, Samuel Maharero's original claim of ownership over the entire country notwithstanding, he accepted a division of his most prosperous territory along a racial color line. In subsequent years, the consequences would be far-reaching for all African societies. While not Samuel Maharero's intention, the agreement signaled his de facto acceptance of the Leutwein system and the structural legal advantages it afforded German settlers. The paramount chief evidently intended to uphold peaceful relations with the colonial regime at any cost. Most significantly, however, the 1894 Okahandja treaty denoted the colonial administration's intent to use juridical and physical acts of violence to maintain its foothold in southern Africa. A clear example of this reality surfaced almost immediately. Only two weeks after the conclusion of their conference, Leutwein confided to Samuel Maharero that any "Herero caught trespassing beyond the southern boundary would be shot at as a last resort."[102]

Though Germany's colonial governor, Leutwein was not the only person to influence and shape the imperial narrative of the colonial state. Perhaps unlike a majority of his fellow colonists, however, he also operated with the knowledge that few people in Germany wanted "a bloody war of conquest."[103] As long as a majority of German settlers and politicians believed that an "occupation through negotiation" provided the best means to achieve success in DSWA, Leutwein could count on public and royal approval for his colonial initiatives. In spite of these intentions, compromise and diplomacy did not mean harmony and peace. Armed conflict and suggestive military displays, he understood, would likely always have a key role in *Heimat* Südwest. For instance, Leutwein showed no reservations when he deployed the *Schutztruppe* against "his friend" Hendrik Witbooi in September 1894. Nevertheless, imperial and metropolitan leaders agreed that their fundamental objective in the colony was economic growth and regional cohesion. Centralized acts of armed aggression usually created more problems than solutions. The only way for unrestrained physical violence to replace the Leutwein system, therefore, was for a majority of white German settlers to lose confidence in its ability to forge what they regarded as sustained peace and stability.

Leutwein also understood that the sovereign interests of German and Ovaherero populations made for a delicate situation. In a missive to Chancellor Hohenlohe-Schillingsfürst shortly after the Okahandja conference, he explained that even though Samuel Maharero had consented to their terms, the Ovaherero still "shrink from two things which are in direct conflict with our colonial ambitions": the sale of land and cattle to white colonists. Such obstruction, in Leutwein's view, hampered Germany's ability to transform Southwest Africa into a protocapitalist settlement. "The whole future of the colony," he continued, "lies in the gradual transfer of the land from the hands of the work-shy natives into white hands." Though this process should occur "gradually and peacefully," Leutwein manufactured a colonial arrangement that favored German priorities above all else but, he knew, stood little chance of permanent success without some level of equity and fairness for their African subjects.[104]

Perception and policy, however, flowed both ways. Leutwein may have fashioned an imperial system that presented a semblance of civil hierarchy and order, but he also recognized that any regional stability rested on an unstable foundation. Their military victories and auspicious diplomacy aside, white German settlers were not the unfettered masters of Southwest Africa in 1894. Administrators appreciated that their imperial declarations garnered favorable responses in sympathetic outlets in the metropole but also understood that such pronouncements only mattered if the imperial government could coerce Africans to follow their agenda accordingly. All Ovaherero polities possessed the same capability as the pre-1894 Witbooi Nama to affect the dynamics of the colonial state. From the size of their cattle herds and knowledge of the region to their reputation as formidable fighters, Ovaherero women and men, even in times of peace, could alter Leutwein's grand plans for German Südwest simply by maintaining their traditional ways of life. Samuel Maharero, more than any other person, used this unspoken leverage to his full advantage.

While the political machinations of one man—in this case the Ovaherero paramount chief—alone do not reflect the importance and totality of this central argument, they do amplify just how much Samuel Maharero's actions determined Leutwein's initiatives during this formative period. Both the imperial governor and the paramount chief, without question, benefited politically from their casual alliance. Leutwein, however, needed Samuel Maharero's compliance far more than the other way around. Like his German counterpart, he understood the hidden value of manipulation. In exchange for cattle and land, for instance, Samuel Maharero convinced Leutwein to recognize and defend his chieftainship against an arguably more legitimate claimant, Nicodemus Kavikunua.[105] Though many of his fellow countrymen perceived his association with Leutwein as problematic, Samuel Maharero was fully aware that the imperial government lacked the means to enforce its overreaching contracts. He could strengthen his position, in the words of the *Koloniales Jahrbuch*, at "minimum cost," while simultaneously giving the appearance of obedience to his supposed German overlords.[106]

Formal encounters of a diplomatic and peaceful nature, much like Witbooi's cattle raids in the 1880s, generated outcomes that pressed officials in DSWA to respond defensively. Africans did not have to lead daring missions against imperial troops in the same style as Witbooi to affect Germany's settler-colonial project. They could instead utilize their soft power to counter and refocus imperial advances in more subtle ways. Leutwein certainly wanted to present himself as a man of action, but the dynamics of the colonial situation still confined German policy-makers inside a reactive framework. Over time, the realities of their position vis-à-vis Ovaherero regional supremacy—or at least the collective fear of its potential—steadily pushed white settlers to seek the same violent recourse against Samuel Maharero as they had against Hendrik Witbooi in Hoornkrans. Whether through acts of open resistance or a continuation of calm ambivalence, Ovaherero women and men preserved their cultural ways of life within an otherwise repressive imperial structure, a circumstance that shaped the political evolution of DSWA drastically between 1894 and 1904.

An important example of this fact occurred shortly after Leutwein and Samuel Maharero concluded their conference in Okahandja in January 1895. Though he authorized the colonial government's wish for a southern boundary, Samuel Maharero knew that Nicodemus Kavikunua, who lived east of Windhoek in Gobabis, would not abide by the strictures of the treaty voluntarily.[107] Leutwein's "divide-and-conquer" strategy provided Samuel Maharero an occasion to outmaneuver both men without any physical display of violence. He could claim that he approved of the boundary but that he did not have the power to enforce it without German soldiers. If Leutwein chose not to commit the *Schutztruppe* to such a hypothetical campaign, the Ovaherero paramount chief could adopt the same passive approach without fear of imperial retribution. On the other hand, if Leutwein confronted Nicodemus Kavikunua militarily, the presence of Okahandja Ovaherero soldiers promised to strengthen the German leader's commitment to him even further. Either way, Samuel Maharero and his people stood to benefit from the arrangement.

As Samuel Maharero predicted, the treaty enraged Nicodemus Kavikunua. When he received the terms of the treaty, he and one hundred armed Gobabis fighters prepared to confront the German boundary commission as it approached Omitara (east of Windhoek) later that same January. When both sides met in Omitara, Kavikunua demanded significant revisions to the settlement contract.[108] In response, Leutwein ordered Friedrich von Lindequist, a high-ranking official in the colonial administration, to survey the contested areas of the boundary with Kavikunua and several of his subchiefs. After inspecting various locations along the banks of the Nossob River, which on paper divided white settler and Ovaherero territory, Lindequist discovered that the natural geography of the region made it impossible for anyone to uphold the integrity of the demarcation. "He who has seen the great density of the Hereros on the banks of the Nossob and their huge herds of cattle," Lindequist wrote Leutwein after the expedition, "will surely find [a granting] of a respite [to Nicodemus] justified. Only a constant bloodletting from the side of German traders, as practiced by Witbooi three years ago, will decrease the herds of cattle to the right size and make the occupation of the whole of the right bank of the Nossob by Germans possible."[109] Leutwein quickly realized the dangerous complexity of the situation after he read Lindequist's report. On the one hand, if he acquiesced to Kavikunua and the Gobabis Ovaherero, he risked losing all of the domestic and international legitimacy that the imperial government acquired from its victory over Witbooi. On the other hand, if German troops tried to force the Gobabis Ovaherero to comply with the Okahandja agreement, they might delegitimize Samuel Maharero's paramount chieftainship and potentially start a war across the entire country.

Faced with no other option, he modified his hardline stance and agreed to a compromise. "I do not want a boundary," Leutwein avowed to Samuel Maharero in February 1895, "that I receive at such a cost. . . . The whole colonial history teaches us that the cry 'The Whites want to take our land!' has always led to bloody uprisings."[110] While a border remained in place, Kavikunua's obstruction and Samuel Maharero's careful manipulation proved, once again, that Germans could not govern the colony without ample consideration for how their so-called African subjects might answer in kind. The implication of this phenomenon is immense, for it further demonstrates how Nama and Ovaherero societies influenced Germany's colonial project in the years before the outbreak of the Herero-Nama war.[111] Most significantly for this study, Nama and Ovaherero resistance campaigns denote just how persuasive colonial encounters were on the national development of *Heimat* Südwest. Where Witbooi used cunning advances and charismatic diplomacy, Samuel Maharero relied upon political manipulation and soft power to challenge Germany's imperial authority. Regardless of the merits or limitations of these strategies, they both shattered the illusion of primordial German supremacy. Colonial enthusiasts and others within the so-called imperial consensus continued to embrace notions of national and racial superiority, of course, but events in DSWA consistently revealed those positions as utter delusions. While neither Witbooi nor Samuel Maharero alone was responsible for Leutwein's increased centralization and reliance on armed persuasion, their efforts exposed the limits of Germany's reach more than any other dynamic. The Okahandja conference and its fallout in the eastern provinces conveyed this argument in clear terms. Even with a legal contract, German settlers were seemingly at the mercy of the local environment and population. The Leutwein system secured a negotiated peace, but not total German supremacy.

Along with the Okahandja meeting, three additional examples during this same period exhibit how local events manipulated the trajectory of Germany's Southwest African settler colony. The first was the deterioration of Samuel Maharero and Leutwein's relationship with Kavikunua and his Ovaherero allies. In the aftermath of Lindequist's setbacks at the Nossob River in February 1895, Leutwein mandated that German soldiers accompany all future settlement and survey commissions in Damaraland. He also directed Samuel Maharero to deploy Ovaherero troops to join these delegations.[112] This tactic almost immediately produced positive outcomes for Leutwein. Throughout the remainder of that year, African leaders who had been opposed to Samuel Maharero's paramount chieftainship withdrew their objections when they faced a united German and Okahandja force. In exchange for Leutwein's military assistance, Samuel Maharero signed treaties that were amenable to the colonial administration, empowering the paramount chief to sell land and cattle to the imperial government without the consent of local Ovaherero leaders.[113]

Though Africans had little choice but to acquiesce to these forced land sales, such involuntary measures generated an intense collective animosity toward the imperial government. Kavikunua, together with Kahimemua

Nguvauva, leader of the Ovambanderu, and Andreas Lambert, leader of the Khauas-Khoi, particularly resented Germany's constant infringements on their daily lives.[114] Leutwein, however, was largely oblivious to these growing tensions. "At that time," he later reflected in his memoirs, "it looked very peaceful in the middle of Hereroland, in which the border question [*Grenzfrage*] was irrelevant. Everywhere troops were greeted with joyful astonishment and everywhere the Hereros swarmed around us unarmed and trusting, just begging for tobacco."[115] Leutwein continued that "the Hereros sensed their impending containment to the periphery [but] made a visible peaceful impression on the outside."[116] Despite their supposedly serene outward appearance, Africans suffered considerably from dispossession and the loss of their traditional homelands. They simply could not accept such blatant disregard for their lives and customs forever.

A significant number of German colonists, however, deemed Leutwein's initiatives as far too accommodating to Africans. Settler representative Carl Weiss, for instance, submitted several complaints to the colonial government about what he regarded as the problems of Leutwein's "mild stance on *Eingeborenen politik*."[117] His objections were terse and laced with civilizational overtones. On more than one occasion, Weiss went so far as to demand the immediate dismissal of any official who did not reflexively favor the rights of German settlers over those of the Ovaherero. Though among the most vocal, Weiss was certainly not alone in his negative views of Leutwein. In January 1896, Hermann Sander, a self-described twenty-two-year-old Welshman, wrote that "the Hereros come over to the whites from the east every day and trouble them in small groups."[118] He could not fathom why the German government tolerated such cavalier acts from their supposed subjects. In a separate petition, Ferdinand Otto, Sander's friend and neighbor, confirmed his statement about the "daily infringements by the Hereros." Otto also included a litany of his own complaints about the "shortsightedness" of Leutwein's policies. Toward the end of his five-page letter, he asked rhetorically why white colonists needed to summon German troops "to ward off native [*Kaffern*] settlers" with such regularity.[119] Otto's verbal attacks against Leutwein seemingly provided a clear answer. Each of these petitions called for Kaiser Wilhelm II to expel Leutwein from the colony. As they testify, tensions over colonial land policy and Africans' sovereignty thus threatened the unstable peace in Damaraland, regardless of Leutwein's subsequent recollections.

Public demonstrations and calls for reform eventually forced German policy-makers to recognize the dangerous situation in the colony. In an effort to avoid another war, Samuel Maharero, Leutwein, and all of the major Ovaherero chiefs agreed to take part in a second conference in Okahandja at the end of January 1896. On the first day of the meeting, Leutwein pledged to shift the southern boundary demarcations once again. Kavikunua, however, was unable to convince the imperial governor to remove the German military garrison in Gobabis. The daily presence of armed soldiers in their territory caused considerable anxiety and frustration for his people.[120] This matter proved decisive. While everyone strove to avoid military conflict, few believed that their revised agreements could permanently alleviate the divisions between German settlers and Africans in Damaraland.

Near the end of March 1896, forces under the command of Kavikunua, Kahimemua Nguvauva, and Andreas Lambert attacked the imperial garrison in Gobabis.[121] After fierce fighting that lasted into April, Leutwein and Samuel Maharero emerged victorious. Despite Kavikunua and Kahimemua Nguvauva's claims of innocence, the German government found them guilty of high treason and sentenced them to death in June 1896.[122] Andreas Lambert fled to Bechuanaland to avoid the same fate. Over the course of that same summer, imperial soldiers placed all remaining enemy combatants in concentration camps in the vicinity of Windhoek, where they worked as forced laborers for the colonial state.[123] While this outcome ushered in a renewed period of compulsory reconciliation in Damaraland, the means German officers used to stabilize affairs in the colony underscored their increased commitment to state violence. A combination of administrative fear and individual desire ultimately pressured Leutwein and white German settlers to seize even more land and resources from "uncooperative Africans." The colonial government, in a similar manner to the 1894 Witbooi campaign, sought to enforce its will over anyone whom German colonists perceived as a potential threat. Perhaps the only difference in 1896 was the government's ability to expand its violent recourse to include systematic imprisonment and capital punishment.

The second major encounter to affect the political and social trajectory of DSWA was the outbreak of rinderpest and typhoid in the colony. An infectious viral disease that causes fever, dysentery, and inflammation of mucous membranes in cattle, rinderpest was, in Leutwein's words, "the most feared animal epidemic in Africa."[124] This particular plague first arrived on the continent in the 1880s. The disease slowly moved southward from the Horn of Africa until it reached the Zambesi River, where present-day Zambia's natural geography sequestered the outbreak until 1895.[125] "At first, it was believed that it could be blocked off. A cattle-free zone of 20 km in diameter," Leutwein penned in his memoirs, "was therefore created along the [northeastern] border and a corresponding increase in the number of border stations was arranged. . . . The invasion of the plague could not be prevented in the long run, however, simply by the fact that it also seized wild game."[126] In spite of the imperial administration's early preventative efforts, rinderpest spread into central Damaraland before the conclusion of 1896. Some studies estimate that the outbreak killed over 95 percent of all African-owned cattle within six months of its arrival in Southwest Africa.[127]

Reports of the outbreak brought the true scale of the crisis to life in shocking detail. Stories about the enormity and swiftness of the epidemic must have seemed unimaginable. According to a group of Rhenish missionaries who departed Otjimbingwe in an ox wagon for Walvisbay in 1897, "It was a gruesome road. It was covered with ox bones. A couple of weeks ago the Finns with 5 waggons lost 82 oxen. The road could not be otherwise, as in one year 880 consignments were transported inland, of these over 500 passed Otjimbingwe. During the past year 10000–12000 oxen passed Otjimbingwe as draught animals."[128] A road covered in potentially thousands of sun-bleached ox bones presented a grisly picture for readers. It also worried German merchants and commercial investors, who feared how the epidemic might impact their business interests in southern Africa and Europe.

After the epidemic crossed into DSWA, Leutwein moved rapidly to confine the outbreak to the colony's border regions. He sent police units to blockade roads, issued temporary bans on cattle importation, and followed the advice of three well-known veterinarians who recommended a statewide inoculation program,[129] including experimental vaccines, enforced physical isolation, and the mass killings of herds whom authorities believed carried the virus.[130] Though the German government, perhaps surprisingly, did not purposely limit these remedies to regions with white-settler majorities, most African cattle owners never received inoculation treatments, either because they lived far away from Windhoek and other colonial centers or because some local leaders regarded such measures as a further extension of imperial domination.[131] Despite these efforts, rinderpest continued to spread throughout the entire country. The outbreak largely spared southern Namaland the worst outcome, but only because of its arid climate and dispersed population centers. Regardless of this one "victory," however, the epidemic caused severe environmental and social damage throughout the entire country.

While rinderpest certainly affected German imperial and economic interests, its impact on Ovaherero polities was devastating and socially ruinous. The loss of their vast cattle herds on such a cataclysmic scale destroyed their traditional modes of life. All at once, the epidemic collapsed the Ovaherero's ox-based transport systems, artificially inflated the price of essential goods and merchandise, and weakened their political sovereignty and cultural independence.[132] In the wake of Samuel Maharero and Leutwein's military triumph in Gobabis, the confluence of destructive events forced Ovaherero communities to rely increasingly on the colonial government for all of their most basic needs. Their situation only worsened the following year, when systemic crop failures, droughts, and outbreaks of typhoid, malaria, scurvy, and anthrax killed as many as ten thousand people.[133] Leutwein's demarcated settlement zones heavily contributed to the swiftness of this biological catastrophe. Never before in Southwest Africa's history had people lived so closely together in such confined spaces. As a result, no amount of inoculation or physical separation could reduce the horrific impact of rinderpest and typhoid in the colony.

The third factor to influence the colony's political and social evolution was white settlers' collective aim of reducing African agency entirely, which eventually pressed Samuel Maharero to call out the dangerous potential of his supposed German ally. Though the rinderpest and typhoid epidemics tied Ovaherero polities ever closer to the colonial state, their most consequential legacy was that they pressured Black Africans to sell enormous tracts of land to white settlers and soldiers. Such an action—inconceivable before 1896—seemingly provided Ovaherero leaders their only means to recover their self-sufficiency. Cattle, regional trade, and landownership had enabled Ovaherero polities to flourish even after the arrival of German colonists in 1884. The sweeping collapse of mercantile activity and mass deaths of their cattle herds and oxen, however, offered them limited means to generate revenue and to maintain their social independence. Within only a short period of time after 1896, German landowners expanded their reach into areas that prior treaties recognized exclusively as Ovaherero territory.[134]

While Leutwein and the imperial government certainly welcomed the *idea* of more territorial control, the *reality* proved far more complicated and hazardous to the long-term development of the colony. Most policymakers believed that Ovaherero cattle herds would eventually recover from the rinderpest epidemic.[135] Leutwein feared that when they did so, questions over land and private property might once again lead Germans and

Africans down a path of conflict. Rhenish missionaries, in addition, spoke out adamantly against these forced land sales. They reasoned that if they could no longer build mission stations or enroll local populations in German-language programs, the RMG's presence in the region might altogether disappear. Rhenish missionaries thus emerged as vocal supporters of the rights of Ovaherero and other African communities in Damaraland. Leutwein and more trustworthy religious agents, therefore, moved to eliminate the Ovaherero's ability to sell land to white merchants, traders, speculators, and military officers and troops. In 1899, the colonial administration passed legislation that forbade German settlers from accepting territory as a form of debt payment. Two years later, Leutwein also introduced plans to create inalienable land reserves for individual African polities throughout the colony.[136] White colonists, unsurprisingly, sharply opposed Leutwein's plans. In their minds, the imperial governor's proposals threatened to cheat them out of their legal land purchases. They also believe that "native reservations" (*Eingeborenenwerften*) endangered their ability to acquire territory in new and potentially resource-rich areas in the future.

For his part, Leutwein chose to ignore the pleas of German settlers and traders. In spite of his position as German governor, he carried deep reservations about the ultimate objectives of his white imperial constituents. Years later, in a report to the AAKA, Leutwein wrote that "the Europeans flooding into Hereroland were inclined, with their inborn feeling of belonging to a superior race, to appear as members of a conquering army, even though we had conquered nothing." He also decried their actions as ignorant "of the protection treaties [that we] signed with the Herero. They did not know that according to article 3 of the treaty, *ratified by the German emperor*, the Germans were pledged to respect 'the particular customs and practices' of the Herero. But at the very least the ruling Herero knew as much."[137] Leutwein cast German colonists in an even more negative light after Kaiser Wilhelm II dismissed him from DSWA in 1905. He went so far as to blame them—and not Samuel Maharero—for regional destabilization and ultimately the outbreak of the *Herero Aufstand*:

> There has never been one individual system in Southwest Africa with regard to indigenous treatment, nor could it have ever existed, contrary to popular public opinion in the metropole [*Heimat*]. Rather, there was only one system in the German motherland, which was the avoidance of a bloody war of conquest, which is why

> our colonization in Southwest Africa began with the conclusion
> of protection and trade contracts with the natives, and thus the
> protection of German trade, as well as the life and property of
> whites living among tribal chiefs. . . . The means of power corre-
> sponded only to this point of view, because without the participation
> of the chiefs they could not offer whites sufficient protection.
> Anyone who thought this system was wrong usually attacked indig-
> enous people and only received lenient treatment. But this was not
> enough to break the system itself. In other words, the change in
> our system had to be preceded by a significant increase in our
> means of power, both materially and in personnel. To answer the
> question "how much," all one needs to do is look over at South-
> west Africa today [1907].[138]

While one must consider this statement in the light of the German Kaiser's
public removal of Leutwein, his words are consistent with policies that he
either enacted or attempted to pass after the rinderpest and typhoid epidemics. Leutwein never wavered in his political career on brokering treaties
that benefited German colonists at the expense of African polities. We
should not, therefore, romanticize him as a humanitarian advocate or as a
sincere friend to Witbooi and Samuel Maharero. On the other hand, he
personified the full extent to which formal colonial encounters influenced
German imperial policy at the turn of the twentieth century. "The change
in our system" he alluded to—that is, white Germans' sweeping control of
DSWA—came about from genocidal warfare, not protection treaties.

The more Africans shattered their racist illusions, the more German
colonists and like-minded enthusiasts embraced violence as a solution for
their economic and social ills.[139] Even before 1903, Leutwein understood
that German settlers—short of "a bloody war of conquest"—could not rule
the protectorate without some measure of diplomacy and negotiation.
When military defeats and biological disasters upended the Ovaherero's
ways of life in seismic ways, he nevertheless strove to honor their prior
agreements with an eye toward posterity. By that time, however, a majority of white traders, soldiers, and settlers did not share the same "tolerant"
perspective regarding German colonial rule in Südwest. In addition to
Leutwein, Samuel Maharero was also well aware that tensions between the
imperial government and individual settlers did not favor the long-term
prospects of his people. Throughout the spring and summer of 1903, frustrated settlers and alcohol-fueled soldiers began to target Ovaherero women

and men in isolated acts of violence throughout the country.[140] Independent commissioners with the support of several patrols in the *Schutztruppe*, meanwhile, tried to revise border agreements with African leaders without Leutwein's direct knowledge.[141] Over the course of that year, rumors of an impending rebellion started to spread throughout the colony as a result. When Lieutenant Ralph Zürn allegedly confirmed their worst fears and fired upon a group of peaceful Ovaherero representatives near Waterberg in January 1904—an action that formally started the *Herero Aufstand*— neither Leutwein nor Samuel Maharero could do anything to quell the jingoistic ambitions of colonists and their metropolitan supporters.[142]

These biological and foreign calamities weakened Ovaherero societies in profound ways. Most detrimentally to their political livelihoods, the consequences of rinderpest and typhoid entangled Africans even more closely with the imperial government. The realities of their condition forced Ovaherero leaders to sell vast stretches of territory to white settlers.[143] A series of systemic misfortunes had thus thrust Africans into a perilous situation. As Ovaherero women and men looked to Leutwein and the government for aid and the hope of returning to some semblance of normalcy, individual German settlers increasingly believed that they could act with impunity toward their African subjects. In the wake of two tragedies, one on the battlefield and one epidemiological, German colonists considered themselves even in the balance of power for the first time in their occupation of DSWA. Leutwein and his associates, despite their own efforts to disenfranchise Africans from their homes and livestock through military action and negotiation, nevertheless regarded constant acts of brutality as a sign of an unsuccessful colonial regime.[144] Germany was in Southwest Africa, or so they thought, for economic prosperity and national glory. "I do not concur with those fanatics," Leutwein asserted in February 1904, "who want to see the Herero destroyed altogether. Apart from the fact that a people of 60,000 or 70,000 is not so easy to annihilate, I would consider such a move a grave mistake from an economic point of view. We need the Herero as cattle breeders, though on a small scale, and especially as laborers. It will be quite sufficient if they are politically dead."[145]

Eliminatory warfare only emerged as a potential solution to Germany's colonial situation when the private aspirations of a virulent nationalist minority seized control of the imperial narrative. No one act of African resistance or formal encounter predicated DSWA's evolution into a genocidal and apartheid state, twin subjects that the subsequent chapter will chronicle in detail. But consistent challenges to their presence in the colony, together with an internal acceptance that German colonial fantasies were indeed nothing more than delusions, ultimately positioned hardline forces—namely white farmers and members of the *Schutztruppe*—to dictate the stakes of victory and defeat. In this group's opinion, there was no longer any room for negotiation. All that mattered was unchecked supremacy. "The change in our system," to quote Leutwein, occurred once the colonial regime received a "significant increase in [its] means of power, both materially and in personnel."[146] When Lieutenant General Lothar von Trotha assumed command of the government in May 1904, he and his supporters were willing to unleash the genocidal potential of the colonial state so as to fashion—once and for all—a white German homeland in their imperial image.

"COUNT UP THE SOULS WHO HAVE PERISHED"

As Germans strove to distinguish themselves as citizens of a newly unified state after 1871, they did so with considerable awareness of the world beyond the European continent. Once Germany entered the "African scramble" in 1884, the colonial sphere slowly grew into an important aspect of national life. Colonial fantasies may have instigated a public fascination with Africa, but formal encounters with Africans exposed the cultural illusions behind preimperial discourses. The realities of colonial rule persuaded supporters to question the necessity of the colonial project. After Caprivi designated DSWA a settlement colony in 1893, enthusiasts subsequently relied on nationalism, geopolitical rivalry, and racial segregation to defend Germany's presence overseas.

Frederick Cooper and Ann Laura Stoler remind us that European empires "were neither monolithic nor omnipotent."[147] They balanced a myriad of political agendas, economic strategies, and systems of control to maintain power in their respective imperial and overseas domains. Germany's occupation of Southwest Africa exemplifies this argument in several notable ways. First, the appearance of German officials in DSWA did not immediately transform the political and social dynamics of the colony so that they favored the colonial government.[148] Even after the first contingent of imperial soldiers in the *Schutztruppe* arrived in 1889, most local Africans, as well as resident German missionary associations, still regarded the Nama and Ovaherero as the most powerful polities in Damaraland.[149] Second, imperial leaders were at a loss over how to confront and overcome the persistent challenges to their authority. Witbooi's refusal to accept German rule and Samuel Maharero's skilled political manipulation, in particular, pressed policy-makers to consider a wide range of strategies. German officials not only tried diplomatic outreach and bribery but also issued blanket threats—all in an attempt to pressure Witbooi and Ovaherero subchiefs to submit peacefully. When those policies failed, they sanctioned the use of armed aggression to drive first the Nama and later the Ovaherero from power.

Neither Witbooi nor Samuel Maharero ever signed a ship manifest or published an editorial in the *Deutsche Kolonialzeitung*. They nevertheless played a decisive role in German colonialism and the evolution of the settler-colonial project. In both their published correspondence and their military confrontations with African rivals and the colonial government, Witbooi and Samuel Maharero made Germans recognize the fallacies behind European precolonial views. Their endeavors necessitated reactions from the colonial administration, as opposed to the other way around. François and Leutwein, most especially, personified this reality in their own separate ways: one responded with bullets, cannons, and murder, while the other sought a balanced approach of negotiation, diplomacy, and military confrontation. Their careers denote the limits of German imperial power, as well as the brutal measures that colonial officials were willing to exercise in order to sustain a presence in southern Africa.

European colonialism was an inherently violent enterprise in all respective cases. In Germany, collective motivations for empire fluctuated as costs rose and conditions grew more brutal. By the turn of the twentieth century, nationalism had gradually evolved into a central factor in German colonial policies. As exclusionary politics and racial segregation became more important to Germany's imperial agenda, Africans found fewer outlets to enjoy their own cultural, religious, and political ways of life beyond the reach of the colonial government.[150] In response, the Ovaherero and later the Witbooi Nama eventually found themselves in another violent conflict in 1904—one that forever shaped their respective cultural and social ways of life.

At the height of the so-called *Herero Aufstand*, Witbooi sent the following lines to Leutwein: "I have for ten years abided by your law, stood under your law, and behind your law—and not I alone, but all chiefs of Africa. For this reason, I fear God the Father. You accuse me of murdering helpless white people and say that eighty of my men are in your custody, but who shall pay for the white people? I beg you, when you read this letter, sit down and quietly reflect [on my words]. Count up the souls who have perished in this country since you arrived, and the weeks and days and hours and minutes since they died."[151] With these words, Witbooi not only justified his decision to join Samuel Maharero in his fight against the *Schutztruppe* but also once again altered the nature of German colonial affairs in DSWA. Though he did not live to see the end of his renewed campaign against imperial occupation, Witbooi's impact on German imperial practices carried into the next violent phase of colonial rule. In particular, he pressed settlers overseas and citizens in the metropole to question the kind of colonial power that they wanted Germany to be in the twentieth century. After the start of the Herero-Nama war, imperial authorities gave their answer in genocidal terms.

PART 3

An Imperial Homeland, 1905–1914

Where has the great vanished people
of the mighty Herero gone? Where are
their hundreds of thousands of cattle? . . .
Major von Estorff, the well-tried and
brave "old African," advanced in October
1904 (two months later) to the east along
the waterless bed of the Eiseb; the lack
of water forced them to turn around. . . .
The assumption that the whole people
were destroyed by thirst and hunger in
the sand of the Omaheke is more and
more likely.
—Anonymous German soldier, 1907

CHAPTER 5

"My Nearly White Wife"

Colonial Citizenship and the Racial Boundaries of Germanness

"ULTIMATE SOURCE OF CONTROL IS VIOLENCE"

In September 1909, Carl Becker, a German cattle farmer living near Vaalgras in southern Namaland, wrote to Bruno von Schuckmann, imperial governor of DSWA,[1] to convey his apprehension over a series of race laws the German colonial administration had passed earlier that same year, specifically paragraph 17f of the Regulation of the Reich Chancellor concerning Self-Government in German Southwest Africa.[2] The regulation revoked Becker's right to participate in all future elections because his wife was a *Bastardfrau* (Rehoboth Baster woman) and also called into question the legal status of the couple's five children, including two who were living in Germany.[3] Before 1909, Becker had probably given little thought to the hazardous potential of the colonial government. Indeed, his family's prior status as German cattle farmers had the advantages of freedom, adventure, and, as the colonial recruitment posters promised, endless potential to fashion an ideal life in *Heimat* Südwest. Paragraph 17f, however, threatened the hopeful optimism and political legality behind the Beckers' colonial fantasies.

Left with no other alternative, Carl Becker pleaded his family's case to Governor Schuckmann. He called the regulation "an illegitimate act designed to deny him civil rights and marriage."[4] Becker also claimed that German authorities had no legal right to subject his marriage retroactively to such a law because his wife was "nearly white."[5] His argument was both logical for the time and overtly hypocritical. Becker endorsed the inferred collective belief of whiteness as an essential component of *Deutschtum* and simultaneously attacked the restrictive nature of race thinking as it applied to his family's legal struggle. He claimed that "§ 17 is born of the following idea: Southwest Africa is white man's land."[6] Though Becker was himself a white man, the colonial government had thrust him into the precarious position of colonial Other. While Becker emphasized his contempt for the new state of affairs in DSWA, he did so with a notable degree of caution. Near the conclusion of his letter, Becker conceded that the government "has all the power" and that its "ultimate source of control is violence."[7] This remark was likely an reference to Germany's victory in the Herero-Nama war two years earlier, a "triumph" that culminated in the genocide of approximately ninety thousand Herero and Nama peoples between 1904 and 1907.[8]

Carl Becker's plight embodies how imperial race policy in DSWA affected the lives of Africans and German settler colonists in the aftermath of the Herero-Nama genocide. He and his family, moreover, demonstrate the elusiveness of German identity, an imprecise construct that wove together individual and shared perceptions of citizenship, culture, language, geographic origin, and race both before and during the imperial age. Finally, Becker and his wife's experiences serve as a clear example of the dangerous capabilities of states in the modern era. In the aftermath of the first genocide of the twentieth century, the colonial government retained the exclusive capacity to decide the Beckers' political orientation in relation to the German polity. Neither their familial background and linguistic aptitude nor their national heritage and devotion to the colonial project merited Becker's family legal affiliation with the German Empire. Carl Becker certainly imagined himself and his family to be part of the national community, but the imperial regime moved to exclude them from it once race evolved into the defining element of German colonial identity.

The Beckers' legal concerns came at a crossroads in Germany's occupation of Southwest Africa. For the first time since 1884, German settlers were the unquestioned masters of the colony. "The change in our system" that Leutwein described in his memoirs had extended unfettered control to colonists who increasingly determined their national station along a racial color line.[9] Nevertheless, questions over the ambiguity of citizenship and the status of so-called mixed-marriage couples continued to torment German judicial bodies in both colony and metropole.[10] Local and national courts had an especially difficult time adjudicating "mixed-marriage" cases that produced children, as the hereditary parentage of the father typically determined citizenship in Wilhelmine Germany.[11] Before 1904, hierarchical dogmas and myths of cultural supremacy pervaded colonial society at every level. The same racial intolerance, for instance, that radiated throughout Dr. Max Buchner's writings in *Die Gartenlaube* also affected colonized peoples' lives in horrific ways that produced equally horrific outcomes. As Gesine Krüger has contended, however, German settlers and soldiers principally relied on these racist postures in the formative colonial period in order to justify treating Africans as "economic assets" that they could exploit for their own benefit.[12] Xenophobic attitudes alone, in other words, did not sanction or even encourage wholesale mass murder *as such*, because white settlers were more concerned with indenturing Black Africans to the colonial state as free labor. Racist practice and rhetoric unquestionably created an atmosphere that made wholesale brutality like the Herero-Nama war a distinct possibility, but they initially served colonists as violent mechanisms that they intended to use for their own financial and personal gain. The Herero-Nama genocide forever changed that worldview. After 1904, German settlers strove to craft a racial state that served the interests and livelihoods of white colonists exclusively. The so-called *Eingeborenenfrage* (native question) and *Frauenfrage* (women question) replaced the so-called labor question. "Racial separation" replaced "cultural education." Ethnic deviancy replaced "noble inferiority." Genocidal warfare pushed racial superiority to the forefront of Germany's imperial lexicon and elevated racial segregation and malice into the primary functions of the colonial state.

Racisms are, admittedly, fluid constructs that adapt to and draw upon perceived situational experiences within domestic, national, imperial, and societal registers. They seldom emerge in isolation and are often the product of biases that familial groups and local communities transmit from one generation to another through sensationalized accounts, myths, and stories. Historically speaking, where racism exists, some form of violence follows. Racists seek to defame, intimidate, or physically attack those whom they deem inferior as a means to avow their own civilizational superiority, to uphold economic inequality, and to defend the so-called biological, cultural, and national purities that supposedly make them a preeminent people. As Benedict Anderson has argued, while "nationalism thinks in terms of historical destinies, racism dreams of eternal contaminations, transmitted from the origins of time through an endless sequence of loathsome copulations."[13] If we accept this premise, then polities that imbue racist logic into their sociopolitical agenda can justify systemic brutality and oppression more easily because the "Other" living amongst them represents a universal threat to their primordial identities.

Segregatory racism in DSWA was no different with respect to its evolution and manifestation among white colonists after the Herero-Nama genocide. As the previous two sections have illustrated, racial prejudice in all its forms heavily influenced precolonial and early colonial explanations for overseas conquest in Germany. While these contemporary rationalities produced horrific outcomes for indigenous peoples in Southwest Africa, ranging from forced encounters and foreign solicitation to land displacement and armed violence, racism alone was not the sole apparatus behind German imperial authority. Individual desires for adventure and wealth, alongside collective advances for glory, power, and national purpose, generally drove colonial and metropolitan enthusiasts to champion imperialism as an essential dynamic of German identity. Once Africans laid bare the mirage of German colonial logic, however, first in the person of Hendrik Witbooi and then during the consequential period between 1894 and the outbreak of the Herero-Nama genocide, eliminatory racism evolved into a preeminent role in the colony. It alone provided cause for Germans to adopt universal solutions to imperial problems that had seemingly plagued the colonial project since its inception.

After the genocide, one's race operated as the only determinative measure in colonial society. White settlers seized control over every aspect of political life and looked to use their newfound power to target African survivors as enemies of enlightened progress. Imperial officials banned and later nullified "mixed marriages," raised the social status of white European women, and forced German politicians to reconsider their position on the colonial project in Southwest Africa. In this manner, institutional racism and state-condoned acts of physical and juridical violence evolved into twin cornerstones of postgenocide DSWA. "Race thinking," an ideological conviction that embraced ethnic belonging and purity as the driver of national politics, assumed social primacy and marginalized all other modes of imperial categorization and governance in DSWA. Most consequentially, it persuaded settler colonists to embrace racial segregation as their main weapon to establish permanent white German rule in the colony.

This chapter traces the evolution of *Heimat* Südwest into an apartheid state between 1904 and 1914. It concentrates on four conditions that shaped this process: (1) the imperial government's adoption of *Rassentrennung* (racial separation) as official policy, most notably through bans on "mixed

marriages" and the construction of *Eingeborenenwerften* (native settlements), (2) an increase in metropolitan efforts to encourage white women
to emigrate to DSWA, (3) the colonial administration's categorization of
Afrikaners and other non-German groups in strictly racial terms, and (4)
the electoral landscape in the metropole, which culminated in the so-called
Hottentot elections of 1907. These four conditions exemplify how hierarchical assertions of race came to define the boundaries of German colonial
citizenship in the wake of the Herero-Nama genocide. The same was true
for supporters of the colonial project in Germany. Colonialists, nationalists, and politicians from across the ideological spectrum used their
perceptions of DSWA as a mirror to replicate what they saw as the essence
of an ideal national-imperial character. By 1914, a majority of white settlers,
together with their allies in Berlin, defined that character in racial terms.

"*RASSENTRENNUNG*": SEGREGATING THE SOUTHWEST AFRICAN *HEIMAT*

On 16 October 1908, Dietrich Reimer, Germany's consul to the Cape Colony,
sent a letter to the AAKA in Berlin to criticize an article that had appeared
in the *Norddeutsche Allgemeine Zeitung* the previous month.[14] Entitled
"Koloniales," the article advocated a plan to grant voting rights to all foreign
and African subjects living in DSWA. Though the proposal enjoyed support
among some white settlers in the colony, Reimer wanted to voice his strong
opposition. He argued that German imperial policy should instead follow
the example of neighboring European colonial powers and severely restrict
voting rights in DSWA. Doing so had the potential to forge permanent
white rule in Südwest, especially since a majority of Herero and Nama in
1908 were either dead or locked away in forced labor camps. Reimer further
argued that the voluntary forfeiture of what he saw as "hard-fought victories" through initiatives such as equal suffrage might lead to dangerous
consequences in the future. "It has been said that the personal character
[*Eigenschaft*] of the community is to be practiced through three classes,
namely Germans, other whites, and natives. The treatment of these classes,"
he asserted, "*should* be different. Only Germans are full citizens, while
foreigners, in recognition of outstanding achievement or special economic
capacity, may only be granted the right of participation (voting rights) by
the community."[15] In Reimer's mind, the current law was not only well-
defined but also fair. If local officials made German authority politically

negligible, the colony might descend into a cosmopolitan wasteland. "Why," he asked rhetorically, "should we give foreigners and natives German privileges, from which we are excluded in English colonies?"[16] Reimer's argument was intentionally polemical, but his sentiments were representative of the attitudes of most white German colonists after the conclusion of the Herero-Nama war. Four years of fighting had soured the attitude of farmers and investors, many of whom now looked upon DSWA's nonwhite populations as nothing more than dangerous enemies capable only of rebellion.

Perhaps the most explicit example of this new reality occurred when the colonial administration adopted *Rassentrennung* as official state policy. Commissioner for Settlement Paul Rohrbach articulated the intentions of *Rassentrennung* in clear terms shortly after his arrival in DSWA. "Our task," he pronounced, "is to divest [the Herero and Nama] . . . of their specific *völkisch* and national characteristics and gradually meld them with the other natives into a single colored work force. . . . This is to be a society based on work."[17] In this effort, German leaders passed an exclusionary "antimiscegenation" act, as well as various other racist laws, and also authorized local officials to construct segregated "native reservations" throughout the colony. Hans von Tecklenburg, vice governor of DSWA, issued the initial legal restriction of "mixed marriages" in October 1905. "Mixed-blood children produced by a native woman become German citizens," he proclaimed, "and are thereby subject to the laws valid for Germans. The male mix-bloods will be liable for military service, capable of holding public offices, and will assume the right to vote sometime in the future, as well as other rights tied to citizenship. Not only is the preservation of purity of the German race and German civilization here substantially impaired because of them, but also the white man's position of power is altogether endangered."[18] The racial motives behind Tecklenburg's security measures were explicit. In his estimation, so-called race-mixing was the antithesis of a prosperous colonial state.[19] It was so dire a threat, he alleged, that it authorized the imperial government to outlaw not only future mixed marriages but also existing ones retroactively.

Though the legality of colonial antimiscegenation policies remained tenuous up to the start of World War I, Tecklenburg ultimately succeeded in the imperial realm because he purposely chose to derive DSWA's racial laws as distinct from German legal precedent. He argued that the German constitution had failed to address marriages "across racial lines" and that the colonial government's prohibition on mixed-race relationships and subsequent redefinition of mixed-race children was juridically legal.[20] Among the most provocative legacies of this debate, however, was the restriction Tecklenburg's decrees placed on the patriarchal rights of white German men. The newfound limitation on white men's sexual escapades and hereditary prerogatives were unforeseen consequences of the 1905 racial ordinance.[21] Several prolonged legal battles emerged in German courts as a result—Carl Becker's among them—and lasted until the start of hostilities in Europe in 1914. Advocates of *Rassentrennung*, nevertheless, forged ahead with additional methods to segregate German and African polities. Tecklenburg informed the AAKA in July 1905 that "half measures will only exacerbate the current situation without breaking the resistance and make future rebellions possible. It is [therefore] necessary to give the [imperial] governor broad political powers."[22] His intentions were straightforward: if the governor could exercise comprehensive executive authority in moments of crisis, the colonial administration could more effectively demonstrate to "natives that they are in the land of the white man and live under German law."[23] Five months after Tecklenburg delivered this statement, a majority of his proposed "broad powers" were the law of the land.

Friedrich von Lindequist, who succeeded Trotha as governor in November 1905, did not hesitate to use his newly won authority. He not only upheld Tecklenburg's prohibition on mixed-race marriages but also authorized the government to seize cattle, land, and other property from Africans who had participated in the Herero-Nama war, issue *Paßmarke* (identity passports) to individuals whom the colonial administration deemed nonwhite, and establish segregated *Eingeborenenwerften* throughout the colony.[24] Imperial officials rooted each measure in a larger policy goal. Lindequist's confiscation of personal property, for instance, aimed to humiliate so-called Ovaherero and Nama belligerents and force them to rely upon the state for their livelihoods. Such initiatives, in Tecklenburg's words, carried the added bonus of having "natives go through a period of suffering," but not at the expense of DSWA's economy.[25] Forced labor had an additional purpose as well: it created a protocapitalist workforce for what was still an emergent colonial economy.[26] Farm owners and German investors strove to establish a regulated system of exploitation that they built on Ovaherero and Nama labor.[27] German colonial leaders expressed optimism for this plan. They reasoned that white business owners needed laborers and Black Africans needed employment.

Governor Schuckmann was among the most prominent proponents of this economic framework. In 1908, he applauded the colony's new strategy before DSWA's government council. "The period after the insurrection is short," he proclaimed, "and the natives, to whom we have extended the hand of peace, need to calm down and get used to order. . . . As far as possible, settlers are penetrating; everywhere creative hands are stirring; look at the cities. Settlements and farms [have] emerged, the resources of the country are explored and development is going forward. It remains the duty of the government to promote this development and forge a way forward."[28] Bernhard Dernburg, Germany's first secretary of state for the colonies, similarly proclaimed that Africans will now "be educated to work" and their labor utilized "for the benefit of the economy of the colonizing nation."[29] *Dienstverträgen* (service contracts) provided the colonial administration a means to force Africans into permanent indentured servitude.[30] As a result, employers often treated African workers with malice and rarely gave them a choice of where they could live and work.

The *Kölnische Zeitung* celebrated this approach and proclaimed that "Blacks are now the 'work animals' of whites."[31] As an additional means to "forge a way forward," the colonial government declared all nonwhite persons without employment to be vagabonds (*Landstreicher*) that same year.[32] In addition to *Dienstverträgen*, German officials also required African workers to carry internal passports and to wear identity badges around their necks at all times.[33] Some employers went so far as to tattoo their indentured African servants with specific insignia in order to identify those who left work without proper authorization.[34] The colonial government furthermore afforded Europeans the right to arrest any nonwhite person that they suspected of illegal activities and also permitted business and farm owners to administer their own legal consequences as they saw fit.[35] Typical penalties for even minor infractions included wage freezes, indefinite detainment, flogging, and death by hanging.

We must acknowledge that the German imperial government did not enact these violent measures inside a political vacuum. Officials regularly justified them with reference to other "civilized empires." In a letter to the AAKA, for example, Tecklenburg wrote that "the United States and England's African colonies have a strict separation between Caucasians and colored Africans. [Even] in the United States, marriages between whites and Blacks are prohibited."[36] A few years later, Dr. Wilhelm Solf, the last colonial governor of DSWA, asked a group of German administrators rhetorically, "What is the 'Negro question' in the United States if not a miscegenation question?"[37] In other words, if the United States was also participating in antimiscegenation programs, why should the German government in DSWA harbor any reservations about passing similar legislative restrictions? As these instances demonstrate, therefore, German colonial race policy was part of an international phenomenon that carried violent ramifications for indigenous and minority populations throughout the world. The imperial administration physically segregated Africans and Europeans as well. The "Regulation of the Governor of German Southwest Africa Concerning Passport Requirements of the Natives" mandated that nonwhite peoples could not live in "white districts."[38] It also divided churches, schools, hospitals, trains, post offices, and legal jurisdictions and forbade Africans from owning firearms, selling large quantities of alcohol, and hunting beyond their district borders.[39]

Perhaps the most disruptive regulation, however, required Africans to live on so-called native reservations. As mentioned in the previous chapter, African reserves were not a new idea in DSWA.[40] Several notable officials proposed that reservations could address various security concerns long before the Herero-Nama war.[41] Leutwein, for instance, argued as early as 1902 that reserves offered the only real chance of permanent peace between Germans and Africans.[42] At that time, however, a majority of German farmers, large estate owners, and private companies spoke out against their construction because they feared that white settlers might lose access to valuable land and resources. White speculators in Europe were opposed, too, worrying that reservations might lead to a negative return on their investments. Genocide and racial warfare, however, irrevocably altered that mindset. After 1904, the same groups that had advocated against segregated reservations fought vigorously for their creation. Apart from security concerns, they justified them for economic reasons. They sought to bind Africans to a capitalist labor system, and decentralized reservations seemed to provide a way to accelerate that process.[43] Among the most violent measures German authorities used to enforce DSWA's transformation was child separation. A dispatch to the Omaruru District Commander in January 1908, for instance, detailed the separation of Emma, an eight-year-old Ovaherero girl, from her parents as they departed from the capital city of Windhoek. It concluded that "she ran after her parents since she belongs with her Omaruru family."[44] Emma's fate remains a mystery to the present day.

The same year German imperial policy callously led officials to separate Emma from her parents, Rohrbach extolled the colony's prospects that racial separation made possible. "The economic question as a whole and the question of native labor in particular," he wrote, "are to be decided in the only natural way for the whole of southern Africa: wherever there is a permanent white settlement, it [must] develop the entire land and be kept free, and the natives [must] be kept on living and bread wages from the government.... The next generation must continue this program, as it will also provide a moral uplift for the Negro, as well as improve his moral and intellectual character."[45] As Rohrbach understood, however, his dream could only come to fruition if white settlers fully controlled the colony. The conduct of the German General Staff embodied that goal in the Herero-Nama genocide, as did the imposition of antimiscegenation legislation beginning in 1905. Racial separation permeated all facets of colonial life by the start of World War I but represented only one major step in Germany's creation of an apartheid state in southern Africa.

"OUR CULTURE-BEARER": EMIGRATION AND THE *FRAUENFRAGE*

"Southwest, sweet land of sun and stars, you land of endless blue horizon, open spaces, and wild field deer, you land of the kudus and range animals; I'll build on your sunbaked earth happily, stone by stone in the native soil."[46] For those who embarked on the long journey to Southwest Africa, enthusiasm was never an issue for concern, as these romantic lines from a contemporary German poem exemplify. Unfortunately for the German colonial administration, the creation of a stable and vibrant colony in DSWA required more than youthful vigor, especially in the aftermath of the Herero-Nama genocide. In that spirit, white German colonists deemed that in addition to racially discriminatory legislation, success in *Heimat* Südwest also mandated the presence of more white women in the colony. As Baroness Adda von Liliencron, chairwoman of the Deutschkolonialen Frauenbundes (German Colonial Women's League), wrote in 1908, "the German soldier conquers the land with the sword, the German farmer and businessman searches for its economic utilization, but the German woman is alone called to and capable of keeping it German."[47] In spite of their passionate rhetoric, supporters of Germany's imperial racial program had ample reason for concern. Only 403 white women lived in the colony in 1900, making up just under 12 percent of the total German population.[48] Six years later, the number rose to 717, but the percentage actually dropped to 11 percent.[49]

Procolonial organizations referred to the dearth of white women as the *Frauenfrage* and considered it among the greatest threats to the imperial project. While German proponents of settler colonialism noted it as a problem before the Herero-Nama war, the advent of apartheid rule in 1905 led imperial organizations to approach the issue with even more determination. That same year, the DKG and the Frauenbund joined together to facilitate the emigration of greater numbers of white women to DSWA. Some benefactors even pledged to subsidize the travel expenses of those who agreed to make the expensive journey.[50] Given the goals of both organizations, colonial officials were optimistic that public awareness campaigns had the potential to entice more individuals to join the imperial cause. The Frauenbund, in particular, had an enthusiastic base whom the organization could rely upon to promote DSWA as an extension of *Deutschtum* overseas. In addition to marketing imperial emigration, members vowed to win the support of women from all social classes, educate white children in German colonies, assist other women when they arrived in their respective destinations, and strengthen the spiritual ties between women living in both colony and metropole.[51] Thanks in large part to these efforts, membership in the Frauenbund swelled to 18,680 by the summer of 1914.[52]

Imperial officers also did their part to persuade white women to seek new prospects in Africa. Their tactics, however, generally focused on the dangers of miscegenation and the threats to German cultural identity and national prestige. German officials such as Leutwein had long feared the consequences of what he deemed improper relationships. Even after Kaiser Wilhelm II forced him to step down as imperial governor, Leutwein complained about the supposed "bad traits" of Black African women and how they were on the verge of turning DSWA into a "bastard colony."[53] Rohrbach voiced similar concerns in his 1909 publication *German Colonial Economy, Cultural-Political Principles for Racial and Mission Questions.* He contended that the present situation "ruined German men" and forced them to keep "a filthy house with the lazy, ignorant, indolent . . . colored wenches."[54] Reich Commissioner Dr. Külz, meanwhile, coined the slogan "No Black woman, no yellow one! Only the German woman is to be our culture-bearer" while on a lecture tour in Germany in 1912.[55] He hoped that his stark language might shock audiences and subsequently rally white metropolitan women to emigrate overseas in large numbers.

The most influential activists on this issue, however, were white German women themselves. As the groundbreaking work of Lora Wildenthal, Krista O'Donnell, Renate Bridenthal, and Nancy Reagin has shown, empire shaped the evolution of German femininity and race in consequential ways during the nineteenth and twentieth centuries.[56] Their studies reveal that at a time of "extensive feminist agitation in the metropole, defining citizenship in the colonies necessarily raised the question of what role women played in the German *Kulturnation*."[57] The elevation of whiteness into the principal measure of German colonial identity answered this question, especially for women who desired greater freedoms in an otherwise patriarchal Wilhelmine system. Clara Brockmann, a white settler and advocate of social equality, for example, championed racial purity as a means to advance white women's station in her 1910 book *The German Woman in Southwest Africa: A Contribution to the Question of Women in Our Colonies*. "I challenge my sisters in the homeland to help with the work [and] make our colonies purposeful and agreeable. Support our cultural tasks on Africa's soil in the homeland to build and establish a new Germany."[58] Brockmann alleged that women were essential figures in the colonial sphere and that during an era when authorities concentrated on racial segregation, "the achievement of the prevention of intermarriage, which signifies the spiritual and economic ruin of the settler, the achievement of a profitable farm cannot reach successful development without the participation of the housewife."[59] In this fashion, the *Frauenfrage* provided white women a forum to promote their own roles in the colonial empire, as well as a means to demand more social representation in the metropole.

Brockmann was not the only woman to advocate a socially progressive but racially exclusive message. Baroness Liliencron disseminated a similar view in her 1912 book *War and Peace: Memories from the Life of an Officer's Wife*. Among her central arguments was that "the hard-won territory [in DSWA] was in danger of going completely to the Boers and Kaffirs . . . because a growing race of mixed-bloods threatened . . . to nip Germandom in the bud."[60] Margarethe von Eckenbrecher, a widely known colonist in Germany, echoed Liliencron's message in her 1913 article in which she asserted that the *Frauenfrage* "in the colonies, especially in Southwest Africa, has a national side, in addition to an overwhelmingly ethical and cultural one . . . which the woman has to fill."[61] Eckenbrecher had made a name for herself six years earlier when she published her autobiography, entitled *What Africa Gave and Took from Me: The Experiences of a German Settler Woman in South West Africa*. Divided into three sections, it detailed her journey to DSWA, her life as a farmer's wife in a "remote village," and the family's experiences in the Herero-Nama war.[62] Such accounts resonated with a wide range of women in the metropole, but most especially unmarried, divorced, or widowed women who sought fresh opportunities away from their hometowns or cramped living conditions in large cities. They also provided a human element in popular contemporary literature that portrayed colonial conquest as the exclusive domain of adventurous German men, such as Gustav Frenssen's best-selling novel *Peter Moor's Journey to Southwest*. In contrast to some stereotypes that continue to press nonacademic audiences to look past their advocacy and participation, German women were passionate believers in the colonial project and used their personal testimonials to illustrate the "other side" of imperial life in southern Africa.

The implication that white women had a biological responsibility to bear German children also made for a powerful message among female supporters of the settler-colonial mission. Germany's war against the Ovaherero and Nama had forever tarnished Africans in the eyes of white settlers, generating a collective belief that racial segregation was the only way to ensure the future stability of the colony. White German women played an active role in disseminating this argument. At the inauguration of the Windhoek Chapter of the German Women's League in 1909, for example, Frau Neugebohrn asserted that the German woman "brings very firm views about order and decency and . . . tries to transfer this to the new [colonial] circumstances. She transplants her entire way of life wherever she goes. Therefore, the woman does important cultural work because she bestows great care on all these small things and through this achieves a great deal."[63] Leonore Niessen-Deiters, meanwhile, argued in her article "Racial Purity!" that "the German woman stands out as the strongest and greatest hope for the spiritual Germanization and enduring preservation of the lands that we have purchased dearly with life and property. At her hot, busy, and dangerous outpost, she stands as a factor, more important than all the gold and gunpowder, in the preservation of the race and nation."[64] Neugebohrn and Niessen-Dieters fostered racist xenophobia in explicit terms for nonwhite members of colonial society. They maintained that a woman's "important cultural work" included the domestication of Germany's "wild African periphery," not just in the home and garden but also as the only element that could render colonial society ethnically German.

Settler colonialism and its preservation in DSWA, therefore, attracted the attention of a wide network of white German women, including many who challenged hypermasculine views of ideal settler society.[65] Most notably, women who wanted to escape the gendered sociopolitical confines of Germany, progressive women who advocated political suffrage, and women who espoused their patriotic duty to fight "race mixing" in the colony favored a colonialism that made them central players in its ultimate success.[66] The elevation of race as a central component of settler society, together with the environmental and everyday conditions of the colonial state, made it difficult for women to sit by as passive observers in both colony and metropole. Even if their male counterparts wished them to remain at home as "culture bearers," settler colonialism required active participation from white German women in the private and public realms for the imperial project to flourish.

Brockmann, for instance, recommended that women should arrive in DSWA prepared to farm, sew, and raise cattle. "One should not fear the danger of becoming countrified [*Verbauern*]," she wrote, "for the woman farmer protects everyone's good upbringing and education."[67] Others celebrated the opportunity to showcase their value to the imperial project in other ways. In her *Where Else the Warrior's Foot Stepped: Farmer's Life in Southwest After the War*, Maria Karow praised how cleanliness separated Europeans from Africans.[68] After her arrival in DSWA in 1908, she contended that "native homes," which she likened to "molehills," stood out from those of white settlers for their lack of "proper doors or ventilation."[69] When she visited the homes of white settlers, however, Karow asserted that "their wives greeted me and showed me their households with pride, in which everything was so clean that it gleamed. If the African servants had not been there, I would have thought myself in Germany."[70] German women evolved into essential partners in colonization as a direct result of the imperial state's effort to forge a white settler colony. Whether as mothers or small business owners, housewives or protectors of the nation, the elevation of race in the colony made white women a vital component of Germany's imperial project in southern Africa.

Near the conclusion of Frenssen's *Peter Moor's Journey to Southwest*, the protagonist states that "it is remarkable how indifferent man is to human life, if that life is of a different race."[71] Though his fictional portrayal of the Herero-Nama war celebrated German imperial expansion, even Frenssen acknowledged the newfound importance of race and its dangerous potential in DSWA. Regardless of Frenssen's veiled warning, German officials and white colonists embraced whiteness as the foundation of settler society after the start of the fighting in 1904. White settlers rejected miscegenation, pledged to safeguard the supposed racial divide between Europeans and Africans, and called for greater collective accountability over social affairs in DSWA. In the process, white women, uniquely situated as "culture-bearers," pledged to keep settler children and "adventurous men" German and to install a more egalitarian political structure for the entire white community in *Heimat* Südwest.

"HARMONY AND PLAGUE": AFRIKANER MIGRATION
AND RACE AFTER 1900

On 22 March 1905, the Pan-German League submitted a report to the *Reichskolonialamt* entitled "Concerning the Boer Question in South Africa." The report sought to verify rumors that Afrikaners in the British Cape Colony looked favorably upon Germany's occupation of DSWA.[72] In that spirit, the Pan-German League's conclusions confirmed the hopes of many in the RKA:

> There are already over 2000 Boers living amongst Germans [in DSWA]. In my opinion the rebellion waged by the Hereros and Witbois in the German Southwest can be a great blessing if we take advantage of the situation. German farmers see their political power destroyed, and their nationality threatened to the highest degree; [Boers] take out for German SW-Africa under mild conditions, and they will be the greatest blessing for our colony. In German SW-Africa, I see the possibility of grafting German culture onto the Boer tribe, as the English do in other parts of South Africa. In no other part of the world does *Deutschtum* have a better chance to spread than in South Africa.[73]

"Cultural cultivation" represented a new and potentially momentous opportunity to reshape DSWA along racial lines. As the descendants of Dutch and Huguenot settlers, Afrikaners offered enthusiasts of a racially demarcated colonial state a resourceful way to address the shortage of white settlers in the region. Advocates contended that Afrikaners could solve the *Frauenfrage*, close the population gap between Germans and Africans, and displace Nama polities in southern DSWA.

Before the turn of the twentieth century, relatively few plans existed to "graft German culture" onto Afrikaner settlers.[74] As emphasized in chapter 3, the German colonial administration initially strove to accommodate moneyed families from Europe in an effort to encourage the growth of large-scale farms and merchant enterprises in the colony. Göring, for example, aspired to see *latifundia* "stretch out side by side to the horizon," generating enough capital for the colony to manage its affairs independently from Berlin.[75] Imperial commissioners like Rohrbach similarly argued that the success of such an initiative first required the support and eventual emigration of wealthy magnates from Germany.[76] Leutwein, a strong proponent of social hierarchy, agreed in no uncertain terms. During his reign as imperial governor, in speeches and official meetings he regularly distinguished between what he deemed "propertied," "lower-middle," and "unpropertied" peoples.[77] As a result, the formative colonial leadership did not regard Afrikaner settlers favorably, dismissing them as old-fashioned "peasant farmers" who they claimed were unsuited to the specific needs of the colony.[78] After the Herero-Nama genocide, however, many white German colonists, especially those who lived near the Cape border, shifted their attitude on what constituted the ideal settler.

From a contemporary outsider's perspective, Germans and Afrikaners seemed like natural allies. They shared a similar language, culture, and religion, as well as a general antipathy toward the British administration in the Cape Colony. Among international newspapers, the *Cape Times* was among the most frequent to acknowledge the potential likenesses between Germans and Afrikaners. An article in September 1903, for instance, asserted that after a recent "great trek," Germany was fortunate to gain "a good type of settler" and that "Boers promised to strengthen" the imperial government's foothold in DSWA.[79] For their part, many Germans also recognized the potential ties between both peoples. The most famous example came from Kaiser Wilhelm II in January 1896. In the so-called Kruger telegram, the German Kaiser publicly congratulated Paul Kruger, president of the Transvaal Republic, for his victory over British forces in the Jameson Raid, an incident that would help incite the Second Anglo-Boer War.[80] The Kaiser's missive signaled not only his political commitment to the Transvaal, but his belief that Germany could benefit from an independent Afrikaner republic.

While the Kruger telegram provoked tremendous indignation in Great Britain, it attracted widespread praise from colonial enthusiasts in Germany and peace advocates from around the world.[81] W. H. Burns of St. Paul, Minnesota, for example, wrote Wilhelm II in April 1900 and asked him to convince his grandmother (Queen Victoria of Great Britain) to remove all British forces from the African continent.[82] Burns declared that such an action "would place [Queen Victoria] at the head of all the men and women that lived on this Earth" and make peace the central component of British foreign policy.[83] In a letter to Chancellor Bernhard von Bülow, another writer, who self-identified as a "German Roman Catholic born in New York," offered a counteropinion that Wilhelm II did not go far enough in condemning the British. He encouraged the chancellor to "overthrow the

Emperor William of Germany and let the people of Germany take a hand of intervention in favor of the Boers in South Africa."[84]

Though the letters offered contradictory opinions of the German Kaiser, both writers evinced a passionate connection with Afrikaners and a desire to see Germandom prosper in DSWA. This attitude became even more pronounced after the start of the Second Anglo-Boer War in 1899. Fritz Bronsart von Schellendorff, an officer in the German armed forces, informed the Foreign Office in January 1900 that "German trade and German industry are England's most powerful enemies in the world and threaten to jeopardize England's purse in the not too distant future. In addition, the German people's strong support for the freedom of the Boers is their greatest worry."[85] In another letter, a self-described "patriot" expressed the "indescribable sympathy [that] people have for the Boers. And what rancor [*Groll*], yes hate against England!"[86] Four years later, similar demonstrations of support appeared in Afrikaner newspapers in the Transvaal as Germans fought the Herero-Nama war.[87] Many Afrikaners even volunteered for the *Schutztruppe* as a sign of their devotion to Germany's cause against the Ovaherero and Nama.[88]

The racial identity of Afrikaners, however, only emerged as the central factor behind German settlers' support for and opposition to immigration during and after the Herero-Nama genocide. As racial standing consumed the attention of more and more individuals on both sides of the immigration debate, Afrikaners' prior affiliation as "lowland farmers" received less and less attention. An article in the *Alldeutsche Blätter*, among the most prominent contemporary channels for *völkisch* ideas, for instance, featured a story about Conrad Rust, a German settler colonist who owned a large cattle farm named Monte Christo near the Cape border. In the story, Rust celebrated what he regarded as a mutually beneficial relationship between Germans and Afrikaners. "I know one Boer woman who shares the greatest sympathies for Germans in the colony. She proudly states, 'My children have to learn German, as they have learned English in the Cape Colony, and my sons should be soldiers! Where we were English subjects, here we want to be citizens of Germany.' With the right tools and necessary conditions, it is only a matter of decades to make Boers in German Southwest Africa real Germans."[89] Rust's account emphasized the ethnic ties that motivated the female subject in his story to emigrate to DSWA. He neither disputed her sincerity nor ignored the possibility that Germans and Afrikaners could one day grow together into a united people.

Rust's narrative was one of several testimonials in the *Alldeutsche Blät-ter* that underscored the potential racial benefits of Afrikaners in southern Africa. Three years earlier, an article entitled "The Immigration of Boers to German Southwest Africa" explained that "over 15,000 Boers were presently trekking into our African colony."[90] The article assured its readers that "their presence would not threaten the ethnic base [*volkliche Grundlage*]" of the region.[91] Many prominent German newspapers also recognized Germany's "sympathetic relationship" with Afrikaners. *Der Tag*, a daily German paper focused on international events, declared that "Boer settlers were welcome in DSWA" and that any "aversion to the Boers in German Southwest Africa is quite unjustified; we can announce that, on the contrary, there has always been a good understanding between the Boers and the Germans, and they would find the same sympathy for them in Germany as in Southwest Africa. . . . It is our hope that Dutch communications [to the contrary] will not disturb Boers and that they will form their own opinion about their prospects in German Southwest Africa."[92] *Der Tag* conveyed a clear desire to see more Afrikaner emigrants in DSWA. Its editors not only drew attention to their shared history in southern Africa but also acknowledged that Germans everywhere harbored a sympathetic view of Afrikaners.

Regional newspapers in southern Africa also called attention to the prospect of Afrikaner settlement. The *African Review*, for instance, exulted that DSWA "undoubtedly has a good future, and is in many ways most suitable for a white farming settlement."[93] In a similar manner, the *Cape Times* portrayed the "great trek movements" as adventurous displays and often emphasized celebratory stories of participants. A feature on Isaac Bosman, a trek leader from the Northern Cape, explained that he "possesses a personality of the most interesting character—connected, as it is, with the thrilling adventures of the bold and hard pioneer who has roamed over every territory south of the Zambesi."[94] The article concluded that "Mr. Bosman is certain to have great results in the development of southern Africa and the planting of a white population on the land of the interior."[95] As each of these stories indicates, the racial identity of Afrikaner settlers was a subject of notable concern for German settlers during and after the Herero-Nama genocide. The supposed ethnic traits that Afrikaners shared with Germans were ultimately all that mattered for proponents who championed their immigration to DSWA.

For many others, however, Afrikaners were a dangerous nuisance that threated the cultural, economic, and racial integrity of DSWA. Governor Leutwein was among the most outspoken opponents of Afrikaner settlement. In his memoir, *Elf Jahre Gouverneur*, he cited what he saw as Afrikaners' lack of education, "tribal weakness," and ethnic inferiority as his primary reasons for concern. "The Boer, generally considered," he wrote, "turns out to be equal to the Low German farmer with all the advantages and disadvantages. He is honest, hospitable, an excellent family man, conservative against excess, and therefore tough on old principles. By living in the intra-Africa grasslands for a long time, [however,] the Boer has evolved to such an extent that it has finally become detrimental to him. The Boer is independent of the pleasures of Europe, his personal needs are therefore lower, while he understands how to utilize better the resources of Africa. However, [the German] will in turn pass the Boer because he is too indolent to advance."[96] Leutwein justified his views in cultural and racial terms, identifying Afrikaners as harmful to the colonial state. He later went on to assert that Afrikaners "went kaffir" (*verkaffern*) and thereby forfeited any claims of cultural superiority over Black Africans in DSWA.[97]

Leutwein was not the only German official to distinguish between "useful and useless" Afrikaners. Rohrbach also shared this perspective and wrote about the topic regularly upon his arrival in the colony. He alleged during the Herero-Nama war that the poor farmer "will not have the means to marry a white woman, and will only produce mixed children [*Bastardkinder*] for the colony."[98] In his opinion, the best settlers were wealthy, highly educated white families from Europe, who could prevent colonial society from "sinking to a more primitive level of civilization."[99] Captain Ludwig von Estorff, an officer in the *Schutztruppe* whom the next chapter will discuss in detail, echoed similar fears in a letter to the Foreign Office. "If Boer immigration continues," he contended, "the small German population [will not be able] to handle the situation through schools or forced conscription. *Deutschtum* is in direct danger of succumbing to the self-confident, well-established Boers if stronger German immigration does not soon take place."[100] In response to Estorff's warnings and Leutwein's provocations, colonial leaders moved to ban newly arrived Afrikaners from owning land in 1905. Governor Schuckmann also forbade Afrikaners from owning farms next to one another. He reasoned that "multiple farms side by side can easily form into associations" and eventually weaken German authority. "Those farms," he continued, "will be reserved for German applications. I would love to see German settlers there with German women."[101]

In spite of this wide spectrum of opinion, proponents and opponents of Afrikaner immigration did agree on one thing, namely that Afrikaners were a separate race and thereby inherently different from Germans. Advo-cates of "cultural cultivation" meant exactly that—graft German culture onto Afrikaner settlers only as a means to augment white immigration from Europe. After all, what the imperial government ultimately desired were settlers like Friedrich Deckert, an agriculturalist from Wolferstadt, Bavaria. In his colonial petition for settlement, Deckert represented Leut-wein's ideal colonialist in every way imaginable. "I am an agriculturalist by profession," he wrote, "and would like to settle in a German colony (as a farmer) with my family: 3 boys and my wife. After selling my business I have 25,000 marks at my free disposal. . . . Where do I go and how best could I comport myself as a settler in the colonies?"[102] A white German farmer with a family, financial flexibility, and personal ambition met the standard of both class-conscious and racial exclusivist officials. So, too, did Carl Hanke. In his petition from January 1905, Hanke declared that he had lived "in the Transvaal for 8 years and mastered English, Dutch, and *Käffern*. The government can use energetic young people in German Southwest Africa after the suppression of the [Herero and Namaqua] uprising."[103] Though Hanke was less financially secure than Friedrich Deckert, his educa-tional background, previous experience in southern Africa, and white German heritage elevated him above a "useless trek Boer" in the eyes of officials like Rohrbach and Leutwein.

Critics of Afrikaner immigration, meanwhile, viewed race as an indis-putable truth and justified their position in stark national terms. Bernhard Dernburg, Secretary of Colonial Affairs and head of the Imperial Colonial Office, looked to other nearby colonies to defend his opinion. "In the Boer States the white man could not dispense with colored labor, while the Blacks could not progress without the whites. [In] the 'Boer countries' and the purely British Colonies, where the Blacks, though legally equal with the whites, [they are] actually oppressed and despised even more [by the whites]."[104] Dernburg's stance was clear: if other imperial states utilized racial hierarchy, so, too, should DSWA. In the immediate period before the start of World War I, colonial authorities were exuberant about the colo-ny's future. In all but one district, Germans outnumbered Boers in large numbers and looked to expand their control even further. As with the social elevation of white women, race policy made the authority of German settlers essential for the growth and preservation of *Deutschtum* in DSWA.

By 1914, Germans owned 1331 large farms in southern Africa, a figure that dwarfed the number of plots inhabited by Afrikaners. For advocates of the colonial dream, this reality was a good and necessary development.

"We must never lose sight that they are gradually to be subordinated to our culture," an exuberant Governor Tecklenburg wrote in 1911.[105] After the Herero-Nama genocide, German administrators endeavored to make Tecklenburg's vision an extension of imperial state strategy. People in the colonial sphere, most especially Africans, felt the impact of this effort in culturally and physically violent ways. Soon after the start of hostilities, however, events in the metropole started to reveal the shared influence of colonial policy on German national politics as well. In particular, debates over the conduct of the Herero-Nama war reconfigured Germany's political spectrum in ways that lasted until the start of World War I.

POLITICS, RHETORIC, AND "WILD PEOPLE" IN WILHELMINE GERMANY

On 17 March 1904, Ludwig Graf zu Reventlow, an outspoken conservative reactionary, voiced his support for Germany's war against the Ovaherero and Nama in a speech before the Reichstag. Given the severity of the military campaign in DSWA, Reventlow advocated swift and unapologetic action: "Of course we are for humanity with respect to human beings of all kinds. But in contradiction to some of the speakers preceding me, I shall conclude by adjuring the interested authorities: do not afford too great a degree of humanity toward the bloodthirsty beasts in human form [in Südwest]."[106] At the same session, August Bebel, the parliamentary whip in the Social Democratic Party (SPD), also spoke about the war in DSWA. A fierce opponent of German colonial expansion, Bebel asserted that the war was "an act of desperation among the Herero."[107] Though he still voiced his displeasure about the imperial project, Bebel approached this speech differently from those he had given in previous years, specifically in his portrayal of Black Africans in the colony. "Let me repeat," he asserted, "I have not given a speech in favor of the Hereros; they are a wild people, very low in culture. . . . My words do not gloss over the barbarous and cruel activities that they commit against murdered soldiers and farmers."[108]

Reventlow and Bebel presented two widely distinct opinions about the necessity of the German colonial empire. And yet both men expressed similar views about the humanity of the Ovaherero after the start of the Herero-Nama war. Reventlow used the image of "the primitive" as proof of its inhumanity, while Bebel ascribed humanity to "the primitive" in spite of its supposed cultural and ethnic inferiority. Taken together, these two arguments reveal the extent to which race thinking had consumed public discussions on DSWA since the start of hostilities in 1904. They also illustrate how German politicians across the ideological spectrum viewed race as a fixed and primordial category. Reventlow and Bebel may have disagreed about the treatment of colonial combatants, but both men nevertheless regarded Germans and Africans as ethnically distinct peoples.

The endemic influence of race thinking in 1904 and thereafter underscores two important realities about the effect of colonial rule on German society. First, German citizens and politicians were keenly aware of events in DSWA. As we have seen, metropolitans fashioned collective impressions of empire through formal and informal encounters with the imperial world. Colonial racial policy, therefore, had a significant effect on the evolution of German national identity in the metropole as well. After the start of the Herero-Nama war, the defense of German culture led some prominent leaders in Germany to accept systemic violence and racial segregation as acceptable solutions to the conflict in DSWA. Reventlow and Bebel were not partisan outliers in an otherwise apathetic parliamentary body. To the contrary, they personified the newfound significance of colonial racism and its sway over German national politics. Karl Schrader, a left-liberal representative from Berlin, for example, declared to the Reichstag in March 1904 that "in the midst of a revolt, one is not inclined to mild treatment of wild people, and, often enough, it is hardly appropriate."[109] At the same session, Eugen Richter, the leader of the left-liberal Freisinnige Volkspartei (Radical People's Party), asserted that "the current moment is inappropriate" to question military conduct in DSWA.[110] Two days later, Martin Spahn of the Catholic Center Party announced that "because we have established a German protectorate in the area, we owe SWA every protection."[111] These attitudes were outgrowths of the rancorous atmosphere the war spread throughout German society and reflected the pressure that leaders felt to address the fighting in definitive terms. The most important aspect of this level of explicit racism, however, is the degree to which it permeated political and social rhetoric. Instead of a "heroic minority" that bravely resisted a "superior power"—words that Bebel had once used to describe African resistance in southern Africa—the Ovaherero had suddenly become a "marauding horde" that threatened enlightened civilization.[112] Rebellion in Africa inspired advocates of colonial rule, in addition to a growing number of its detractors, to measure cultural and racial difference on a universal scale, an evolution in action and discourse that was on full display in the deserts of DSWA and in the halls of the Reichstag.

FIG. 11 Herero and Nama prisoners of war under German guard during the so-called Herero-Nama uprising, ca. 1905. In the aftermath of the genocide, German authorities established an apartheid state in Southwest Africa. White officials relied upon systemic violence, juridical and social racism, and arms as their principal instruments to maintain their control of the colony. Photo: Wikimedia Commons / Jonund.

Second, the fact that racial epithets and pejorative overtones saturated civic debate in 1904 is hardly coincidental. From Rohrbach, who stated that Africans "lacked the ability to be educated to moral independence," to Ernst Müller-Meiningen, a member of the Radical People's Party who wanted the imperial state "to build reservations for the natives in the cultural interests of native groups," war in DSWA elevated colonial racial policy into an issue that transcended customary political and socioeconomic divisions.[113] Lieutenant General Trotha's *Vernichtungsbefehl* provided the clearest example of this new political reality. On 2 October 1904, Trotha declared that the Ovaherero were "no longer German subjects [and] must now leave the country. If it [the Ovaherero nation] refuses," he continued, "I shall compel it to do so with the great cannon. Any Herero found inside the German frontier, with or without a gun or cattle, will be executed. I shall spare neither women nor children. Such are my words to the Herero people."[114] The language in this genocidal order provided clear insight into Trotha's intentions for all Africans, as well as his vision for postwar society. News of both the massacre and Trotha's "annihilation decree," setting out his "peace of the graveyard strategy," proliferated quickly throughout Germany. Though politicians in the Reichstag were aware of the violence, most did not speak out publicly against the actions of the *Schutztruppe*.

In the few instances where leaders drew attention to Germany's military conduct in DSWA, they typically couched their disapproval in cynical terms. Georg Ledebour, a member of the SPD, for instance, warned against German soldiers "sinking down to the moral level of the Hottentots [through] bestial and uncivilized" acts of murder.[115] Others, such as Rohrbach and Chancellor Bülow, expressed their unease about the violence in the colony but articulated their displeasure in economical prose. How, they questioned rhetorically, could German settlers establish an affluent colony in southern Africa if there was no "human material" to exploit?[116] Due in large measure to these complaints, Kaiser Wilhelm II rescinded Trotha's annihilation decree on 8 December 1904.[117] Unfortunately for advocates of the colonial empire, the war in DSWA did not end in 1905. Nor did it end in 1906. To make matters worse for the German government, the Maji Maji war broke out in German East Africa in June 1905, and Kaiser Wilhelm II's trip to Tangier in March caused the First Moroccan Crisis.[118] These foreign policy calamities prompted the SPD and Center Party to reject Chancellor Bülow's supplementary request for 29 million marks to fund the war in December 1906. In response, Bülow dissolved the Reichstag and called for new national elections.

The so-called Hottentot elections of 1907 evolved into nothing less than a referendum on Germany's colonial occupation of DSWA. They also represented a watershed moment in the history of German national politics. These elections were not about women's suffrage, tax reform, or social mobility. Nor did they contrast Prussian Junkers or the industrial "New Right" against the urban electorate of the SPD. Instead, these elections concerned Germany's honor overseas and the status of white-settler authority in Africa.[119] For members of the German "New Right," which included industrialists, pan-German nationalists, and champions of the colonial project in Africa, these concerns were especially prominent. In an effort to galvanize support for the imperial empire, Chancellor Bülow's government, the German Colonial Office, and the political Right attacked Left and Center politicians for their supposed betrayal of German soldiers in their fight against what they called "Herero and Namaqua savages."[120] The "Bülow Bloc," as their devotees called them, orchestrated an electoral campaign that associated colonial conquest with German patriotism and the anti-imperial German opposition with cowardice, deviancy, and racial betrayal.

In the weeks before the election, the Bülow Bloc distributed racist leaflets that emphasized Ovaherero and Nama acts of violence and regularly referred to their opponents as the "Black-Red League for the Defense of

Kaffirdom Against Germans."[121] An article in Nuremberg's *Frankischer Kurier* decried what its disciples regarded as the fundamental shortsightedness of the anticolonial opposition. "[They] deal quite thoroughly with the colonial scandals objected to by all parties, and with the costs of German colony policy," the article accused, "but entirely conceal that the Center and Social Democracy refuse the means necessary to maintain the military readiness of the German troops standing against the savage and cruel enemy."[122] In a similar manner, Colonial Secretary Dernburg argued that the justifications for colonization in DSWA spoke for themselves. "The exploitation of the soil, its natural resources, the flora and fauna, and above all the people benefit the economy of the colonizing nation."[123] Dernburg also asserted that German imperial practices were much more humane than those of other rival powers, including the United States. "Man has previously engaged in colonialism through merchants, [and] through adventure companies that sold natives what they wanted most, schnapps, the "firewater," and firearms," he claimed. "They served as the foundation for the destruction of large masses. There is no doubt that some native tribes degenerate just like some animals in civilization, and become dependent on the state. Fortunately we are not too heavily loaded with these elements in our German colonies. But the history of the United States, which engaged in the largest colonial undertaking that the world has ever seen, almost completely destroyed the native population with these methods."[124] If "policies of destruction" were representative of a civilized colonialism, Dernburg concluded, then so must "agents of conversion, which include the missionary as well as the doctor, the railroad, which serves as the engine, as well as the advanced theoretical and applied sciences in all areas."[125] Dernburg failed to mention Trotha's peace of the graveyard strategy in his speech. He instead cast the agents of anticolonialism as socially inept, unpatriotic allies of Black Africans who threatened "the entire colonial project [and] its inherent benefits."[126] Thanks in large part to messages like those of Dernburg and the colonial press, the "Hottentot elections" produced a decisive outcome. Though the SPD received nearly a quarter of a million more votes than it had in 1903, the party lost exactly half of its preelection seats in the Reichstag.[127] The SPD, Center, and Bülow Bloc parties all recognized this electoral defeat as a sign of the new influence of colonialism on the German electorate. A national consensus that enthusiasts built on race successfully diffused the power of oppositional groups who had traditionally focused on issues of class and social mobility.

The outcome of the 1907 elections signaled that colonial racism had moved into the political lexicon of Germany's national electorate. This development was only possible because the Herero-Nama war presented a legitimate challenge to the colonial project in DSWA. In colonial and national politics, "the beast," as the conservative parliamentarian Graf Ludwig zu Reventlow referred to the Ovaherero in January 1904, replaced "the subject." Like Trotha's peace of the graveyard, the racist atmosphere promoted by politicians like Reventlow encouraged officials in DSWA to pursue segregationist policies against the Ovaherero and Nama, populations that Germans now regarded as inherently dangerous and inferior to the white settler class.

"THE FATHER'S WORTHINESS"

In 1914, German settler colonists exemplified a national character that celebrated exploration, scientific discovery, and overseas conquest. As exponents of culture, *Auslandsdeutschen* stood as agents of Germandom in a land that they claimed was otherwise devoid of "modern achievement." And yet freedom did have its limits. After the start of the Herero-Nama war, racial apartheid dictated political and social policy totally and without remorse. It justified Governor Tecklenburg in banning and nullifying "mixed marriages," raised the cultural status of white women, and forced politicians in the metropole to reconsider their views on the colonial empire. Germans of "mixed race" and other nonwhite populations, meanwhile, found themselves at the mercy of the colonial state. The infusion of race as a category of German national belonging represents the most consequential legacy of Germany's imperial project in Southwest Africa. After the conclusion of the Herero-Nama genocide, the means through which settler colonialists justified imperial domination depended entirely on racial segregation. Carl Becker's confrontation with the German colonial administration in 1909 was emblematic of this shift in German imperial politics. Indeed, the culmination of his family's legal dispute exposed the newfound primacy of race in questions of national identity.

In October 1909, Governor Schuckmann responded to Becker's petition that began this chapter. Schuckmann agreed that Becker's situation warranted special attention and pledged to support his case against the new marriage law. He proposed an alternative draft of §17f that spoke "in favor of those who had married a Rehoboth woman in a civil ceremony, or if before 1890 an ecclesiastical one, and had carried on a normal European household."[128] Schuckmann forwarded this proposal to his superiors in Berlin and awaited their reply. After a month of deliberation, Colonial Secretary Dernburg rejected Schuckmann's revision on the basis that "the reasons for which the exclusions in §17 were enacted still exist today."[129] Dernburg, however, did concede one point. He authorized Schuckmann to restore the franchise "in those cases where a marriage with a native admits the particular respect from a moral point of view and where, in the light of the whole way of life of the family in question, the father's worthiness to be entrusted with civic rights is beyond all doubt."[130] Dernburg nevertheless urged Schuckmann "to make exceptions of this nature only in the most compelling cases and to report them to Berlin."[131] Becker and his family may have won a partial victory in their legal confrontation with the colonial government, but the verdict represented an even larger triumph for advocates of racial hierarchy. As the edict made clear, the imperial administration and German colonial office together retained the exclusive right to decide a person's national status—regardless of merit or individual desire—in all cases.

In her powerful commentary "Race-Thinking Before Racism" from January 1944, Hannah Arendt postulated that "racism sprang from experiences and political constellations which were still unknown" to most people in the nineteenth century. "It is highly probable that the thinking in terms of race would have disappeared in due time together with other irresponsible opinions of the nineteenth century, if the 'scramble for Africa' and the new era of imperialism had not exposed Western humanity to new and shocking experiences."[132] While it is doubtful that collective views of civilizational hierarchy and racial prejudice might have disappeared entirely if not for colonialism, imperial conquest certainly helped promote race thinking as a necessary and justifiable action in a world that Europeans increasingly framed in zero-sum terms. There were no passive bystanders to imperialism, for overseas conquest consumed substantial attention and support among contemporary European "great powers" and influenced metropolitan society in a myriad of ways. No one, most especially those in academia, finance, and other high-profile positions in late nineteenth-century Europe, could sincerely claim that events in the world's so-called peripheries did not affect them in some way.

The advent of colonial racial states such as DSWA is a clear example of this argument. Perhaps, as Arendt claimed, "an abyss" did exist between "men of brilliant and facile conceptions and men of brutal deeds and active bestiality."[133] But if we accept this premise, we must willingly ignore the transnational exchanges between colony and metropole that fashioned race thinking as a driving political and social force in Europe's continental and overseas empires. So-called brilliant men like Arthur de Gobineau and Benjamin Disraeli, whom Arendt cites as contemporary champions of the "race idea," may not have fully understood the consequences of their arguments, but we certainly can today. Once Africans shattered the façade of German colonial fantasy, eliminatory racism provided white settlers with a convenient solution to what they considered the most pressing issue in DSWA—white dominance. In the period between the start of the Herero-Nama war and the inception of World War I, white German settlers transformed their racial fantasies into political reality. The same was true for supporters of the imperial project in Germany. Colonialists, citizens from across the socioeconomic spectrum, and politicians weighed their own perceptions of German national identity against those that emanated from colonial Africa. After the conclusion of the Herero-Nama genocide, German settlers, together with their allies in the metropole, defined that identity along a racial color line.

In a similar fashion to their white female fellow citizens, white German men also drew upon postwar DSWA's racist and violent atmosphere to inform their masculinity in imperial and metropolitan society. The consequences of this undertaking, as the following chapter will illustrate, produced a national environment that increasingly favored bravado, independence, racial hierarchy, strength, and violence as the principal constituents of German manhood.

CHAPTER 6

"A Little Bit of the Devil in His Body"

Imperial Masculinity and the Ideal German (Settler)

"THE BLACKS, LIKE COWARDS"

In the immediate years before and after the Herero-Nama war, German settler colonists envisioned themselves as the standard-bearers of the nation. Though a majority of those who made the long journey to DSWA viewed conquest in an adventurous light, the terms of Germany's imperial occupation changed markedly in the wake of the first genocide of the twentieth century. Diplomacy and negotiation, essential tenets of the Leutwein system, were no longer requisites for imperial rule. Racial separation, mass imprisonment, and ethnic segregation successfully created an environment in which white settlers could occupy with total supremacy.[1] Even before 1904, few German officials considered how their African subjects might react to their political and social mandates. If colonial leaders thought of Ovaherero, Nama, and other nonwhite polities at all, they did so in a context of labor, forced servitude, and racial apartheid.[2] Though Kaiser Wilhelm II dismissed the architect of Germany's "war of annihilation" from the colony, Trotha's proclamation that Africans "were no longer German subjects" still served as the juridical foundation of postwar Südwest.[3]

Not every colonist overseas or citizen in Europe, of course, viewed ethnic and social segregation in positive terms. Neither did every white German woman or man interpret their identity along a primordial and fixed color line. The ferocity of the fighting and constant flow of information between colony and metropole, however, compelled citizens to question their Germanness and its global reach in a racially oriented framework. Much like the informal encounters of the previous century, official testimonies, memoirs, published diaries, and personal accounts from southern Africa made the human consequences of the Herero-Nama genocide palpable for a European audience. In clear and direct terms, eliminatory warfare stirred both colonists and metropolitans to consider the centrality of empire in the Kaiserreich's national progression. From political battles over the makeup of the German Reichstag to queries over civil belonging and citizenship, imperial conflict demonstrated just how entangled DSWA and Germany were after the turn of the twentieth century.

Genocide and the circumstances it created also affected how Germans *thought* about empire and their particular connection with the settler-colonial world. As discussed in the previous chapter, a significant number of white women looked upon racial apartheid in DSWA as an opportunity to attain greater independence in an otherwise patriarchal Wilhelmine system. Whether as "priestesses" of the domestic hearth or as business owners, farmers, and mothers of the nation, white women incorporated the postwar consequences of the Herero-Nama genocide into their perceptions of femininity. Though most white men did not face the same occupational and social limitations as their female compatriots, violent conquest nevertheless shaped how they constructed an image of German masculinity. When news first reached the metropole in January 1904 that "the Blacks, like cowards, murdered all the farmers and their wives and children," a surge of patriotic fervor spread throughout broad cross-sections of German society, as it did for the young men in *Peter Moor's Journey to Southwest*.[4] The *Schutztruppe's* total victory three years later seemingly confirmed the merits of their nationalist mission and prepared the triumphant settler army to transform Südwest into a pillar of Germandom.

In the throes of military euphoria, white German men merged their private convictions about the consummate citizen and settler to justify their place in colony and metropole. The following chapter traces how imperial masculinity developed into the ultimate measure of German manhood between 1900 and 1914. Genocide, mass imprisonment, and the colonial government's enforcement of a racial color line created an environment that championed bravado, self-reliance, strength, and cultural hierarchy as the foundation of Germany's authority in DSWA. As contemporary settlers proudly declared, if a man did not exhibit these qualities, then he did not belong in "our Südwest."[5] This sentiment arose chiefly from farmers', soldiers', and travelers' experiences as participants in imperial conflict and the proliferation of discourses on imperial violence's meaning and legacy.[6] Whether on the battlefield or in everyday life, the inherent brutality of their actions provided a lived authenticity to Germany's murderous encounters with Africans.

White German men no longer concerned themselves with questions about why Africans wanted to challenge their hegemony, or about Germany's ultimate purpose in the colony. Instead, their triumphs motivated them to reflect on what they could accomplish as the unrivaled masters of DSWA. Regardless of whether Africa started as a momentary adventure or a meaningless escape from their otherwise muted metropolitan lives, white men now looked upon Südwest as their future. The past did not matter, only posterity. Dominance and racial hierarchy developed into an essential part of the colonial experience, a process that ultimately shaped the sociopolitical framework of DSWA, as well as the contours of German manhood throughout the entire African empire and European metropole.

It is ordinarily impossible to measure the private aspirations of historical agents with any certainty. White German men and their hopeful brethren, however, created an archive of materials where they conveyed their innermost imperial desires. In explicit language, diaries, illustrations, and letters from settlers in Südwest exhibit the characteristics that men perceived as ideally masculine in the wake of Trotha's "annihilation order." One venue where male supporters contemplated their masculinity was in their colonial *Eingaben* (petitions) to the AAKA. Across the metropole, white men from diverse backgrounds and political persuasions saturated these applications with complementary rhetoric. Regardless of their financial affluence or views on the *Schutztruppe*'s pursuit of genocidal warfare, almost every prospective settler evinced a zeal for imperial rule, provided evidence of their mental and physical acuteness, and championed DSWA as a future German India. Masons from Hamburg envisaged innovative architectural projects in a so-called uncultivated land, industrial laborers fantasized about endless horizons and mountainous terrain, and fathers spoke for their daughters' dreams of finding love and increased standing as "culture-bearers" of the nation. Though these documents exude an expectant naïveté about life in DSWA, they illustrate how aspiring colonists accentuated the same masculine notions of Germanness that they read about in memoirs and newspapers. From the imperial fantasies they confessed in official petitions to violent recollections in colonial mission statements, white German men framed their identity in fervent masculine overtones and a civilizational worldview.

We must acknowledge that imperial conceptions of "model men" produced horrific outcomes in Africa during the totality of Europe's colonial age, most notably for African women, men, and children. Germany's colonial project was no different. Racism begat violence. Virulent gendered tropes begat greater acceptance of hypermasculine perceptions of German manhood. This fact did not change even in the aftermath of World War I. Indeed, the same perspectives that fashioned an imperial German masculinity continued to influence metropolitan society long after Germany entered its postcolonial era. Though Weimar Germany never had a formal empire in its fourteen years of existence, civilizational illusions of Africa continued to shape how many white German men regarded themselves in contrast to their imperial past. *Heimat* Südwest might have been gone, but for a majority of former colonists and imperial enthusiasts, the "right man" for Southwest Africa remained the right man for Germany.

"THE MAN WITH UNYIELDING WILLPOWER"

"So far it has rained badly (twice) today. The field is still very dry, water is scarce. If we do not get a good rainy year this year, it will look very bad in the protectorate. Otherwise nothing happens here. I live alone here in Hamakari. . . . I have two cats now because of the mice. They were so strongly represented in the old house that I had to put out bread for them so they would not nibble on the commercial goods."[7] So wrote Hans Warncke, a thirty-two-year-old German settler colonist, from his farm in Hamakari (Waterberg) in November 1903. Born in Neustrelitz the same year that Bismarck and his liberal allies unified Germany in the Hall of Mirrors, Warncke looked curiously upon the world at an early age.[8] When he turned thirteen, he started to keep a diary, a private place where he could escape and note his observations on the local wildlife, the topography of nearby forests, and his desire to emigrate overseas to the United States. Like many young German girls and boys, Warncke brought his exploratory fantasies to life in two-dimensional form as well. He drew at least twenty-seven illustrations of a variety of scenarios, such as a gold-mining camp in California, explorers huddled around a warm campfire cooking fresh meat on a spit, and pioneers surveying new territory in wagon trains and on steam engines.[9] Thoughts of excursions like these consumed his childhood, as his father noted to his friends, family, and teachers regularly.[10]

After he finished school, he began to prepare in earnest for a new life in Germany's overseas empire. In December 1893, the twenty-two-year-old aspiring colonist boarded the *Maria Woermann* and departed for DSWA. "Tomorrow we will probably reach Monrovia. I am currently sitting on a bench on the middle deck," Warncke likely wrote eagerly, "sitting and holding a piece of cardboard and paper on my knees. It is only 7:30 in the morning, but still very hot. . . . We are all excited for the next portion of the journey."[11] Later in the letter, which touched on his lodgings, conditions at sea, and the "quiet, still night air," Warncke described the demeanor of his fellow travelers. "*I know* for sure," he declared, "that all the settlers on the previous ships are still sitting idly in Windhoek for fear of Witboi [Witbooi]. We here on this ship: Schurzens, Mauer, and I decided to stick together and possibly settle close to each other as a result. They are simple, honest, hardworking people and understand the limitless possibilities in front of them. We are all farmers, blacksmiths, locksmiths and mechanics, gunsmiths, watchmakers, and gardeners."[12] Each man seemingly had a common background and general sense about what awaited them in DSWA. They accepted the inevitable hardships and also celebrated the romantic simplicity of their situation—from the looming dangers of Witbooi to the "quiet, still nights" at sea.

Shortly after he arrived in Südwest, Warncke found a small settlement near Otjimbingwe. In a subsequent letter to his parents, he portrayed "the vast country" with its "heavy ox-wagons . . . plate tobacco [and] stingy people" as the geographical and social antithesis of the Kaiserreich.[13] His early correspondence shows that he took great amusement in noting the familiar pleasures from home. In May 1894, for instance, Warncke explained that a certain "Herr Wilke regularly calls me for coffee and to share his fabulous Pentecost cake, which he bakes himself with lots of raisins."[14] He also delighted in the curious and exotic foods, such as *Dickmilch*.[15] Warncke devoted almost an entire letter to a meal he ate in Windhoek, consisting of "salted pickled meat, smelly stockfish, half-raw ox meat, 3–4 potatoes per man, and salty vegetables."[16] Though he appreciated the new experience, he explained that he did not find "the presentation all that appetizing."[17] He also often mused on German colonial policy in these formative years, most especially on the imperial government's confrontations with Witbooi. "The Major von François went to the field against Witbooi, and the new Major Leutwein traveled up to Windhoek 14 days ago. I should be wondering how things are going, for François has made mistakes, especially in attacking Hoornkrans and letting Witboi escape on his horse."[18] Though he was critical of François's actions, Warncke's sympathies remained firmly with the imperial government and his fellow German settlers. He merely wanted regional stability, so that he could enjoy "goose meat, sausages, and bacon" each day without having any serious cause for concern.[19]

The following year, 1895, Warncke's father began publishing his letters in the local *Neustrelitzer Zeitung*. Each one, filled with detailed notes on DSWA's sundry landscapes and prospects for employment, attracted widespread attention throughout Mecklenburg-Schwerin.[20] Perhaps most importantly, Warncke's excitement about life in the colony was palpable to his metropolitan audience. Each illustration of and narrative about Südwest figuratively leaped off the page, creating an informal encounter that manifested a genuine human element for his readership to embrace. "I still praise the moment," he wrote in a letter in 1895, "when, following my inner drive, I decided to go to Southwest Africa. To my German brothers at home, especially you young countrymen, who do not have enough resources to become something where there is too little property, and you young craftsmen, especially wheelwrights, cobblers, bricklayers, and brickmakers, if you want to make a prosperous life but cannot at home, then follow me! . . . Our young colony is becoming the exalted German Southwest Africa!"[21] As in the fanciful tales of the preimperial era, Warncke cast Germany's only settlement colony as a place for everyone, so long as they accepted the hardships of colonial occupation and were willing to work toward one common goal: the cultivation of a prosperous and stable society.

While he never pretended that the situation overseas was easy, his optimism and zest for Germany's imperial mission permeated his letters. Warncke regarded the colony as "a land of freedom" and opportunity, most especially for young Germans trapped in filthy tenements and stationary livelihoods "in daheim."[22] Though he never used the phrase "imperial masculinity," his initial correspondence held up courage, strength, and national pride as essential elements of an ideal German settler. The colony did not simply provide colonists with land and resources. Much to the contrary, German men had to seize and defend territory in a dangerous, isolated, and unforgiving environment. Warncke may have framed this process in optimistic prose, but he was also careful to fashion narratives that appealed only to men who shared the same passion and inner devotion for Germany's imperial cause.

As time passed and Warncke acclimated to his station as a German colonist, however, both his language and his general outlook started to transform. The emotional demeanor of the model German settler remained a focal point in his correspondence, but he steadily began to emphasize culture and race as essential principles for worthy colonists to uphold. Warncke also increasingly characterized Black Africans in derogatory and racist terms, a rhetorical staple that was absent from his formative correspondence. Finally, he started to represent imperial leaders and other Germans with whom he disagreed as "crazy fools."[23] In July 1903, for instance, Warncke shared his displeasure with Leutwein and other imperial officers in a letter to his father. "Now we hear that a police station is coming to Waterberg. District chief Zörn [Zürn] from Okahandja will most likely leave," he wrote, "which is good as he is very unpopular. People have already written poems about him. Leutwein is getting crazier. Soon a law will probably come out of his mouth that forbids the government from supporting a [white] merchant in matters over debt collection with the Hereros."[24] Warncke had previously complained to his parents about his money problems and confrontations with several Ovaherero communities that supposedly reneged on a trade agreement.

Later in the same letter, he criticized German missionaries for what he considered their hypocritical nature. "Those people [the missionaries] tolerate the greatest uncleanliness and meanness among their [Ovaherero] members. Only when a white man takes a native woman into his house," Warncke snapped, "do they tear their snouts open and scold him for his behavior."[25] One month later, he lamented how the death of Kambazembi wa Kangombe, chief of the Waterberg Ovaherero (and Samuel Maharero's cousin), created a heavy strain on his finances. "Kambazembi, the old Herero captain of Waterberg, has died recently. Now there is a great funeral service from all sides over there [Waterberg]," Warncke complained, "and big oxen are slaughtered and fatty liver is made every day. In a way it is very bad for us because we wanted to collect debts and now because of the solemnity of the occasion nobody hears us. That is why I do not know if I can send money to Germany this time."[26] Before Kambazembi's passing, he and other local German colonists had a relatively friendly relationship with Ovaherero polities in the region. That changed, however, once the imperial government intervened and stopped white settlers from acquiring territory as a form of debt collection.

Warncke's letters from this period portray just how much Leutwein's policies incensed white colonists in the region. In October 1903, he confided to his parents that he could not understand why politicians were preventing white Germans from taking advantage of their hegemony in the colony. "You write that complaints have gone to the chancellor from [Südwest]. That is right. Why do people complain? Because the conditions here are so bad. Why are they so bad? Because the government in Germany and the local administration are working to make it difficult for settlers to move forward by force." He also bemoaned the fact that "all essential materials are heavily taxed," which allegedly did not happen in other German colonies.[27] Warncke never directly stated the principal reason for his frustrations. The narratives in his messages and the context in which he wrote them, however, betray his irritation. Ten years after his arrival in southern Africa, he and his fellow German colonists still had to negotiate with their supposed Black African inferiors. Though military victories and outbreaks of disease had reduced the ability of Nama and Ovaherero leaders to resist imperial encroachment, Leutwein forbade German settlers from seizing cattle and land from their unfortunate subjects. Such a diplomatic and passive approach, in Warncke's mind, ran contrary to everything that he and other white settlers had worked so hard to achieve in southern Africa.

In the immediate period before the start of the Herero-Nama war, Warncke aspired to disenfranchise Africans from their regional positions of power and to reduce the scope of the imperial government. He suggested that if weak and "crazy fools" like Leutwein could not achieve this outcome, then "determined settlers" might need to seize the initiative and forge a real colonial state on their own.[28] Warncke refused to accept that white German settlers had to coexist with "lazy, stingy, and tricky" people in *their* colony.[29] In this particular regard, his prejudice knew no bounds. While Warncke focused much of his attention on Nama and Ovaherero polities, he also viewed Afrikaners as an especially dangerous and vile population. "What this Rust v.M. Lhisto [unknown] writes about Germans and Boers is nonsense," Warncke wrote to his parents in October 1903. "Of all the Boers who are here, 2/3 are bankrupt. And they are lazy, by no means better than the Germans! The Boers are undemanding, however; they live just like a Kaffir, and also share the same moral and social ideas." Warncke also took offense at any notion that Germans and Afrikaners shared any cultural or ethnic similarities. To the contrary, he viewed them as a social plague and strove to articulate this racist "fact" to anyone who might read his dispatches in the metropole. "On the whole," he sneered, "Boers are much worse than a native; they absolutely lack a moral standard for their actions. Despite their stinginess and trickery, they also do nothing. They are harmed further by their laziness and stupidity. Almost all people who have worked with them for a long time share my view (here in the country). The bad ones always come here . . . nothing but cowards, rogues, traitors, and wretches."[30] Civilizational and racist stances had overtaken his perspective on the ideal colonist. In Warncke's eyes, all that seemingly mattered now was a person's ethnic orientation.

Warncke played upon these racial stereotypes fervently during this period. In his final letter to his parents in November 1903, he intimated the prospect of a future rebellion in the colony. "The Hottentots near Warmbad [southern Namaland] shot at the police and killed 4 men. A patrol with 14 men and a lieutenant has also disappeared, which has not been seen in 14 days. The German batteries from Omaruru and Karibib have gone to the war zone." Though he tried to calm his family by claiming that "everything in Hamakari is quiet," Warncke did acknowledge that "unsavory" people lived in his vicinity. "Hopefully the poor Kaffirs will soon go away, which would [open up the land] only to those who either have cattle or work with the white man or the servants of their grandparents."[31] Here again, Warncke stressed the value of a person's work ethic and racial background over all other qualities. Südwest needed real men to create an environment that all Germans could regard favorably. Diplomacy and government interference, he believed, merely created an illusion of success. Formal expressions of strength and military supremacy were the only methods that settlers could rely upon to craft an idyllic state in Southwest Africa.

Several years later, near the bottom of this same handwritten message, Hans Warncke's brother Paul inscribed the following note: "My brother Hans's last letter. A few weeks later he was murdered on 14 January 1904."[32] Despite rumors in Neustrelitz that same spring, the AAKA did not officially notify Warncke's family about Hans's fate until four months after his death.[33] In the immediate aftermath of this announcement, local German newspapers published numerous and heartfelt articles about Warncke's contributions to the colonial project in Southwest Africa. One of the most notable pieces appeared under the title "Einer von vielen" (One of many) in the *Landeszeitung*. "One will like to hear [Hans Warncke's] story as an example of German life," the article began, "with its many tribulations and the quiet joys on German-African soil. It is up to us to ensure that he did not become a victim for nothing."[34] Instead of solely calling for revenge, the article shared excerpts from his descriptions of the colony. "The landscape is often beautiful," read one. "You can see so far because the air is so clean. It is especially extraordinary in the evening when the sun goes down and the whole horizon is covered with fire, it is enchantingly beautiful. . . . There is nothing but endless sandy and stony surfaces. And that is exactly what I like because nature is not desecrated here and there are only a few people."[35] The *Landeszeitung* also quoted several other instances where Warncke portrayed Südwest as a German oasis. Only in the piece's final paragraph did the contributors discuss his death. "The Herero uprising was fatal to Warncke, like so many of our compatriots," they declared mournfully. "Warncke was murdered by the Blacks on 14 January of this year. . . . Insolence towards the whites, great mendacity and thievery, drunkenness when [the Ovaherero] get schnapps. It certainly proves that fifty years of Christian influence on such a raw natural people means little for its inner transformation."[36]

A consummate pioneer and lover of nature, at least in his own mind and his family's, Hans Warncke aspired to live his best life in Germany's *Heimat* abroad. His correspondence provides a detailed lens on the principles that guided his imperial desires, as well as the gendered and spiritual qualities that defined his worldview. Perhaps the most remarkable aspect of Warncke's approach to colonialism was his initial optimism and sense of purpose. His sanguine attitude did not adhere to a strict racial color line, at least in comparison to the views he harbored at the end of his life. Much to the contrary, his copious writings projected a general egalitarian sentiment toward *nearly* all people in Southwest Africa. For Warncke, strength, reliance, and hard work were all that separated failure from a prosperous colonial occupation. DSWA did not need *Arbeitsscheu* (work-shy) women and men who were afraid to relinquish the comforts of modern society. Instead, the formation of a self-sufficient colonial state demanded settlers whose prior experiences infused them with a candid sense of patriotism and an appetite for adventure, governance, and sobriety. Warncke's masculinity was not a restrictive identity that he constructed within a primordial racial framework but rather a succession of personality traits he deemed essential for the formation of an imperial homeland. Though he did not reveal an inherent racism or cultural superiority in his first years in southern Africa, we should not mistake Warncke's imperial impulse for a sincere sign of tolerance or romantic colonialism. He emigrated to Southwest Africa as a German settler colonist without invitation, a fact that no amount of superficial compassion can erase. Racial separation and desires for total domination may not have incited his colonial ambitions, but Warncke still maintained a sense of national entitlement that he believed gave him the right to colonize African territory against the collective wishes of local populations.

On the other hand, we need to distinguish his reflections in the 1890s from those in the period immediately before the Herero-Nama war. Warncke's attitude about his station as a German colonist underwent an intense evolution the longer he lived in the colony. Along with physical power and inner determination, he increasingly looked upon cultural enlightenment and ethnicity as markers of civic belonging and self-worth. Warncke's letters after 1900 describe the colonial domain in zero-sum terms, a way of thinking that demanded minority rule in favor of the colonizer at the expense of the colonized. In order to build such an imperial state, capable men needed to embrace their masculinity and suppress all forces that threatened the civil and racial integrity of their realm. DSWA deserved nothing less than a population of white men who had the mental stamina and physical means to take aggressive action against weakness, tolerance, and racial difference. Leutwein's diplomatic outreach and shallow charity toward Black Africans were antithetical to this line of thinking, eventually compelling Warncke to identify exclusively with white colonists, whom he deemed the only real Germans. Though Warncke probably did not recognize any change in his own conduct, metropolitan audiences could easily trace how colonialism affected German settlers like him in their letters and published articles. Over time, these same individuals in Europe began to adopt similar perceptions of what virtues distinguished exemplary men from their fallible neighbors. If an acceptance of cultural hierarchy and displays of toughness were necessary to cultivate a German homeland in southern Africa, they reasoned, it was likely no different for men in the metropole. Hans Warncke's life, both as a young idealist and as a formal colonist, exhibits how colonialism altered one man's views on German masculinity over eleven years.

Though his personal story was not necessarily a universal experience, Warncke was hardly the only white male settler to undergo such an evolution in his identity. Eberhard Rosenblad, a former lieutenant in the Swedish navy, for instance, also experienced a personal transformation while "adventuring" in DSWA. After the untimely death of his daughter in February 1894, he departed for Southwest Africa with the same Swedish trader mentioned in chapter 2, Axel Wilhelm Eriksson. The bereaved Rosenblad sought to participate in an arduous undertaking as a means to redefine himself. While in the colony, he recorded almost everything that he experienced in a journal, which he later published under the title *Adventure in South West Africa*. Rosenblad believed that once he faced the adversarial conditions of DSWA's environment, the masculine impulses that defined his days as a seaman might once again take hold of his character.[37] His diary begins with a detailed overview of what he regarded as the dangers, both hidden and overt, that he and his fellow travelers faced in Africa. "The road which goes over the coastal mountains and down their eastern slopes was not created by nature alone. The work of human beings has had to be employed at particularly difficult places to remove the rocks and even out the slopes. . . . You have to go up and down steep mountain slopes, often with precipices on either side. It has frequently happened that the traces have broken, with the result that the heavy wagon has tumbled down into the depths."[38] Later in the same section, he describes his first encounter with a lion. "A scream of terror! We rush out and just glimpse a large lion that has leapt at the leader of the ox team and is now rushing away with the man between his wide jaws. . . . We have our guns out in a moment. . . . I have been told that people who survived such an incident have said that it is quite a pleasant feeling to be carried away over stock and stone at frantic speed, but I doubt the pleasantness of the situation."[39] While these and numerous other anecdotes present a thrilling account of his first weeks in southern Africa, they also denote the central premise behind Rosenblad's journey to the colony. Above all, he wanted to regain his virility alongside other men whom he regarded as the epitome of European civilization.

Though he had never traveled to Africa before 1894, his notes indicate that contemporary literature and newspaper accounts had filled him with hyperbolic depictions of German Südwest and what he could expect to discover once in country. Interactions with local populations, audacious excursions into uncharted territory, and dangerous confrontations with lions, hyenas, and other wildlife, in other words, promised to make him a man once again. He simply needed to shed the luxuries of so-called modern civilization to recover his vibrant nature and verve as a white European. Despite his intentions, however, Rosenblad's search for a strenuous life brought him face to face with Black Africans, the rightful inhabitants of the region, whom he looked upon with disdain and malice. As a white European traveler with proimperial sympathies, Rosenblad espoused primordial notions of cultural superiority and race that shaped his encounters with Ovaherero and Nama peoples from the very beginning of his sojourn. Page after page, he filled his notebook with illustrations and racist portrayals of local inhabitants. Shortly after he arrived in central Damaraland, for instance, Rosenblad commented on what he perceived as the "vagabond nature" of the population. "In addition to our ordinary servants, our company had more than doubled because of hangers-on who followed the wagons like jackals. Eriksson had strictly forbidden unauthorized persons to accompany us, but during a short journey that he had undertaken with his boys [*gossarna*], he had acquired a whole crowd of jabbering and babbling concubines of all ages and types."[40] Several weeks later, while relaxing under an "enchanting African moonlit night," Rosenblad described Ovaherero dancing rituals in racist, derogatory terms. "Negro dancing is not particularly attractive to watch and does not seem to be very difficult to learn. Generally men, women, and children hop rhythmically round the fire with a kind of polka step while singing a monotonous tune and clapping their hands. They can spend all night doing this without getting tired, and they seem to be enjoying themselves enormously."[41]

Like Warncke, he did not limit his discriminating attitude to one particular polity. While Rosenblad interacted with the Ovaherero more consistently at the start of his expedition, he also perceived southern Africans, especially Nama communities, in the same prejudicial way. In November 1897, during his first safari in Namaland, for example, he shared a story about a violent engagement between a group of "Hottentot scoundrels" and his hunting party. "A friend has written that the Swartbooi Hottentots had risen up in rebellion against the German government, and his advice was that I should join him immediately . . . as they would doubtless try to steal the livestock entrusted to me. . . . As soon as darkness fell, we moved to our allotted places which nobody was allowed to leave before sunrise. I was in charge of the men at the shooting-places on one side of the kraal and had the wagon driver as my partner."[42] All members of the encampment remained in this position for several days, when new information suggested that an attack was imminent. "Since it was now beyond doubt that violence could be expected, our lives were again at stake. Guns and cartridges were examined carefully, the wagons were brought close to the kraal. . . . Sofi and the other servant women were allowed to stay in their 'pondoks' with fires lit outside. . . . The black beauties would not be in any greater danger there, as the battle would certainly be fought over the cattle and would therefore take place around the kraal."[43] Rosenblad's likely sensationalized account reduced all Nama, including the women in his company, to lowly thieves who were too cowardly to confront the hunting party outside the cover of darkness. The racist phrase "black beauties," moreover, denoted the hierarchical and hypersexualized nature of his relationship with African women. His manhood, in other words, was based in overt racism and hierarchical perceptions that elevated his station at the cost of all others in his party.

When Rosenblad boarded the Union Line ship *Mexican* for his return trip to Europe in 1898, he knew that he had accomplished his mission. "Now, as I lay down my pen after this unpretentious description of my adventures in the hunting fields of south-western Africa, my thoughts return to all those who helped me in times of danger and illness. . . . I want to express my warm and sincere thanks to my friend Axel Eriksson: a man with unyielding willpower, who understood how to gain the respect of both the German government and the Portuguese rulers [of Angola], and of the natives of the country."[44] Rosenblad clearly considered himself such a man at this juncture. "Despite all the hardships and dangers, I [will] look back to the free and unfettered life still prevailing in that part of the world. . . . It now belongs to the past, the dark side upon which I have touched."[45] German Südwest invited Rosenblad to shape his masculine fantasies into an adventure that refashioned his character and outlook on the world. His encounters not only elevated his perception about what he could accomplish as a proud and strong man but also affirmed his racial predispositions as a white imperialist. In Rosenblad's mind, he could now go forward and represent himself proudly as a virile member of a superior culture. DSWA's milieu of so-called dangerous Africans, sun-scorched landscapes, and menacing wildlife tested his manhood in a way that "modern" Europe could never replicate. Men must struggle, he believed, either to discover their innate masculinity for the first time or to retain it over the course of their lives. Colony and metropole, in this manner, folded together into a conceptual space where men could seek out and perform their manhood. Episodes of imperial violence such as Rosenblad's early morning encounter with Nama "bandits" merely gave aspiring enthusiasts more reason to "take up their burden" as white men in German Südwest.

Colonialism was not an undertaking for everyone. While individual German men generally retained the right to make such a decision for themselves, a significant number of white colonists, through their correspondence and travel literature, tried to control who might aspire to live overseas. As Warncke, Rosenblad, and many others asserted, if white men wanted to secure a place in the *Heimat* abroad, they needed to exhibit the same masculine qualities that they manifested on a daily basis. Hubert Janson, a white German settler farmer in Franzfontein (northwestern Damaraland), exemplified this argument.[46] In the popular contemporary periodical *Kolonie und Heimat: Im Wort und Bild*, he contended that "the man who easily loses the desire, who is fearful and accustomed to good living and social life, who always must have spiritual refreshment and cannot endure loneliness and exertion, [should] remain at home with Mother." In DSWA, "one must be everything, gardener, livestock breeder, farmer . . . hunter, trapper, smith, cartwright mason, plumber, glassblower, yes even photographer. . . . The man who does not shun work and who has a little bit of the devil in his body, he is the right man for our Southwest!"[47] Male enthusiasts throughout Germany regarded Janson as the model German man. He represented not only what Germans could accomplish in southern Africa but also how conquest could shape the social outlook and national demeanor of citizens in the metropole.

Though his colonial situation was certainly not universal, the romantic sentiments his narrative evoked made a clear impression on the public, most especially among those who longed for their own plot of land in German Südwest. As we have seen, official and unofficial organizations circulated imperial propaganda that portrayed empire in heroic and serene terms. Concomitantly, descriptions like Janson's honest and unapologetic narrative promoted an organic image of rugged masculinity, one with the power to tame Southwest Africa's "rebellious landscapes" and "defiant populations" for the collective good of the German nation. Such a person, seemingly capable of constructing an imperial homeland through his sheer force of will, thus emerged as the personification of German masculinity both overseas and in the metropole.

"AN ESSENTIAL PART OF THE COLONIAL EXPERIENCE"

As much as the imperial government relied upon white men to create the social conditions for absolute rule, German officials depended upon troops in the protection and police forces to uphold their decrees. German commandos, in particular, regularly articulated their actions in a hyper-masculine lexis due to this circumstance. As Gesine Krüger has shown, the protection force was neither "a machine of cool killers" nor an "Aryan fighting organization" that unleashed eliminatory warfare out of a "Eurocentric desire" for bloodshed.[48] Those who joined its ranks were instead a combination of young men who were away from home for the first time, hardened veterans of previous military campaigns in other German colonies, and farmers, merchants, miners, and volunteers whom the imperial government conscripted into service after the start of the Herero-Nama war. Though a majority of them had no formal knowledge of colonial warfare, they accepted their charge on behalf of the German nation-state. Formal encounters in a setting seemingly in a constant state of upheaval pressed white German would-be farmers into becoming combatants in the Kaiser's imperial protection force. Increasingly, warfare taught these men how to forge an empire on and off the battlefield. Combat, drought, exhaustion, and partic- ipation in genocidal policies over time inspired in them a personal relationship with the open savannahs that they were fighting to preserve for white settler rule.

In the wake of their military experiences, veterans looked at German Südwest's future through a lens of exclusionary violence and cultural hier- archy. Their military exploits between 1904 and 1908 not only motivated them to defend their actions in memoirs and various other publications but also permanently bound them to the mythology and success of Germa- ny's only African settler colony. In vivid detail, imperial soldiers worked to inspire only those metropolitans whom they regarded as "the right men for Südwest" to emigrate overseas. The measure of German masculinity everywhere, as a result, increasingly aligned with what white colonists in DSWA regarded as the model man. From bookstores and newspaper stands in Berlin to the so-called desolate terrain that the *Schutztruppe* struggled to overcome, imperial masculinity framed what German men compared themselves against during the first decade of the twentieth century.

Ludwig von Estorff, a combatant and eventual commander of the protection force in German Südwest, personifies this argument. Born into a noble family in Hamburg in 1859, Estorff grew up idolizing the Prussian army. He enrolled in Berlin's prestigious *Kadettenhaus* (Lichterfelde) and upon graduation started his career as an officer in the First Thuringian Infantry Regiment of the German army.[49] After receiving several promo- tions, which brought him temporarily to the War Academy and German General Staff, Estorff sought a post in the imperial *Schutztruppe* in June 1894. Before embarking for southern Africa, Estorff enumerated his moti- vations for seeking this command to his father. "Such an opportunity to see the world," he wrote, "would never be offered to me again. The climate [in Südwest] is the most favorable in all of Africa, and even if the stay will have some downsides, I still believe that I would be in my perfect place. The prospect for advancement, no matter how magnificent, would only stop me for a moment now that the life of soldiers and hunters in the colo- nies has beckoned me. Many of our great generals have also looked around the world in their younger years, Moltke, Grolman, Werder, and others."[50] Confident and filled with youthful ambition, Estorff embraced the oppor- tunity to follow in the footsteps of his military heroes.

Shortly after he arrived in DSWA, Estorff's superiors sent him into the country's interior to face Hendrick Witbooi. He started to keep a diary and documented his exploits during the campaign, which he eventually published under the title *Migration and Fighting in Southwest Africa, East Africa, and South Africa.*[51] His entries indicate that he was already well acquainted with the Nama captain's exploits against German troops, including some of the same men who were now under his command. "In Swakopmund," Estorff wrote, "the Gouverneur Major Leutwein welcomed us and discussed the situation and our task. The government had been at war with the Wittboi-Hottentot tribe and their chief Hendrik Wittboi for more than a year. [We need] to drive him out of his safe mountainous hiding place, [which] is a vast mountain range near Naukluft."[52] Estorff wanted to bring the war to a quick conclusion so that Germans could take full advantage of the colony's vast resources and agricultural promise. As a civilizational corollary to this aspiration, he looked upon Black Africans as natural sources of labor. He reasoned that the *Schutztruppe* must secure a decisive victory without inflicting immense bloodshed on the Nama (and later the Ovaherero). In order to achieve this goal, Estorff structured his regiment into small formations that had the ability to deploy and attack rapidly.[53]

When he was not formulating military strategies alongside his fellow officers, Estorff found time to sketch his impressions of Southwest Africa. Like other contemporary German settlers and travelers, he filled his diary with hand-drawn maps, illustrations, and rich portrayals of what he saw as the colony's harsh terrain. "The land on the coast receives almost no rain. The dry east winds, however, heat up the sun-drenched ground and arrive on the coast with a blaze of desert wind, which carries lots of loose, fine sand and is a terrible nuisance that we all can still fully taste."[54] His words form a clear image of a desolate and at times hazardous landscape. Nevertheless, Estorff's portrayal of Südwest's rugged beauty evidences a sincere appreciation for southern Africa. Though sun-scorched and tired, with mouths full of dry sand, he and his troops sustained their disciplined march against their "formidable foes" with a deep-seated commitment to the settler-colonial project. In their minds, they were fulfilling their national duty, both as Germans and as men, in the deserts of Southwest Africa.

Among the most descriptive sections in Estorff's diary are those that portray his African allies. "The [Rehoboth Basters] had been involved in the long-standing struggles of the Hottentots and the Hereros by themselves, until they reasonably joined the Germans and provided us with local leaders and fighters. The Basters are crossbreeds [*Mischlinge*] of whites and

Hottentots and look very different. Most of them look like southern Europeans, others very much like the Hottentots, and a few with blond hair and blue eyes could hardly be distinguished from Boers or Low Germans [*Niederdeutschen*]." Most "had adopted the names of the Boers: van Wyk, Wimmert, Diergardt and others . . . some are also rich in herds of cattle and sheep, horses and ox wagons. . . . They were far superior to us in knowing the country and in getting used to the climate, the rigors of which they could easily endure physically and more efficiently."[55] Though his style does not employ the rhetorical bombast of Warncke's final letters, Estorff's observations demonstrate that he viewed imperial society through a racial lens as well. In his mind, the Rehoboth Basters' cultural and ethnic features made them natural partners. DSWA's so-called forsaken landscapes and unruly populations required a strong presence that could protect Germany's national interests in southern Africa for the foreseeable future.

We can additionally read these narratives as private musings on one person's identity under siege. His relentless attempts to frame Südwest in foreboding language perpetuated a colonial storyline that looked favorably upon courageous white male protagonists in a campaign against "cultural barbarism" and "sloth." The combination of DSWA's environment and "hostile populations" coerced Estorff to seek refuge in his identity, an exclusionary space where he found legitimacy as a colonial occupier. White masculinity operated as a mechanism for Estorff to distinguish himself from Black Africans on his terms. The more he retreated into his colonial identity, the more Estorff's anxieties about "white masculinity and racial robustness" shaped his views about the ideal German settler.[56] Similar to Hubert Janson, he believed that a man who could not endure material deprivation and hardship "should remain home with mother" and leave colonialism to the real men.[57] Imperial hegemony eventually made Estorff's conception of the idyllic German settler "ripe for export" to the German metropole, where favorable audiences could incorporate the same beleaguered mentality in their own processes of identity formation.[58] Estorff's views about imperial masculinity only grew deeper the longer he stayed in colonial Africa. After he and his fellow fighting men helped Leutwein defeat Witbooi in 1894, he remained in Windhoek until 1896, when he left to participate in Germany's campaign against Nicodemus Kavikunua. Estorff's superiors transferred him briefly to German East Africa in 1900, but he returned to DSWA only a year later to assume the role of deputy commander of the *Schutztruppe*.

When the Herero-Nama war started in January 1904, Estorff's singular identity as a white imperial officer steered his convictions even more intensely, most especially in how he regarded Ovaherero and other African polities. Shortly after the beginning of hostilities, Estorff, now a lieutenant colonel, took control of the First Regiment, which played a central role in Trotha's assault at Waterberg in August 1904. Trotha ordered Estorff's regiment to pursue all Ovaherero survivors into the Omaheke Desert (*Sandveld*) as a measure in his eliminatory campaign. Estorff later depicted the entire operation in victorious terms.

> Through a violent march I succeeded in finding them [the Ovaherero] by a large rain pond and fought them back in battle. They were forced to turn south again as a result, but this time through a great thirst march [*Durstmarsch*] on which they lost a lot of cattle. . . . The thirsty cattle lay around [the wells] after they reached them with the last of their strength, but could not be watered in time. The Herero then fled ahead of us into the *Sandveld*. . . . They fled from one [dry well] to the other and lost almost all of the cattle and many people. The people shrank to scanty remains.[59]

Despite his triumphant tone, Estorff disagreed with Trotha's genocidal strategy. "It was a cruel and foolish policy to smash the people so much," he confessed privately. "We could have saved a lot of them and their herd wealth. . . . I suggested this to General von Trotha, but he wanted their total annihilation."[60] In Estorff's mind, a systematic "punishment through defeat would have sufficed" and would have enabled German colonists to reap the material spoils of their victory.

While he committed his disapproval of Trotha's tactics to the pages of his diary, Estorff carried out the annihilation order to the fullest extent possible. We should, therefore, regard his privileged sentiments not as an expression of regret but rather as a difference of opinion on the totality of Germany's military engagement against its African enemies. Estorff believed that German settlers had a justifiable right to seize property and to live in a manner consistent with his hierarchical perspective on white colonial rule. He may have disagreed with Trotha's approach, but he celebrated its sociopolitical results when the fighting came to its violent end. In 1907, members of the German General Staff recognized Estorff's conduct against the Ovaherero in highly favorable terms. "The enemy was chased from water station to water station half-rushed to death," they boasted, "until he finally became a victim of the nature of this own country. Südwest's water-less Omaheke [Desert] was supposed to complete what German weapons had started: the destruction of the Herero people."[61] The General Staff's words reflect the full measure of their intentions for the colony. They also signify how imperial conflict pressed even distinguished soldiers in the elite officer corps to compare themselves with men like Estorff. Whether a combatant in the German army or colonial *Schutztruppe*, male enthusiasts embraced imperial masculinity as an exemplar for how to perform one's duty in both colony and metropole. Südwest provided them—either formally or informally—with a space where they could evolve into their best selves and permanently sew Germandom into the colony's cultural and spatial fabric.

Gottreich Hubertus Mehnert, a self-proclaimed "knight of the *Schutztruppe*," also celebrated the value of masculine prowess in his memoir, *With Sword and Ploughshare in Saxony and Southwest Africa*. The son of an aristocratic landowner in Saxony, Mehnert enjoyed a life of privilege during his childhood. When he turned eighteen, he enlisted in the German Nineteenth Field Artillery Regiment in Erfurt, where he served for one year.[62] After completing his military service, Mehnert returned to the family estate as a senior agricultural inspector but soon left after an explosive altercation with his father. In August 1904, Mehnert volunteered for the imperial *Schutztruppe* and joined 812 soldiers and 32 officers aboard a steamship headed for DSWA.[63] "I had a chance to carve out my own corner in Africa. And so, against the wishes of my father," he wrote, "I emigrated to Africa, the sunny land that was to become my new *Heimat*."[64] Shortly after their ship docked in Swakopmund, Mehnert and his company began their long march into the colony's interior. "In the beautiful Swakop valley," he wrote, "the squadron moved further into the country, with music. On the right and left in the rugged mountain walls sat the countless masses of lizards that sang to the beat of our musicians: gecko, gecko, gecko, and the crickets sang in unison."[65] Later during the same advance, Mehnert questioned why "some parties hostile to the fatherland in the Reichstag" could oppose Germany's imperial project in southern Africa.[66] Quite simply, Mehnert's new environment overwhelmed his sensibilities. He was convinced that Germany's defense of the colony was worth any trial that existed beyond the horizon. In his mind, the likely deprivation, hunger, illness, and death that awaited them had the power to join colony and *Heimat* together forever.[67]

As his armed detachment approached Okahandja, his attention quickly shifted from Southwest Africa's natural orchestra and serene beauty to the war against the Ovaherero. "These people have endured two hard years of war with us, and have touched every rider at least once. In Okahandja the picture was quite warlike. When we moved in, another company brought in a few hundred captured Herero warriors, followed by a gun with 12 oxen. 'If you think you are going to war, you have to write [about it].' These were the words you heard everywhere."[68] Mehnert's diary, above all, glorifies the cavalry and its role in Germany's subjugation of the Ovaherero. On multiple occasions, he portrays horses and riders in mythic prose, as if they alone could secure victory. "[The squadron leader] and I have two stocky, unassuming Masurian mares, which like their riders are not afraid of death and the devil. We march almost daily," he boasted, "for weeks and months and already in the Herero uprising, through bush-covered grass steppes and forest-like tree populations, toward the insidious enemy, who likes to launch surprise attacks from hidden points."[69] In the same section, Mehnert gave voice to the connection between a soldier and his four-legged companion. "Take care on the left, Schilling [deputy sergeant], I am doing this on the right. I then patted my brown mare, Bertha, nicely on the neck. Because what both riders do not see, the horses' sensitive smell often alert us to the enemy. [We] speak little and only whisper when we do. Our eyes, accustomed to the environment, sweep forward, left and right, searching the red Kalahari sand for fresh traces."[70] In addition to several promotions, he received numerous decorations for his conduct in the Herero-Nama war.

Mehnert's service in the *Schutztruppe* instilled in him a deep-seated love for the colony and Germany's imperial mission. At the war's conclusion, he chose to stay in southern Africa and assumed the role of settler-farmer. Mehnert's special relationship with the land arose primarily from his experience in what he perceived as a justified conflict. He believed that others, most notably men with the same "conviction and soldierly stamina," could also find an agreeable life in German Südwest.[71] "Large landowners get by with much less land," he affirmed, "and there is room for new farmers. New cities are springing up out of the ground, because in addition to agriculture and animal husbandry, the mineral treasures are processed on site. All people find enough bread, thousands and thousands of people flock to the country. . . . Mother Germany shelters her hungry children in the safe womb of her colony."[72]

Lieutenant Erich Friedrich Oscar von Schauroth's involvement in the Herero-Nama war led to a very similar outcome. After growing up in an aristocratic family in East Prussia, Schauroth enlisted in the famous Queen Augusta Guard, where he remained for three years.[73] In April 1905,

Schauroth's superiors transferred him to the imperial protection force in DSWA. One month after his arrival, he received a promotion to serve as Lieutenant Colonel Estorff's adjutant. In this capacity, Schauroth partici- pated in numerous engagements against the Nama and Bondelswarts over the next two years. When not encountering Africans in combat, he composed at least thirty-six letters to his father in Germany, who subse- quently published them in a short book entitled *Dear Father: Letters from the Nama Uprising, 1905–1906*. Schauroth offered his unvarnished perspec- tive on a number of topics in these missives, including his impressions of the campaign, the Nama's use of guerrilla warfare, and how he felt about his comrades and superiors. As Estorff's adjutant, however, he mostly noted the valiant deeds of Germany's imperial soldiers. In a letter of 1 July 1905, for instance, Schauroth provided a detailed summary of an encounter with the Nama near Sandfontein (southern Namaland). "No sooner had we formed the marching column and the point had not yet taken 800 steps when it was popping on all sides. Two point men had been shot in the head. The usual picture, everything apart, artillery and machine guns opened and in 5 minutes the thing was in full swing."[74] Schauroth explained that he "was with members of the Ninth Company [at the time], where the others were nobody knew. The Hottentots apparently had their shipyard pretty safe and left unseen after a one-hour battle. We buried our dead and then followed very carefully. From now on, our advance was such that there were always two guns on one bend and the avant-garde on the heights at the next bend."[75] Surprise attacks, forced marches, and a determined enemy pushed Schauroth to his physical limits.

Though an arduous trial, his war against the Nama shaped him into the type of man—at least in his mind—whom Germany could rely on in the future. After his many triumphs in DSWA, Schauroth returned to the Queen August Guard in Berlin, where he eventually earned the rank of captain. His experience as a colonial soldier, however, left him with memo- ries and experiences that weighed heavily upon his mind. Upon his retirement from the German army in 1913, Schauroth returned to Südwest as a settler colonist. For him, the toils of battle gave him a permanent attach- ment to the imperial landscape.[76] Regardless of his time away from the colony, he felt bound to its future. One made the other whole. Colony and *Heimat* were more than two mutually exclusive locales, at least for men like Schauroth. Imperial warfare tied his identity to the colonial hemi- sphere, forging colonial Africa and metropolitan Germany together into one cohesive homeland.

Another officer in the *Schutztruppe*, who chose to remain anonymous, offered a similar narrative about the conditions that connected him to the colony. The author originally published his diary, entitled *My War Experiences in German Southwest Africa*, with the help of an anonymous veteran of the Franco-Prussian War. The older officer relied closely on notes from the anonymous soldier's diary and contributed short annotations throughout the piece as well. The memoir begins with a romantic overview of the conditions that inspired him to join the imperial protection force. "I struggled with fate. A year ago [1903] I had signed up for the *Schutztruppe* in Africa in order to get out of the constant monotonous garrison service [in Germany], where I could stand on my own feet over there in the mysterious black continent, and create with my own strength a new German colony as a cultural pioneer. . . . Thank God!"[77] His joy leaps off the page and makes his experience tangible for the reader, as is also evident in Warncke's letters to his father and Janson's enthusiasm for imperial life.

After the first chapter the Franco-Prussian War veteran takes his turn. His opening words make clear just how much the fighting in Südwest affected his own views about the courageous men sacrificing to defend *their* overseas domain and Germany's place in the world. "Now I want to speak about our Africa! What can we old people from 1870 truly say, do the dangers, efforts and deprivations we suffered even remotely compare to those of our young comrades in Südwest? I went through the whole campaign in France from the first to the last day and can honestly say: no! [Their bravery is purer.] . . . As the war continued, a positive mood among broader sections of the German people, who still had a heart for the welfare and woe of the thousands of children of their country, who went into battle with joyful sacrifice, increased more and more."[78] His commentary confirms the degree to which events overseas influenced audiences in the metropole. In no uncertain terms, he asserted that Germany's imperial mission in Südwest was just as nationally significant as their victory over France in 1870. Each conflict was necessary, in his estimation, to create a sovereign, strong, and vibrant German Empire, one that started in Central Europe and then expanded to southern Africa.

Through the anonymous author's formal encounters, readers learned about the busy atmosphere that greeted soldiers when they first disembarked in the harbor at Swakopmund, about the so-called "Black Southwest African beauties" who titillated the male German onlookers, and about "the heroes of Waterberg."[79] In a chapter he entitles "Our Heroes at Waterberg," for instance, the author portrays the Ovaherero as "nothing more than skillful cowards" in the face of the superior protection force. "On 11 August . . . the Hereros began to close on the wings of the Germans. But soon the artillery that could only follow on the sandy floor arrived and opened fire. The firefight was extremely violent in the front. Both wings were clutched by a superior enemy, and numerous black figures appeared in the back of the Germans in the bush. A new front was quickly formed, however, so that the German division now formed two half circles with the small gap in the middle."[80] The author then advances the story forward to illustrate the gallantry of the protection force. "The Hereros pressed harder and harder on the brave German band. The wilder and faster their fire became, the calmer and safer that the Germans became. 'Aim quietly— every shot must be a hit,'" Captain [Harry] Puder ordered right before the charge."[81]

Later in the same chapter, the anonymous officer details the scale of their victory. "The total number of Hereros was estimated at 60,000, but later expanded to 100,000 heads. The number of prisoners was around 15,000 with those added after Waterberg, August 1904. A small number, who fled east across the border with the chief and instigator of the uprising, Samuel Maharero, were disarmed at the Ngami by the English, reduced to a single small gang, without cattle and weapons. There is now peace and quiet and the small farmers have largely resumed their businesses."[82] Astonishingly, the author follows this celebratory account with a discussion of the fate of the Ovaherero in the Omaheke Desert. This is especially notable given his intended audience in the metropole. While he, of course, does not use the word "genocide," the officer openly admits that German soldiers strove to destroy the Ovaherero once and for all. "Where has the great vanished people of the mighty Herero gone? Where are their hundreds of thousands of cattle?" he asks rhetorically. "It was a long time before the puzzle was solved. Major von Estorff, the well-tried and brave 'old African,' advanced in October 1904 (two months later) to the east along the waterless bed of the Eiseb; the lack of water forced them to turn around. . . . The assumption that the whole people in the sand of the Omaheke was destroyed by thirst and hunger is more and more likely."[83] In a chapter where he dubs imperial troops the "heroes of Waterberg" and romanticizes their valiant conduct, the author undoubtedly wanted to cast eliminatory warfare as a necessary undertaking to preserve Germany's imperial foothold in Africa.

A stable colony, at least according to this interpretation, required resolute fighting men to create a social climate for German colonists at the physical expense of everyone else. The *Schutztruppe*, therefore, was correct to carry out a systematic campaign of annihilation, an opinion that both authors expressed openly in *My War Experience*. As "arbiters of culture," white German soldiers and settlers were in southern Africa to create a new German homeland beyond the shores of Europe.[84] Their formal experiences together on the battlefield inculcated this belief even more firmly in their hearts and minds. German Southwest Africa was *German* thanks to their service and sacrifice. If men in the metropole wanted to participate in colonialism, they first needed to embrace an imperial worldview that recognized comradeship, patriotism, and whiteness as the cultural foundations of postwar Südwest.

In addition to the protection force, men in the *Landespolizei* (imperial police) also espoused a favorable view of hypermasculinity and its necessity for the creation of a hierarchal social order. As Jakob Zollmann and Marie Muschalek have shown, a significant majority of the police's personnel came from artisanal and agricultural backgrounds.[85] When men arrived in the colony, either as soldiers or as artisans, the imperial police immediately offered them the chance "to escape the strain of modernity" that they felt negatively affected them in the metropole.[86] Not only did these men have a chance to earn a decent salary and establish themselves in colonial society, but they also relished their capacity to affect the legal contours of the imperial state through the use of juridical and physical acts of violence.[87] As it had for white German miners and small farmers who joined the *Schutztruppe* in 1904, the feel of a uniform and a position of purpose left lasting impressions on their identities as colonists and men. For the first time in their lives, they had power over others. Their station as white imperialists already afforded them considerable authority in postgenocide DSWA. But now, as members of the imperial police, they were in a position to establish themselves as masters of the colony.

Members of the *Landespolizei*, as a result, regularly treated African communities with contempt and malice, most especially in the aftermath of the Herero-Nama genocide. Over time, individual policemen strove to prove their masculine honor through public displays of brutality. Sergeant Emil Hirschmüller, for instance, wrote in his police exam that "the best administered remedy [to achieve atonement for wrongdoings] is an immediate, really palpable punishment. . . . Besides the withdrawal of foodstuffs, drinks, and tobacco, the Herero recognize only a palpable beating as real punishment."[88] The racial overtones in this statement are both overt and purposeful. Policemen like Hirschmüller genuinely believed that "uncultivated peoples" such as the Ovaherero and Nama possessed only the most basic means of social interaction. In this manner, their infliction of physical acts of violence on African "criminal deviants" was the only method that German police could use to inspire sincere behavioral change. White authorities, therefore, seized upon corporal punishment as a tool to manifest control throughout imperial Südwest.[89] Fierce interrogations, physical beatings, public shaming, food depravation, and the use of batons, metal shackles, and whips also permitted policemen to validate their masculine prowess to their peers and supervisors. Such actions, like the experiences of their settler-colonial brethren in the *Schutztruppe*, cultivated an atmosphere that celebrated patriarchal and racial archetypes as model police officers. Regular acts of brutality, in this way, evolved into common practice. Violence begat violence; imperial masculinity begat colonial hierarchy.

Military service in Germany's only settler colony afforded men a chance to forge a new life for themselves in a locale where they were recognized as social elites, often for the first time. Whether on the battlefield or in the streets of Windhoek or Okahandja, their experience as soldiers and members of the imperial police connected them to DSWA. Their exploits in forced marches, training facilities, and battle, most notably between 1904 and 1908, also granted them occasions to chronicle the dangers and hardships that they overcame in letters, newspaper articles, and memoirs. In most cases, these men prepared their accounts for a European audience. "I have finished my descriptions," the anonymous soldier wrote at the end of *My War Experience*. "If my coauthor and I succeeded in showing what I was trying to show, readers now have a picture of war in Southwest Africa, [and can see] that we old soldiers, who were able to help in the great war of 1870/71 in building a strong German Empire, are able to look proudly and confidently at the young generation, and furthermore to set an honorary monument in the hearts of readers for the brave fighters, as well as the dead. If we succeeded, then this book served its purpose!"[90]

In illustrative detail, veterans of imperial conquest tried to inspire metropolitans whom they regarded as "the right men for Südwest" both to support their cause and to consider a life overseas. The measure of German masculinity aligned more and more with what white colonists regarded as the model man. Imperial masculinity, in this way, framed how white German men in Europe and Africa analyzed themselves in the context of empire. The normalcy of imperial violence, moreover, produced a firm sense of "what it meant to be a man."[91] From their collective suffering in the waterless Omaheke to their adoption of systemic brutality as members of the *Landespolizei*, a significant collective of white men believed in the value of strength, hierarchy, and the ability to wield such power reflexively and without remorse. In this manner, *Heimat* Südwest was as much a laboratory for brutal statecraft as it was a conduit for the imperial consensus to incorporate colonial life into national affairs in the metropole.

"THE STRENGTH AND INNER UNITY OF *DEUTSCHTUM*"

Extreme visions of adventure and colonial violence evolved into essential features of German imperial masculinity. In addition to the writings of white farmers and soldiers in DSWA, we can also trace this development in the colonial *Eingaben* that aspiring settlers submitted to the AAKA. From across the metropole, men from diverse social backgrounds and with dissimilar political persuasions filled these applications with similar rhetoric and notions of German nationalism. Regardless of their financial affluence or views on annihilatory warfare, almost every prospective settler stressed a zeal for imperial rule, provided evidence of his mental and physical acuteness, and championed DSWA's national potential. Many also believed that Germany required men of action to succeed on the global stage. In their minds, the formative history of colonial rule in Southwest Africa made that fact abundantly clear.

H. Lane, a resident of Hamburg, exemplified this experience. In February 1912, he wrote the AAKA about his desire to emigrate overseas with his wife and children. "My family consisting of five people has the desire to emigrate to German [South] West Africa. I am thirty-nine years old, healthy, big and strong, with a thirty-four-year-old healthy wife, fifteen-year-old strong son, eleven-year-old daughter, and young three-year-old baby."[92] Though neither he nor any member of his family had ever traveled to Africa, Lane insisted that they "were familiar with the land and society in colonial German [South]West Africa."[93] Lane's family simply wanted to assist in the construction of a new *Heimat* ideal that stretched from metropole to colony and back. Colonial *Eingaben* such as H. Lane's corroborate the extent to which hopeful imperialists used jingoistic language to justify their involvement in the colonial project. In addition to occupational proficiencies, academic credentials, military service, and general background information, hopeful settlers chronicled their dreams of economic independence, national security, and adventure in these petitions.

In 1902, the German Colonial Office opened the Zentral-Auskunftstelle für Auswanderer (Central Information Bureau for Emigrants, ZAfA), a state-funded association under the auspices of the DKG. The ZAfA quickly emerged as the central resource for hopeful German settlers. In its first year of operation, the ZAfA received over 3,300 petitions from factory workers, artisans, shopkeepers, and farmers who were interested in colonial emigration. Those figures stayed constant until the conclusion of the Herero-Nama genocide, when the number of petitions tripled to over 9,500. In the final months before the start of hostilities in 1914, 19,714 prospective German colonists inquired about Germany's overseas territories in Africa, China, and New Guinea. One such applicant who filed a petition with the ZAfA was Rud Erpf, a twenty-year-old self-described "healthy and strong" student from the Hohenheim Landwirtschaftliche Hochschule in Stuttgart. In his *Eingabe*, he concentrated especially on his desire to work on a "Southwest African farm or plantation" and stated that "plenty of opportunity awaited" in Germany's African empire.[94] As a way to demonstrate his commitment to DSWA, Erpf requested that the German government allow him to fulfill his military conscription duties in the colonial *Schutztruppe*. That same year, Karl Freimüller, a dentist from Mannheim, contacted the ZAfA on behalf of two families who "longed to get to German Southwest Africa."[95] Freimüller explained that an article in the *Mannheimer Tagesblatt* portrayed a "positive outlook for settlers in DSWA" and inspired him to contact the ZAfA as a means to speak in favor of their application. Karl Cremer, a barber from Düren, Westphalia, meanwhile, looked to Germany's first African colony as a land of limitless promise. Though he was "only twenty-nine years old [with] one thousand marks in savings," Cremer believed that he had the ideal qualities necessary for settlement overseas.[96] So, too, did Julius Asser, an upholsterer and decorator from Hamburg. In his *Eingabe*, Asser emphasized that he was "not timid" in the face of "hard work in D.S.W. Africa" but wanted an opportunity to succeed in a new social environment.[97]

These authors all shared more than a general curiosity about Germany's first colony. In each case, DSWA represented a place where they could reach their fullest individual potential. Though they never articulate it explicitly, Erpf, Cremer, Freimüller, and Asser's letters imply an inner restlessness for change. The repetitive nature of their occupations and the financial constraints of a working-class socioeconomic station compelled them to look elsewhere for fulfilment. Colonial Africa offered them an escape from the cramped and uneventful circumstances of their daily lives in Germany. New occupational prospects, however, were only part of the story. The allegation that their lives lacked purpose implied a sense of disunity and loss, two sentiments that conflicted with a traditional *Heimat* rhetoric that promoted community, family, and common national tenets. Erpf, Cremer, and Asser expressed an emotional detachment from their local environment and aspired for a home that was devoid of the industrial, urban, and social conditions they felt thwarted their attempts at happiness. DSWA afforded them a chance to rediscover themselves outside their homeland, but in a place that still seemed culturally familiar and within the political strictures of the German Empire.

Exposés on career prospects and desires for personal fulfillment were not the only ways prospective settlers participated in the construction of a global *Heimat* ideal. Many also appealed directly to the strength of the German nation and the necessity of European imperial domination. J. Christ, a resident of Nuremberg, for instance, wrote the ZAfA about his desire "to establish a new *Heimat* in Southwest Africa" in October 1910.[98] Christ explained that he and his family "had enough practical experience with field work" in Germany and could easily adapt to the environmental conditions in southern Africa. In particular, Christ tried to assert his nationalist commitment to the colonial project. "We would like to establish a new German livelihood [*Existenz*] and work to create a foundation in Germany's new [colonial] possession." He concluded that "we will leave no stone unturned to be German and remain German."[99] Ludwig Eckstein, meanwhile, articulated a desire to "return to the Southwest [African] *Heimat*" as a *Kleinsiedler* (small landowning settler).[100] Eckstein wrote that his experience as a soldier in the Herero-Nama war had opened his eyes to the realities of colonial life and inspired him to start a new life in German Südwest.

Johann Andrae, a former soldier in the *Schutztruppe*, advanced a similar appeal in his *Eingabe*. Andrae stressed his "excellent health" and remarked that "he never once contracted a disease during his entire period of service." He attributed his demeanor to "youthful vigor and a general healthy disposition." Andrae's petition, however, primarily emphasized his desire to help Germanize DSWA through settlement. "I am currently on military leave [in Hamburg]," he explained, "and would like to return to Southwest Africa for the purposes of settlement before my conscription expires on 20 October 1907." Overcome with "duty and devotion," Andrae wanted to embark for DSWA "as soon as possible!"[101] Georg Andler, another member of the *Schutztruppe*, was even more forceful in his *Eingabe*. "I beg your pardon to ask whether or not the colonies are still seeking pastors, craftsman, and the like and if the government supports such feeble groups in this manner. I was in the imperial *Schutztruppe* for 2 ½ years and fought in the insurrection against the Hottentots in Southwest Africa and would like to return to the colony."[102] Andler's assertion that "pastors, craftsmen, and the like" were nothing more than "feeble groups" underscored his rationale for settlement. The success of Germandom overseas required strong, able-bodied men to defend the hard-fought territorial gains in the wake of the Herero-Nama genocide. Andler's colonial petition argued that it was his sacred duty to secure DSWA for the nation and future generations of prospective German settlers.

Christ, Andrae, and Andler all fortified their *Eingaben* with appeals to German nationalism and collective impressions of duty and honor. Each petition suggested an urgency about the future of the colonial project and advocated increased settlement so as to counteract the so-called negative indigenous and "weak" elements already present in DSWA. In addition, they asserted a patriotic commitment to the success and development of a new German *Heimat*. Christ's pledge to "leave no stone unturned to be German and remain German" was not an empty phrase. To the contrary, it embodied the spirit of aspiring colonists who fixated on communal values, language, and customs as a cultural fabric that bound DSWA to the German nation and the *Heimat* ideal. Perhaps most noteworthy, however, is how closely these *Eingaben* emulated the mission statements of procolonial organizations, specifically those that championed overseas expansion using nationalist rhetoric. "For centuries, a heavy stream of German emigration flowed across the borders of the empire into foreign lands," began the program for the Gesellschaft für Deutsche Kolonisation (Society for German Colonialism, GDK), one of several German associations that promoted settler colonialism in DSWA. "In every land and among all peoples it was the Germans," the program continued, "who have, in outstanding numbers, taken part in the great cultural task of civilizing and cultivating our earth. . . . Germandom across the whole world begins once more to think seriously of its common fatherland, and the urge for a closer union with their countrymen at home brings everything to life."[103] The GDK spoke for a broad cross-section of society, from rural farmers and urban industrial workers to pan-German nationalists and colonial advocates, who were tired of émigrés "culturally fertilizing" areas of the world and forfeiting their primordial bonds to the German state.

German citizens who never imagined a life in colonial Africa often shared similar sentiments about the overseas empire. Though the emergence of unofficial movements like the Heimatbewegung (*Heimat* movement) illustrates the importance of national issues in German collective discourses on identity, we should also view them as symptoms of the growing national importance of the overseas empire after the turn of the twentieth century. Indeed, the societies that comprised the Heimatbewegung typically made no formal distinction between Germany and Southwest Africa. The language of their various programs and informational pamphlets cast DSWA as an integral part of the Kaiserreich. In December 1901, the *Berliner Neueste Nachrichten* wrote that "Southwest Africa would not in and of itself be considered a German colony . . . if not for the excellent strength and inner unity of *Deutschtum* at the southern end of the old world."[104] Hermann Hesse, a colonial official stationed in German Qingdao, meanwhile, fantasized about the colony's territorial potential. He wrote in 1905 that "the basis of state power is the territory, both at home and in the colonies. Who owns the land is lord, the medium of political force."[105] Hesse also encouraged citizens to look to posterity. "Faith in a prosperous future," he urged, "will increase the determination to keep the country and to develop and build a strong bulwark of *Deutschtum* in South Africa."[106] Whether for land, prosperity, or the sanctity of *Auslandsdeutsche*, citizens in the metropole determined that DSWA was worth the financial and human cost of imperial occupation.

Public awareness of the overseas empire, therefore, went a long way toward defining the composition of a model German man and settler. Aspiring colonialists took care to accentuate their mental and physical health in their *Eingabe* and often included a detailed financial and employment history. In addition, all applicants listed their prospects for work in the colony.[107] Walther Heinemann, a merchant from Erfurt Nord, for example, emphasized his educational credentials and youth.[108] Along with being "free from the military," Heinemann explained that he was also a recipient of a "graduate certificate [*Zeugnis*], including seven classes in university."[109] He even shared the name of a friend "who had the same credentials," in the hopes of aiding his application.[110] Gustav Engelke, a machinist and member of the Northern Railway Service in Cologne, meanwhile, emphasized his technical abilities in his *Eingabe*.[111] A husband and father of five, Engelke wrote that he had been encouraged to apply for colonial settlement after meeting with representatives from the Deutsche Frauenbund.[112] He was careful to note that he had been "with the Northern

Railway Service since 1893 and [was] particularly knowledgeable about working with machines and possesses very good credentials."[113] All Engelke needed was financial assistance to bring his entire family to DSWA. These men spoke for the thousands of aspiring colonialists in search of adventure, new opportunity, and national prosperity, but who still wanted "to be and remain German."

Otto Seyfarth, a field worker from Malheim, was among the many who fit this description. In his *Eingabe*, Seyfarth conveyed that he had the "greatest interest in our Southwest African colony [and] wished to see activity in the protectorate come to fruition." Seyfarth also wrote that he viewed "colonialism in terms of enlightenment" and that a powerful nation like Germany deserved colonies in Africa. He provided descriptions of his "excellent health," listed several occupational qualifications, and said that he was "happily married with three children."[114] What makes Seyfarth's *Eingabe* significant is its utter lack of uniqueness. Like many hundreds before him, Seyfarth believed that his white German identity was enough to ensure success in the *Heimat* abroad. It did not matter that neither he nor any member of his family had ever traveled to southern Africa. The cultural and national dynamics that bound DSWA to the metropole had already familiarized Seyfarth's mental picture of imperial life and how the colony fit within the *Heimat* ideal.

As a result, many proponents of overseas expansion looked to DSWA as an extension of national prosperity. Indeed, empire was far from a marginal interest for Germans during the imperial era. Rather than an inconsequential enterprise of the few, conquest inspired hopeful German imperialists to define their identity and national belonging in global terms. For many of these individuals, DSWA's Orange River had become as familiar as the Rhine, or the harbor in Swakopmund as integral to German national prosperity as Kiel and the Jutland Peninsula. "We see in Germany a powerful agitation and hear the loud call for a definitive solution to the colonial question," Timothy Fabri wrote in the *Colonialpolitisches Correspondenz*. "Here a great field of action has opened up for all, irrespective of party position, and this high end seems to us attainable without the complications posed by war or the sacrifice of human life."[115] Among those who made up the imperial consensus, Germany's occupation of Southwest Africa in 1884 represented that "great field of action." No longer the dominion of fantasy, a formal colonial empire expanded the geographic perspective of *Deutschtum* and simultaneously gave voice to *Auslandsdeutsche* in Germany's national conversation.

"THE ULTIMATE MEASURE OF GERMAN MANHOOD"

In an age of seeming boundless opportunity, both actual and aspiring colonists saw themselves as the vanguard of the German Empire. From the hopeful father and the despondent artisan to the struggling factory worker and the prospective farmer, colonialism expanded the scope of German masculinity to include much of the imperial domain. Memoirs, diaries, newspapers, and colonial *Eingaben* all document the extent of this development in clear terms. DSWA was a place for those with "a little bit of the devil in their bodies," as well as for any white German man who embodied the attitudes, convictions, and sentiments that characterized the imperial *Heimat* ideal. Imperial violence created a colonial setting that championed self-reliance, strength, and cultural hierarchy as the foundation of Germany's dominance in southern Africa. If a man did not exhibit these qualities, he did not belong in "our Südwest." This sentiment arose chiefly from farmers', soldiers', and travelers' own experiences as participants in imperial conflict and their creation of imperial discourses on its legacy.

Their respective diaries, memoirs, and correspondence all narrated a variety of self-explanatory accounts of what they construed as justifiable acts of retribution against Nama and Ovaherero combatants. The inherent brutality of their actions provided colonialism a lived authenticity that over time pressed German colonists to project their imperial gaze exclusively to the future. White settlers during and after the Herero-Nama genocide, in other words, no longer concerned themselves with questions about why Africans wanted to challenge their imperial hegemony, or about Germany's ultimate purpose in the colony. Much to the contrary, their military and political victories motivated them to reflect solely on what they could accomplish as the unrivaled masters of Southwest Africa. Dominance and racial hierarchy developed into essential parts of the colonial experience as a result, a process that ultimately shaped the sociopolitical framework of DSWA, as well as the contours of masculinity throughout the empire.

While this development was not due to an inherently genocidal character, yearnings for empire persisted long after German guns fell silent in Europe in November 1918. In spite of their new postcolonial reality after the Paris Peace Conference, repatriated citizens and fervent nationalists continued to maintain that "the right man for our Southwest" was the right man for Germany—a consequence of colonialism that later helped bring about disastrous outcomes in a defeated and embarrassed country.

Conclusion

After Empire—Heimat *Südwest and German Identity*

"WHAT ATTRACTED AND SEDUCED ME"

Young as weaver bird children,
old as Welwitschia,
full of sheep, zebras, cattle,
I saw South West Africa. . . .
. . . .
I saw desert, waterholes,
the jackal, the desert dog.
I saw Windhoek with the sources
and on the sea Swakopmund. . . .
. . . .
I saw Nama,
I saw [Damaras].
What I saw and what I heard
whether on farms, in the veldt,
what attracted and seduced me
comes from the beginning of this world. . . .
. . . .
Old country of the young, will
wax and bloom again![1]

So wrote the popular German children's author James Krüss, long after Germany's forfeiture of Südwest in 1919. Though he never personally visited the former colony, Krüss based many of his whimsical imaginaries on the African imperium. His poem "Südwest ist Gross," much like the fanciful descriptions from the precolonial and imperial eras, heavily emphasized the so-called exotic traits of the country. From zebras, cheetahs, and the dry sand veldt to Nama, Damaras, and Ovambo, Krüss's imagined nostalgia signaled a deep, almost permanent relationship with *Heimat* Südwest. The empire was gone, but its memory continued to linger in private conversations, public celebrations, and jingoistic reveries.

Germany's thirty-one-year occupation of Southwest Africa forged tangible connections between Wilhelmine society and what Krüss characterized as the land of the kudus, springboks, and desert dogs. In the immediate aftermath of World War I, these relationships were especially resilient, most notably among white metropolitans and expatriates who looked upon Südwest with an irredentist gaze. For them, Southwest Africa remained German, an obstinate reality that no so-called diktat could extinguish. The victorious entente powers may have changed official designations on world maps and reorganized entire countries under the guise of "population politics," but erstwhile imperial administrators, business owners, and farmers remained resolute in their conviction that Southwest Africa was German land.[2] Though spiritually palpable, we must acknowledge here that collective yearnings for a return to empire after 1919 were not indicative of a historical *Sonderweg* or a unique genocidal character. Instead, they signify just how important Southwest Africa was to German women and men between 1884 and 1915 and why the former colony continued to factor into their considerations about Weimar Germany's political legitimacy. This argument does not abjure or ignore the brutal legacy of Germany's imperial project but rather places it in the context of Europe's imperial age. Just as concentration camps in the British Cape Colony or French declarations of martial law in Algeria alerted citizens to the violent potential of their African colonies, the inherent cruelty of white rule in DSWA compelled Germans to scrutinize the purposes behind their only settler colony in stark terms. In doing so, they expanded their impressions of *Heimat*, justified genocide, rationalized apartheid, and learned to look upon Südwest as an overseas extension of Germandom.

When Europe's guns fell silent and the Paris Peace Conference ushered in Germany's postcolonial era, repatriated citizens, discharged soldiers, and fervent nationalists looked to reclaim what they believed the League of Nations' mandate system stole from them unjustly.[3] Lydia Höpker was one of many contemporary Germans to vocalize their revanchist spirit and personal sorrow in the wake of German military defeat. In her memoir, *As a Farmer in German Südwest: What I Experienced in Africa*, Höpker lamented what Germany had lost in Southwest Africa, using her own—likely sensationalized—memories as rhetorical ammunition. "Everything was so dewy fresh and untouched, round about loneliness and quiet," she remembered. "Only from afar did the call of a bird resound now and again. We hiked silently through the beautiful morning. A dreamlike feeling enveloped me, and I felt enchanted, as if in another world."[4] Seeing herself as a victim of the Union of South Africa's repatriation program, Höpker felt homeless in a German metropole that neither she nor a majority of her fellow expatriates recognized or trusted. They instead longed to return to *Heimat* Südwest, the only place that they still deemed truly German.[5]

Former colonial officers voiced similar displeasure about the loss of Südwest. Heinrich Schnee, a former governor of DSWA and prominent colonial revisionist, for instance, routinely emphasized what he observed as Germany's proud imperial history throughout the Weimar era. In an effort to present Germans as so-called civilized members of what he regarded as a superior European culture, Schnee compared Germans' violent actions in Africa to those of Great Britain, France, and Belgium.[6] In his book *German Colonialism Past and Future: The Truth About the German Colonies*, he pleaded for Europeans to "admit that episodes [of violence] will always occur so long as 'man's inhumanity to man' is a factor to be reckoned with. The record of every colonizing country is stained with dark blots, for the most benevolent colonial administration in the world cannot wholly protect all its Black subjects against harshness and abuse. . . . That this was done by the German government, especially in the years preceding [1914], can be disputed by no one who is conversant with the actual facts."[7] Schnee believed that if he could convince the international community that Germany's colonial atrocities were commonplace, then perhaps the League of Nations might return Südwest to its forlorn metropole. While this gambit ultimately failed, Schnee's revanchist stance amplified the appeals of many enthusiasts and former settlers throughout German society. Internationally, individuals who comprised this new imperial consensus championed what they saw as the legitimacy of their cause; domestically, they looked to forge solidarity with anyone who praised foreign conquest and imperialism in a romantic light. Such assertions, together with the heroism white expatriates claimed to have displayed in the face of Ovaherero, Nama, British, and South African soldiers during the war, inspired this vocal population to recapture what they saw as their rightful place as a bastion of Germandom in Africa.

In the decades before and after the Kaiserreich entered the "African scramble" in 1884, the overseas world steadily evolved into a central factor in German life. Whether in Southwest Africa itself or in missionary pamphlets, colonial exhibitions, dramatic literature, and newspaper accounts, German citizens embraced their opportunity, in the aforementioned words of Goethe, to "wander beneath palm trees" and experience the overseas world for themselves. As Germany's first protectorate and only settlement colony, DSWA exposed metropolitans to the realities of colonialism. Thus, imperial rule forced citizens to consider their orientation in a global context. Though women, men, and children shared disparate perspectives on colonial settlement, as well as numerous opinions about the necessity of imperialism, we cannot deny the essential role that overseas conquest played in their lives during the nineteenth and early twentieth centuries.

When Germans started to contemplate how a distant colony with seemingly dissimilar cultures, ecologies, and social dynamics fit into their national future and memory, the geographic demarcations of *Deutschtum* expanded beyond the confines of Central Europe. Formal and informal encounters ushered in this evolution. From missionary activity, treaty negotiations, and eliminatory warfare to vivid correspondence, travel literature, and colonial exhibitions, colonial encounters expanded the scope of Germans' worldview to include the Southwest African imperium. Citizens did not have to support the empire or harbor latent desires to emigrate to Windhoek or Okahandja. Much to the contrary, colonial encounters pressed them to confront the authenticity of imperialism as a part of their daily lives—from kitchen tables and participation in political gatherings to general conversations at local bars, clubs, and cafés. In this manner, formal and informal encounters acted as conduits that linked colony and metropole together in a shared national discourse.

The significance of this reality is paramount within the scope of modern German history. Above all, this study has endeavored to show that Africans were as integral to Germany's national development as the merchants, missionaries, soldiers, and settlers who first ventured overseas in the early nineteenth century. In doing so, it has sought to expose the "other side" of imperial domination, most notably how Africans challenged colonial rule and the degree to which transnational entanglements altered German identity in Europe. The appearance of Germans did not immediately transform Southwest Africa into a space that inherently favored their interests, whether as Protestant missionaries, employees in Adolf Lüderitz's corporatist enterprise, or lowland farmers in search of freedom and fresh air. Even after the imperial government commissioned soldiers from Germany to establish a protection force, Witbooi Nama and the Ovaherero still dictated their actions far more than the other way around. Governors, merchants, and most of all settlers were at a loss over how to resolve the situation. When protection treaties and overt threats failed to secure total supremacy, white colonists looked to the imperial government to establish stability in the form of juridical and military violence.

Africans played an essential role in this political transformation. Their refusal to accept colonial domination, an imperial fantasy that most white citizens had not contemplated previously, forced Germans to question the purpose behind their occupation of Southwest Africa. As calls to suppress Witbooi and Samuel Maharero grew louder in the colonial and national press, the Reichstag pledged to defend Germany's imperial presence through force of arms. In this manner, what had started as a minor commercial enterprise had grown into an important extension of the German state by the turn of the twentieth century. Colonial encounters shattered the illusion of German cultural superiority. While imperial fantasies certainly inspired a general curiosity about the world beyond Europe in the early nineteenth century, they in no way represented any semblance of truth about what Germans could expect to face as colonizers in the future. After 1884, white settlers and officials discovered that they could not govern merely on the basis of their place of birth or the color of their skin. In response, they increasingly relied on nationalism, geopolitical rivalry, racial segregation, and systemic violence to retain their authority in DSWA. Though not every German citizen supported overt or covert acts of racial or eliminatory violence, structural apartheid emerged as the principal instrument of control for German authorities in the decade before the start of World War I.

From Carl Becker in DSWA to the halls of the Reichstag during the so-called Hottentot elections of 1907, this outcome preoccupied everyone throughout the German Empire after the turn of the twentieth century. The colonial project had a significant impact on the lives of demographically and socially diverse citizens, permanently shifting the boundaries of German national identity away from isolated pockets in Central Europe. In stark contrast to the wistful dreams that fashioned Germans' precolonial discourses and racist stereotypes, Black Africans were neither culturally submissive nor uncontrollably aggressive and dangerous. This reality inspired white colonists to embrace "race thinking" as the fundamental essence of German identity overseas. In doing so, racial belonging over time pushed citizens and settlers to question the kind of colonial future they aspired for Germany in the twentieth century. Whether through the adoption of total warfare or the acceptance of *Rassentrennung*, Germans provided their answer in sweeping eliminatory terms in the Omaheke Desert and their establishment of an apartheid imperial state in 1905. From colony to metropole and back, race evolved into the principal measure by which Germans defined their identity. While the consequences of this phenomenon were never inevitable, the emergence of exclusionary political movements after 1919 could look to their former imperial homeland as a site where nation and race forged state policy in catastrophically violent ways.

Notes

INTRODUCTION

1. "Die deutschen Fremdenlegion," 47.
2. Goethe, *Die Wahlver-wandtschaften*, quoted in Buch, "No One Wanders," 233.
3. Ibid.
4. Ciarlo, "Picturing Genocide."
5. Ibid., 70, 80.
6. Bowersox, "Boy's and Girl's Own Empires."
7. Zimmerman, *Anthropology and Antihumanism*.
8. Frenssen, *Peter Moors*.
9. See Naranch, "Inventing the *Auslandsdeutsche*"; Conrad, *Globalisierung und Nation*; Maxwell and Davis, "Germanness Beyond Germany."
10. Kalb, *Environing Empire*.
11. Steinmetz, *Devil's Handwriting*.
12. See Walther, *Creating Germans Abroad*; Aitken, *Exclusion and Inclusion*; Eley, "Empire by Land or Sea?"; Zimmerer, *Kein Platz an der Sonne*; Blackler, "From Boondoggle."
13. Zantop, *Colonial Fantasies*.
14. Applegate, *Nation of Provincials*; Confino, *Nation as a Local Metaphor*; Lekan, "German Landscape."
15. Zantop, *Colonial Fantasies*.
16. Drechsler, *Aufstände in Südwestafrika*; Bley, *Kolonialherrschaft*.
17. Bley, *Kolonialherrschaft*, 282.
18. Grosse, *Kolonialismus*; Zimmerer and Zeller, *Völkermord*; Hull, *Absolute Destruction*; Zimmerer, *Deutsche Herrschaft*; Zimmerer, *Von Windhuk nach Auschwitz?*; Zimmerer and Zeller, *Genocide in German South-West Africa*; Madley, "From Africa to Auschwitz"; Madley, "Patterns of Frontier Genocide"; Olusoga and Erichsen, *Kaiser's Holocaust*; Kundrus, *Phantasiereich*; Kundrus, "Kontinuäten, Parallelen, Rezeptionen"; Baranowski, *Nazi Empire*; Kuss, *German Colonial Wars*; Bachmann, *Genocidal Empires*.
19. Hull, *Absolute Destruction*, 227; Zimmerer, *Von Windhuk nach Auschwitz?*.
20. Olusoga and Erichsen, *Kaiser's Holocaust*.
21. Baranowski, *Nazi Empire*; Langbehn and Salama, *German Colonialism*; Sandler, *Empire in the Heimat*.
22. El-Tayeb, *Schwarze Deutsche*.
23. Ibid., 8.
24. El-Tayeb is careful to acknowledge three studies that preceded her own: Pommerin, "*Sterilisierung der Rheinlandbastarde*"; Martin, *Schwarze Teufel*; Oguntoye, *Eine afro-deutsche Geschichte*. I will also highlight Opitz, Oguntoye, and Schultz, *Farbe bekennen*.
25. Campt, *Other Germans*; Mazón and Steingröver, *Not So Plain*; Honeck, Klimke, and Kuhlmann, *Germany and the Black Diaspora*; Aitken and Rosenhaft, *Black Germany*; Michael, *Black German*; Lennox, *Remapping Black Germany*; Eggers, "Knowledges of (Un-)

Belonging"; Florvil and Plumly, *Rethinking Black German Studies.*

26. Eckert, *Herrschen und Verwalten*; Conrad, *German Colonialism*; Sandler, "Colonial Education"; Kallaway, "German Lutheran Missions"; Murphy, *Colonial Captivity*; Kuss, *German Colonial Wars.*

27. See Conrad, *Globalisierung und Nation*; Osterhammel, *Die Verwandlung der Welt*; Eckert, "Afrikanische Nationalisten"; Dickinson, "German Empire"; Jaeger, "Colony as *Heimat?*"; Perraudin and Zimmerer, *German Colonialism*; Lerp, *Imperiale Grenzräume.*

28. Eley, "Empire by Land or Sea?" 30.

29. Ibid.

30. Fitzpatrick, *Liberal Imperialism*; Short, *Magic Lantern Empire.*

31. Wempe, *Revenants of the German Empire*, 4.

32. Conrad, *Globalisierung und Nation*, 4. See also Osterhammel, *Die Verwandlung der Welt.*

33. Osterhammel, *Die Verwandlung der Welt*, 234.

34. Zimmerman, *Alabama in Africa.*

35. Ibid., 3.

36. See also Prein, "Guns and Top Hats"; Moyd, *Violent Intermediaries*; Pugach, *Africa in Translation*; Blackler, "From Boondoggle"; Pugach, Pizzo, and Blackler, *After the Imperialist Imagination.*

CHAPTER 1

1. Weber, *Die Erweiterung*, 65.

2. Ibid., ii.

3. Ibid., iii.

4. Fitzpatrick, *Liberal Imperialism*, 27.

5. Naranch, "Inventing the *Auslandsdeutsche*"; Naranch and Eley, *German Colonialism.*

6. Several notable exceptions include Zantop, *Colonial Fantasies*; Fitzpatrick, *Liberal Imperialism*; Kundrus, "From the Periphery."

7. C. Hahn, *Tagebücher*, 243.

8. Dernburg, *Zielpunkte*, 5.

9. Zantop, *Colonial Fantasies*, 7.

10. Tellkampf, in Wigard, *Reden für die deutsche Nation*, 309. See also Vick, "Imperialism, Race, and Genocide," 11.

11. Fitzpatrick, *Liberal Imperialism*, 33.

12. Tellkampf, in Wigard, *Reden für die deutsche Nation*, 309.

13. Weitz, "From the Vienna."

14. Vick, *Defining Germany*, 40.

15. Ibid., 19–47; Nipperdey, *Deutsche Geschichte*, 286–300; Fitzpatrick, *Liberal Imperialism*, 12–17.

16. Vick, *Defining Germany*; Hochman, *Imaging a Greater Germany.*

17. Herre, *Friedrich Wilhelm IV.*

18. Zantop, *Colonial Fantasies*, 25.

19. Fitzpatrick, *Liberal Imperialism*, 27; Short, *Magic Lantern Empire.*

20. Short, *Magic Lantern Empire*, 2–3.

21. List, *Das nationale System*, 57.

22. Ibid., 57–58.

23. See W. Smith, *German Colonial Empire*; W. Smith, *Ideological Origins of Nazi Imperialism.*

24. Hundeshagen, *Die deutsche Auswanderung*, 1.

25. Ibid.

26. Herre, *Friedrich Wilhelm IV.*

27. Nipperdey, *Deutsche Geschichte*, 608–12.

28. Adalbert, *Denkschrift über die Bildung*, 24.

29. Ibid., 25.

30. Ibid., 22.

31. Wigand, *Die beiden deutschen Reichsverfassungen*, 111.

32. Tellkampf, quoted in Fitzpatrick, *Liberal Imperialism*, 39.

33. Ibid.

34. Wigard, *Reden für die deutsche Nation*, quoted in Fitzpatrick, *Liberal Imperialism*, 41.

35. Ibid.

36. Anderson, *Imagined Communities*.

37. Ibid., 6.

38. Belgum, *Popularizing the Nation*, 1–2.

39. Hamouda, *Der Leipziger Verleger*.

40. Keil, *Der Leuchtthurm*.

41. Belgum, *Popularizing the Nation*, 13.

42. Feißkohl, *Ernst Keils*, 14.

43. "An unsere Freunde und Leser!," 1.

44. "Die Transvaal-Republik im Kafferlande," 14.

45. "An unsere Freunde und Leser!," 1. See also Paletschek, "Popular Presentations of History."

46. Koch, *Nationale Identität*. See also Fitzpatrick, "Narrating Empire."

47. Barth, *Zeitschrift für Alle*, 473.

48. Ibid.

49. Belgum, *Popularizing the Nation*, 16.

50. "Ein Morgen auf der Götterburg der Athener," 123.

51. Ibid.

52. Ibid., 126.

53. "Robinsons Insel—eine deutsche Ansiedelung," 224.

54. Ibid.

55. Ibid.

56. "Dem Andenken zweier deutschen Eroberer," 185.

57. Ibid.

58. Brehm, "Die deutsche Expedition nach Mittelafrika," 74.

59. Naranch, "Global Proletarians," 172.

60. Andree, *Geographische Wanderungen*.

61. Andree, foreword to *Globus*, iv.

62. *Globus*, xviii, 65.

63. T. Hahn, "Die Buschmänner," 65.

64. Said, *Orientalism*.

65. "Baumwolle in Afrika," 160.

66. "Deutsche Weihnachtsfeier in Californien," 143.

67. "Vom Vorgebirge," 208; "Goldwäschereien in Finnland," 320; "Die bengalische Provinz Assam," 16; "Eisenbahn über das Hochgebirge," 46.

68. Belgum, *Popularizing the Nation*, xi–xxx.

69. See especially Reimann-Dawe, "Time, Identity, and Colonialism"; Unangst, "Men of Science and Action."

70. Rohlfs, *Quer durch Afrika*.

71. Meissner, *Durch die sengende Glut*.

72. Rohlfs, *Quer durch Afrika*, 195–219.

73. Ibid., quoted in Reimann-Dawe, "Time, Identity, and Colonialism," 25.

74. Rohlfs, *Quer durch Afrika*, 26.

75. Di Maio, *Gerstäcker's Louisiana*, 2–4.

76. Ibid., 2.

77. Ibid., 3.

78. Ibid., 4.

79. Ibid.

80. Gerstäcker, *Unter den Penhuenchen*, quoted in Fitzpatrick, *Liberal Imperialism*, 195.

81. Weber, *Die Erweiterung*.

82. Weber, *Vier Jahre in Afrika*.

83. Ibid., 10.

84. Weber, *Die Erweiterung*, 63.

85. Weber, quoted in Perras, *Carl Peters*, 33.

86. Ratzel, *Anthropogeographie*.

87. Weber, *Die Erweiterung*, 64.

88. Ibid., 63.

89. "In den Steppen von Afrika," 11.

90. Ibid.

91. Ibid.

92. Bismarck, "Rede im deutschen Reichstag," quoted in Poschinger, *Fürst Bismarck*, 54.

93. Bismarck, quoted in Fitzpatrick, *Liberal Imperialism*, 116.

94. Canis, *Bismarcks Außenpolitik*, 85–108.

95. Wehler, *Bismarck und der Imperialismus*, 115.

96. Wolf, *Vom Fürsten Bismarck*, 16.

97. Strandmann, "Domestic Origins," 145.

98. "Die neue Aera der Kolonialpolitik," 805.

99. "Die Kongokonferenz zu Berlin," 307.

100. "Congo Free State," 304.

101. "Die neue Aera der Kolonialpolitik," 807.

102. Baranowski, *Nazi Empire*, 29–30.

103. Peters, "Deutsche Kolonialpolitik," quoted in Perras, *Carl Peters*, 36.

104. Ibid.

105. "General Act."

106. Article 35, in "General Act," 25.

107. "Official slogan" of the *Deutscher Kolonialverein*, quoted in Fitzpatrick, *Liberal Imperialism*, 109.

108. Peters, "Deutschtum in London," *Die Gegenwart*, 13 October 1884.

109. Jung, "Deutschlands Colonialbestrebungen," *Die Gartenlaube*, quoted in Fitzpatrick, *Liberal Imperialism*, 193.

110. "Deutschlands erster Kriegshafen," 136.

111. Ibid., also quoted in Fitzpatrick, *Liberal Imperialism*, 193.

112. Simonsfeld, *Die Deutschen*, 49.

113. Weber, *Die Erweiterung*, 69.

114. Ibid.

CHAPTER 2

1. Vereinte Evangelische Mission (VEM) / Rheinische Missionsgesellschaft (RMG) 1.577a, "Hahn, Carl Hugo, 1841–1866," Carl Hugo Hahn, "Betr. Hugo Hahn und die Wesleyaner auf Windhoek," 8 July 1844, 2.

2. VEM/RMG 1.577a, Richard Haddy, "Letter to Messre, Hahn, and Kleinschmidt," 12 August 1844, 11.

3. C. Hahn, *Tagebücher*, 1:2.

4. VEM/RMG 1.585, Heinrich Schöneberg, "Otjikango," *Berichte der RMG* 10 (1853): 241. See also Steinmetz, *Devil's Handwriting*, 131.

5. Best, "Godly, International, and Independent."

6. Warneck, "Die christliche Mission," quoted in Best, "Godly, International, and Independent," 586.

7. C. Hahn, *Tagebücher*, 1:17.

8. Ibid., 4–5. Emphasis added.

9. Richter, quoted in Menzel, *Die Rheinische Mission*, 26. Emphasis added.

10. Loth, *Die christliche Mission*, 9.

11. Drechsler, *Südwestafrika*, 18.

12. Loth, *Kolonialismus unter der Kutte*.

13. Vedder, *Das alte Südwestafrika*.

14. Best, *Heavenly Fatherland*.

15. "Statuten einer Deputation der Rheinischen Missionsgesellschaften," 11–13, quoted in Menzel, *Die Rheinische Mission*, 24.

16. Ibid.

17. Ibid., 27.

18. Hartmann, "Sexual Encounters," 42.

19. "Statuten einer Deputation das Seminar," quoted in Menzel, *Die Rheinische Mission*, 27.

20. Menzel, *Die Rheinische Mission*, 27.

21. Oermann, *Mission*, 33.

22. Deputation of the RMG/Barmen, *Allgemeine Vorbedingungen*, quoted in Oermann, *Mission*, 38.

23. Ibid., 34.

24. Oermann, *Mission*, 39.

25. Pugach, *Africa in Translation*, 6–13.

26. E. Hahn, *Letters*, i.

27. Ibid., i–ii.

28. VEM/RMG 1.577a, Carl Hugo Hahn, "Betreff Hugo Hahn und die Wesleyaner auf Windhoek," 8 September 1844, 2–3.

29. Hartmann, "Sexual Encounters," 56.

30. E. Hahn, *Letters*, i–iv.

31. VEM/RMG 1.577a, Carl Hugo Hahn, "Abschrift eines Schreibens von C. Hugo Hahn an die Deputation," 5 February 1863, 21.

32. Menzel, *Die Rheinische Mission*, 56.

33. Trüper, *Invisible Woman*, 7.

34. VEM/RMG 1.573, Franz Heinrich Kleinschmidt, "Blatt, 006a."

35. Trüper, *Invisible Woman*, 65.

36. Zimmermann and Kellermeier-Rehbein, *Koloniale*, 58.

37. Kleinschmidt, *Jonker Afrikaner*.

38. VEM/RMG 1.573, Franz Heinrich Kleinschmidt, "Deputation," 16 August 1854, 85–86.

39. VEM/RMG 1.573, Franz Heinrich Kleinschmidt, "Brief nach Herr Inspector," 15 July 1854, 84.

40. VEM/RMG 2.598, Franz Heinrich Kleinschmidt, "Deputation," September 1842, 225.

41. C. Hahn, *Tagebücher*, 80.

42. VEM/RMG 1.577a, Carl Hugo Hahn, "Abschrift eines Schreibens von C. Hugo Hahn an die Deputation," 5 February 1863, 20.

43. C. Hahn, quoted in Oermann, *Mission*, 50.

44. C. Hahn, *Tagebücher*, 77.

45. Steinmetz, *Devil's Handwriting*, 125.

46. VEM/RMG 1.577b, Carl Hugo Hahn, "Meine Heimreise," quoted in Steinmetz, *Devil's Handwriting*, 128.

47. C. Hahn, *Tagebücher*, 80.

48. Ibid.

49. Ibid., 89.

50. Ibid., 95.

51. Vedder, *Das alte Südwestafrika*, 241.

52. Kleinschmidt, *Jonker Afrikaner*, 1855. See also Vedder, *Das alte Südwestafrika*, 242.

53. Willem Swartbooi, quoted in Vedder, *Das alte Südwestafrika*, 242.

54. Ibid., 243.

55. VEM/RMG 1.573, Franz Heinrich Kleinschmidt, "Blatt, 009."

56. VEM/RMG 1.573, "Bericht an Bruder Eggert," 16 August 1854, 407.

57. C. Hahn, *Tagebücher*, 96–98.

58. Ibid., 96–97.

59. Hartmann, "Sexual Encounters," 58.

60. C. Hahn, *Tagebücher*, 190.

61. Ibid., 188–92.

62. Vedder, *Das alte Südwestafrika*, 243.

63. Ibid.

64. Wallace, *History of Namibia*, 63.

65. C. Hahn, *Grundzüge*.

66. Wallace, *History of Namibia*, 55.

67. Oermann, *Mission*, 48–49.

68. Wallace, *History of Namibia*, 63.

69. C. Hahn, *Tagebücher*, 194.

70. Ibid., 243.

71. Ibid.

72. Ibid., 727.

73. Hartmann, "Sexual Encounters," 58–59.

74. VEM/RMG 1.577a, Carl Hugo Hahn, "Abschrift eines Schreibens von C. Hugo Hahn an die Deputation," 5 February 1863, 18–24. See also Hartmann, "Sexual Encounters," 60.

75. C. Hahn, *Tagebücher*, 1116.

76. VEM/RMG 1.577a, Carl Hugo Hahn, "Abschrift eines Schreibens von C. Hugo Hahn an die Deputation," 5 February 1863, 19.

77. Ibid., 21–22.

78. Engel, "Die Stellung," 50.

79. Oermann, *Mission*, 49–50.

80. VEM/RMG 1.577a, Carl Hugo Hahn, "Aus dem ersten Ovamboreisetagebuch," 26 July 1857, 25.

81. C. Hahn, *Tagebücher*, 1133.

82. E. Hahn, *Letters*, 431.

83. Johannes Rath, *Otjimbingwe: Stationschronik 1840–1924*, quoted in Hartmann, "Sexual Encounters," 80–81.

84. C. Hahn, *Tagebücher*, 1083.

85. Henrichsen, *Herrschaft und Alltag*, 167–68.

86. Oermann, *Mission*, 50.

87. "Otjimbingué," *Berichte der RMG* 21 (8, 1865), quoted in Steinmetz, *Devil's Handwriting*, 127.

88. "Hereroland Mission Conference," 1867, cited in Oermann, *Mission*, 50.

89. Hartman, "Sexual Encounters," 106; Steinmetz, *Devil's Handwriting*, 113–14.

90. E. Hahn, *Letters*, 401.

91. VEM/RMG 1.611 b B/c II 38, Carl Büttner, "Die ersten Eindrücke von Volk und Land," ca. April 1873. See also Pugach, *Africa in Translation*, 53–54.

92. VEM/RMG 1.611 b B/c II 38, Carl Büttner, "Die ersten Eindrücke von Volk und Land," 3 May 1873.

93. VEM/RMG 1.611 b B/c II 38, Carl Büttner, "Die ersten Eindrücke von Volk und Land," 20 February 1873.

94. Carl Gotthilf Büttner, quoted in Pugach, *Africa in Translation*, 54.

95. Carl Gotthilf Büttner, "Letter to the Rhenish Mission," 21 December 1873, quoted in Pugach, *Africa in Translation*, 55.

96. Carl Gotthilf Büttner, "Letter to the Rhenish Mission," quoted in Menzel, *C. G. Büttner*, 26.

97. Büttner, *Das Hinterland*, 280.

98. Bade, *Friedrich Fabri*, 68–79.

99. Wallace, *History of Namibia*, 109.

100. Bade, *Friedrich Fabri*, 108.

101. Fabri, *Bedarf Deutschland der Colonien?*, 180–81.

102. Fabri, "Brief an die Auswärtiges Amt," 3 June 1869, cited in Oermann, *Mission*, 55.

103. Bade, *Friedrich Fabri*, 102–5.

104. Oermann, *Mission*, 31–32.

105. Hartmann, "Sexual Encounters," 107.

106. Een, *Memories*, 14. See also Hartmann, "Sexual Encounters," 107–9.

107. Ibid.

108. Ibid.

109. Rohden, *Geschichte der Rheinischen Missions-Gesellschaft*, 10.

110. "Die Rheinische Mission," *Missionsblatt* 15 (August 1857): 60.

111. Conrad, *German Colonialism*, 23–35.

112. VEM/RMG 1.576, Friedrich Fabri, "Brief an Bruder Carl Hugo Hahn," 28 May 1870, 75–84.

113. Wallace, *History of Namibia*, 68.

114. Oermann, *Mission*, 52.

115. C. Hahn, *Tagebücher*, 1131.

116. Wallace, *History of Namibia*, 72.

117. Oermann, *Mission*, 52.

118. Ibid., 52–53.

119. Wallace, *History of Namibia*, 109.

120. Ibid.

121. Hahn, *Jahresbericht*, quoted in Steinmetz, *Devil's Handwriting*, 128.

122. Ibid.

123. Oermann, *Mission*, 50.

CHAPTER 3

1. BArchB R 1001/2058, Wilhelm Külz, "Die Organisation der Schutzgebietsverwaltung," 27 January 1909, 52.

2. Ibid., 12.

3. Ibid., 15.

4. BArchB R 1001/1532, G. von Bleichröder an die Reichskanzler Fürsten von Bismarck," 30 March 1885, 3.

5. Jung, "Deutschlands Colonialbestrebungen," 614.

6. BArchB R 1001/1134e, Dr. Heinrich Bokemeyer, "Ueber Ansiedelungsverhältnisse in Südwest-Afrika vom Gesichtspunkte der organisierten Kolonisation," *Deutsche Kolonialzeitung*, no. 26/27 (1890): 309.

7. BArchB R 1001/1134e, Baron B. E. von Üchtritz, "Bericht aus Windhoek," 2 August 1891, 2–3.

8. Bowersox, *Raising Germans*, 18–53.

9. Applegate, *Nation of Provincials*; Confino, *Nation as a Local Metaphor*.

10. Confino, *Nation as a Local Metaphor*, 4.

11. Jaeger, "Colony as *Heimat?*"

12. "Fünfundzwanzig Jahre Deutsch-Südwestafrika," 314–16.

13. Ibid., 315.

14. "Unser Programm," *Deutsche Kolonialzeitung* (1884): 1.

15. Drechsler, *"Let Us Die Fighting,"* 33–34.

16. Büttner, "Deutschland und Angra Pequena," 303.

17. Kirchhoff, "Deutsch-Afrika," 333.

18. "Wie soll man kolonisieren?," 337.

19. Deutscher Kolonialverein, "Deutscher Kolonialverein," 417.

20. BArchB R 1001/1532, Bismarck, "Bericht des Kaisers und Königs Majestät," 12 April 1885, 16–20.

21. Drechsler, *"Let Us Die Fighting,"* 30.

22. BArchB R 1001/1532, "G. von Bleichröder an die Reichskanzler Fürsten von Bismarck," 30 April 1885, 3–6.

23. BArchB R 1001/1524, "Deutsche Kolonialgesellschaft für Südwestafrika an den Bundesrat," 6 July 1885, 105.

24. Jaeger, "Colony as *Heimat?*," 468.

25. Naranch, "Inventing the *Auslandsdeutsche*."

26. Weitz, *World Divided*, 206.

27. Gründer, *Geschichte*, 88–89.

28. Blackler, "From Boondoggle," 450–52.

29. BArchB R 1001/1522, Dr. Göring, "Bericht an Fürst von Bismarck," 15 May 1887, 74–75.

30. BArchB R 1001/1134e, Dr. Göring, "Bericht an Auswärtiges Amt—Kolonial Abteilung," 7 July 1890, 20–21.

31. BArchB R 1001/1522, Dr. Göring, "Bericht an Fürst von Bismarck," 15 May 1887, 74.

32. Ibid.

33. BArchB R 1001/1134e, Dr. Göring, "Bericht an Auswärtiges Amt—Kolonial Abteilung," 7 July 1890, 20–21.

34. BArchB R 1001/1134e, Ansiedlung insbesondere deutsche Bauern in Deutsch-Südwestafrika, Adolph von Hansemann, "Bericht von Deutsche Colonial-Gesellschaft für Südwest-Afrika," 23 October 1890, 31.

35. BArchB R 1001/1134e, Ansiedlung insbesondere deutsche Bauern in Deutsch-Südwestafrika, Franz Weller, "Vorschläge für Gründung von Ackerbau Kolonien," 27 December 1890, 40.

36. BArchB R 1001/1134e: Ansiedlung insbesondere deutsche Bauern in Deutsch-Südwestafrika, Franz Weller, "Etwas Soziales und Koloniales," undated, 42.

37. Ibid., 43.

38. Buchner, "Wie lebt man auf einer Afrikareise?," 232.

39. Ibid.

40. Buchner, "Reitochsen in Südwest-Afrika," 432.

41. Ibid.

42. BArchB R 1001/1134e, Major Curt von François, "Brief an die Reichskanzler von Caprivi," 25 August 1890, 22.

43. Ibid., 23.

44. BArchB R 1001/1134e, Major Curt von François, "Brief an die Reichskanzler von Caprivi," 26 August 1890, 29.

45. Jonker Afrikaner and the Orlam were the first to establish a permanent settlement on the site in 1840.

46. Blackler, "From Boondoggle," 454.

47. BArchB R 1001/1522, 1001/1522, *Statut der Deutschen Colonial-Gesellschaft für Südwest-Afrika*, 7 April 1885, 18–24.

48. Ibid., 20–21.

49. BArchB R 1001/1532, Hugo Fürst zu Hohenlohe, Herzog von Ujest, Dr. Hammacher, and W. Weber, "Bericht an die Geheimen Ober. Regierungsrat Rommel," 10 April 1885, 13–16.

50. Mogk, *Paul Rohrbach*.

51. BArchB R 1001/1138, Dr. Paul Rohrbach, "Bericht an AAKA," 28 October 1903, 224, 227.

52. Aitken, *Exclusion and Inclusion*, 57.

53. Rohrbach, *Der deutsche Gedanke*, 127.

54. Rohrbach, "Bericht des Ansiedlungskommissars," quoted in Aitken, *Exclusion and Inclusion*, 57.

55. BArchB R 1001/1138, "Zur Besiedlung Deutsch-Südwestafrika," *Der Tag*, 16 June 1903, 96.

56. BArchB R 1001/2151, Heinrich Vogelsang, "Bericht an die AAKA," 4 March 1885, 3–4.

57. Marvin, "English-Africa," 123.

58. BArchB R 1001/1147, "Southwest Africa," *Cape Argus*, 19 May 1892, 106.

59. *Koloniales Jahrbuch*, vol. 2 (1889), quoted in Drechsler, *"Let Us Die Fighting,"* 38.

60. "Die Lage im Hererolande," 533.

61. Short, *Magic Lantern Empire*, 79.

62. BArchB R 1001/1136, "Eine Stimme aus Deutsch-Südwestafrika," *Berliner Tageblatt*, 23 November 1891, 90.

63. Blackler, "From Boondoggle," 462.

64. François, "Exposé Concerning the Southwest African Protectorate," quoted in Aitken, *Exclusion and Inclusion*, 54. Emphasis added.

65. Preuss, *Kolonialerziehung des deutschen Volkes*, 5.

66. BArchB R 1001/1136, "Deutsches Reich," *Rheinische-Westfälische Zeitung*, 16 September 1902, 215.

67. Ibid.

68. National Archives of Namibia (hereafter NAN), "Woermann-Linie," *Deutsch-Südwestafrikanische Zeitung*, no. 1 (1 October 1901): 27.

69. Ibid.

70. Warburg, "Die Deutsche Kolonialausstellung," 307.

71. Ibid. See also Short, *Magic Lantern Empire*, 44–45.

72. Schreiber, "Bericht am AAKA," quoted in Zimmerman, *Anthropology and Antihumanism*, 28.

73. BArchB R 1001/1137, Alfred Kirchhoff, "Eine neue Zeitschrift über die Verbreitung des Deutschtums auf Erden," *Deutsche Kolonialzeitung* 40 (October 1902): 400.

74. For more on German colonial newspapers in DSWA, see Rash, *German Images*, 130–68.

75. BArchB R 1001/1136, "Sprachverwilderung in Deutsch-Südwestafrika," *Norddeutsche Allgemeine Zeitung*, 3 May 1902, 151.

76. Riegel, *Ein Hauptstück*, 2.

77. Ibid.

78. BArchB R 1001/1136, author unknown, "Bericht an den Allgemeinen deutschen Sprachverein," AAKA 4915/02, 21 March 1902, 157.

79. BArchB R 1001/1136, "Sprachverwilderung in Deutsch-Südwestafrika," *Norddeutsche Allgemeine Zeitung*, 3 May 1902, 151.

80. BArchB R 1001/1136, "Die Zukunft Deutsch-Südwest-Afrikas," *Deutsche Warte*, 23 October 1902, 63.

81. Ibid.

82. BArchB R 1001/1139, "Die Aussichten in Südwestafrika," *Kölnische Zeitung*, 1 September 1902, 64–65.

83. BArchB R 1001/1139, "Die wirtschaftliche Entwicklung unserer westafrikanischen Kolonien," *Deutsche Kolonialzeitung* 24 (June 1903): 244.

84. Bebel, "Gold, Gold und wieder nur Gold," quoted in Gründer, *Geschichte*, 80–81.

85. Conrad, *German Colonialism*, 35.

86. BArchB R 1001/1135, Ansiedlung insbesondere deutscher Bauern in Deutsch Südwestafrika, "Fürst Bismarck und die deutsche Kolonialpolitik," *Deutsche Kolonialzeitung* 27 (6 July 1889): 68.

87. "Bismarck an Göring," quoted in Walther, *Creating Germans Abroad*, 10.

88. BArchB R 1001/1139, Ansiedlung insbesondere deutscher Bauern in Deutsch Südwestafrika, "Die wirtschaftliche Entwicklung unserer westafrikanischen Kolonien," *Deutsche Kolonialzeitung* 24 (June 1903): 246.

89. Nyhart, *Modern Nature*, 259.

90. Bohrdt, "Die Nordwestdeutsche," 308.

91. Nyhart, *Modern Nature*, 260.

92. Bohrdt, "Die Nordwestdeutsche," 682. See also Ciarlo, *Advertising Empire*, 43.

93. *Leipziger Illustrirte Zeitung*, 20 September 1890, quoted in Ciarlo, *Advertising Empire*, 48.

94. *Ausstellungs-Zeitung, Bremen*, 10 June 1890, quoted in Ciarlo, *Advertising Empire*, 48.

95. Lührs, "Vor hundert Jahren," 9–20.

96. Prager, *Die deutsche Kolonialgesellschaft*, 119.

97. Short, *Magic Lantern Empire*, 44.

98. Neisser, "Das Leben und Treiben der Eingeborenen," 42. See also Zimmerman, *Anthropology and Antihumanism*, 24.

99. Neisser, "Das Leben und Treiben der Eingeborenen," 42.

100. Zimmerman, *Anthropology and Antihumanism*, 27–28.

101. Short, *Magic Lantern Empire*, 51.

102. Ibid.

103. Zimmerman, *Alabama in Africa*; Rohrbach, *Der deutsche Gedanke*, 127.

104. For more on toys, games, and the colonial imagination, see especially Bowersox, *Raising Germans*, 18–53.

105. *Kolonialgeschichte im Kinderzimmer*, cited in Bowersox, *Raising Germans*, 38.

106. "Einleitung," *Deutschlands Kolonien-Spiel: Eine Reise durch Deutschlands Kolonien* (ca. 1890).

107. "Spielregeln," *Deutschlands Kolonien-Spiel*.

108. Numbers 2 and 5, *Deutschlands Kolonien-Spiel*.

109. Numbers 12, 29, 15, and 18, *Deutschlands Kolonien-Spiel*.

110. "Einleitung," *Deutschlands Kolonien-Spiel*.

111. See especially Schultz, *Die deutschsprachige Geographie*; Schultz, *Die Geographie*; Sperling, "Zur Darstellung"; Brogiato, "*Wissen ist Macht.*"

112. Volz, *Leitfaden*, cited in Bowersox, *Raising Germans*, 68.

113. Schultz and Brogiato, "Die 'Gesellschaft für Erdkunde zu Berlin'"; Bowersox, *Raising Germans*, 60–62.

114. Büttner, "Über das Erbauen," 23.

115. "Fünfundzwanzig Jahre Deutsch-Südwestafrika," 316.

116. After Bismarck forced him to sell his territorial rights, Lüderitz organized another gold expedition in 1886. While

sailing near the conjunction of the Fish and Orange Rivers, Lüderitz's boat capsized and he drowned in the rough waters.

117. Rupp, *Soll und Haben*, 1, 6.

CHAPTER 4

1. Witbooi, "14. Witbooi an Göring vom Hornkranz." The Nama called Witbooi Knaob !Nanseb / Gabemab, which means "The captain who disappears in the grass." His Herero name was Korota.

2. *Koloniales Jahrbuch*, vol. 2, 1889, quoted in Drechsler, *"Let Us Die Fighting,"* 27.

3. Gewald, *Towards Redemption*.

4. Steinmetz, *Devil's Handwriting*, 120.

5. Bochert, "Witboois and the Germans," 45. See also Steinmetz, *Devil's Handwriting*, 45, 148.

6. Werner, "Brief History of Land Dispossession," 138.

7. See Gewald, *Towards Redemption*, 28–46.

8. Four principal Herero leaders and factions lived in central Southwest Africa in 1884: Maharero Tjamuaha (Okahandja), Manasse Tjiseta (Omaruru), Kambazembi (Otjozondjupa), and Kahimemua (Gobabis).

9. BArchB R 1001/2100, Hereroland (Damaraland) und Namaqualand (June 1885–April 1891). See also Pool, *Samuel Maharero*, 61.

10. Gewald, *Herero Heroes*, 32.

11. On the course of settler-colonial violence in the colonies before and during World War I, see Moyd, *Violent Intermediaries*; Kuss, *German Colonial Wars*; Hull, *Absolute Destruction*; Muschalek, *Violence as Usual*.

12. Zimmerer, "Krieg," 60. See also Madley, "From Africa to Auschwitz"; Hull, *Absolute Destruction*; Kiernan, *Blood and Soil*; Bachmann, *Genocidal Empires*.

13. Ibid., 62.

14. Zimmerer, *Von Windhuk nach Auschwitz?*.

15. Zimmerer, "Krieg," 62.

16. Arendt, *Origins of Totalitarianism*; Fanon, *Wretched of the Earth*; Sartre, *On Genocide*; Platt, *Reden von Gewalt*; Moses, "Hannah Arendt."

17. Olusoga and Erichsen, *Kaiser's Holocaust*.

18. Zimmerer, "Colonialism and the Holocaust," 60.

19. Wolfe, "Settler Colonialism."

20. BArchB R 1001/1486, "Hendrik Witbooi," *Berliner Neuesten Nachrichten*, 29 August 1894, 121.

21. Gewald, *Towards Redemption*, 26–27.

22. Steinmetz, *Devil's Handwriting*, 112.

23. C. Hahn, *Tagebücher*, 77–78; Heywood and Maasdorp, *Hendrik Witbooi Papers*, 196.

24. Witbooi's wife's name was Katharina (!Nanses). See "20. Witbooi an J. Olpp," 3 January 1890, in Witbooi, *Afrika den Afrikanern!*, 73–77.

25. Olpp, "Zur Charakteristik der Namas (Namaquas)," cited in Steinmetz, *Devil's Handwriting*, 119.

26. Heywood and Maasdorp, *Hendrik Witbooi Papers*, iii.

27. Witbooi, "20. Witbooi an Olpp."

28. Olpp, "Beitrag zur Geschichte des Witbooistammes," iii. See also Menzel, *"Widerstand und Gottesfurcht."*

29. Heywood and Maasdorp, *Hendrik Witbooi Papers*, 196.

30. Ibid., 34.

31. BArchB R 1001/2103, "Schutz- und Freundschaftsvertrag zwischen dem

Deutschen Reiche und Manasse zu Hoachanas," 7 April 1886, 12–13.

32. Ibid. Emphasis added.

33. BArchB R 1001/2103, "Schutz- und Freundschaftsvertrag zwischen dem Deutschen Reiche und den Hereros," 23 October 1885, 14–15.

34. Ibid.

35. Göring, "8. Göring an Witbooi," cited in Olusoga and Erichsen, *Kaiser's Holocaust*, 50.

36. Walvis Bay was an extension of the British-controlled Cape Colony in 1884.

37. Witbooi, "Witbooi an Nels," 27 September 1886, quoted in Olusoga and Erichsen, *Kaiser's Holocaust*, 50. See also Drechsler, *"Let Us Die Fighting,"* 34.

38. Göring, "Göring an Bismarck," 21 June 1888, quoted in Drechsler, *"Let Us Die Fighting,"* 34.

39. Afrikaners considered Khoikhoi's click language a linguistic stammer and used the term *Hottentot* (stutters) to refer to the entire group. German colonialists later adopted the term and embraced its derogatory connotations.

40. Göring, "8. Göring an Witbooi."

41. Göring, "24a. Göring an Witbooi."

42. Witbooi, "68. Witbooi an die Engländer in Walfischbucht."

43. Witbooi, "26. Witbooi an Maharero."

44. Witbooi, "25. Witbooi an Göring."

45. Ibid.

46. Kuss, *German Colonial Wars*, 80–87.

47. Bley, *Kolonialherrschaft*, 3–15; Drechsler, *Südwestafrika*, 81–114.

48. BArchB R 1001/1532, "Bericht an den Kaiser und Königs Majestät," 12 April 1885.

49. BArchB R 1001/1522, "Statut der Deutschen Colonial-Gesellschaft für Südwest-Afrika," 7 April 1885.

50. Bley, *Kolonialherrschaft*, 3.

51. "Die Lage im Hererolande." See also Drechsler, *Südwestafrika*, 33.

52. Short, *Magic Lantern Empire*.

53. *Stenographische Berichte des deutschen Reichstags (SBVdR)*, vol. 128, 1 March 1893.

54. Olusoga and Erichsen, *Kaiser's Holocaust*, 56.

55. François, "François an Krauel," quoted in Drechsler, *"Let Us Die Fighting,"* 43.

56. Ibid.

57. BArchB R 1001/1134e, "Bemerkungen zu der Denkschrift der Deutschen Kolonial Gesellschaft: Die Ansiedelung einer Deutschen Gemeinde in Süd-West-Afrika," 3 March 1891.

58. Tabel, "Die Literatur der Kolonialzeit Südwestafrikas," 78.

59. François, "François an Bismarck," quoted in Drechsler, *"Let Us Die Fighting,"* 63n159.

60. François, *Deutsch-Südwest-Afrika*, 153–54.

61. François, "59. Gespräch zwischen von François und Witbooi," 127.

62. Ibid., 127–28.

63. François, *Deutsch-Südwest-Afrika*, 153–54.

64. BArch R 1001/1486, "The Hottentot Power: Fighting in the North-West," *Cape Times*, 18 April 1892.

65. François, *Deutsch-Südwest-Afrika*, 155–57.

66. François, "François an AAKA," 70.

67. Bülow, *Deutsch-Südwestafrika*, 286–88.

68. BArchB R 1001/1483, "Colonization by Bullets," *Diamond Fields Advertiser*, 23 May 1893, 80.

69. BArchB R 1001/1483, "Damaraland," *Cape Times*, 16 May 1893, 23. The *Frankfurter Zeitung* and

its affiliates published the same story the following day in Germany.

70. BArchB R 1001/1483, no title, *Norddeutsche Allgemeine Zeitung*, 18 May 1893, 31.

71. Ibid.

72. Rash, *German Images*, 138–42.

73. BArchB R 1001/1483, no title, *Frankfurter Zeitung*, 16 May 1893, 21.

74. BArchB R 1001/1483, no title, *Hamburger Nachrichten*, 21 January 1894, 74–75.

75. Blackler, "From Boondoggle," 466–67.

76. BArchB R 1001/1483, *Vossische Zeitung*, 22 August 1893, 83.

77. Leutwein, *Elf Jahre*, 411–12.

78. Ibid., 412.

79. BArchB R 1001/1138, Leutwein, "Berichte an die Auswärtiges Amt—Kolonial Abteilung," 13 June 1903.

80. Leutwein, "110. Leutwein an Witbooi."

81. Leutwein, "96b. Leutwein an Witbooi."

82. Witbooi, "97. Witbooi an Leutwein."

83. Leutwein, *Elf Jahre*, 414.

84. Leutwein, "108a. Leutwein an Witbooi."

85. Witbooi, "111. Witbooi an Leutwein."

86. Leutwein, *Elf Jahre*, 57.

87. BArchB R 1001/1487, "Africa," *Kölnische Zeitung*, 20 April 1895, 97.

88. National Archives of Namibia (NAN) / Zentralbureau des Kaiserlichen Gouvernements (ZBU) 2028, W.II.D.16, vol. 3, "Schutz- und Freundschaftsvertrag zwischen dem Deutschen Reiche und Hendrik Witbooi," 15 September 1894, 45.

89. Ibid., 47.

90. Ibid., 48.

91. BArchB R 1001/1487, Theodor Leutwein, Hendrik Witbooi, et al.,

"Schutz und Freundschafts-Vertrag," 12–14.

92. Fenchel, "Letter to Rhenish Mission," 42.

93. NAN/ZBU J.XIII.b.6, vol. 3, "Leutwein an Reichskanzler," Windhoek, 13 December 1894, 161. See also Pool, *Samuel Maharero*, 113.

94. Pool, *Samuel Maharero*, 113.

95. Gewald, "Colonization," 192. See also Zimmerer, *Deutsche Herrschaft*, 23.

96. BArchB R 1001/2100, Theodor Leutwein, "Bericht an RKA," 17 June 1894. See also Gewald, "Colonization," 192; Zimmerer, *Deutsche Herrschaft*, 23.

97. Leutwein, *Elf Jahre*, 60. See also Pool, *Samuel Maharero*, 113.

98. Ibid., 162.

99. NAN/ZBU J.XIII.b.6, vol. 3, "Leutwein an Reichskanzler," Windhoek, 13 December 1894, 162.

100. Pool, *Samuel Maharero*, 115.

101. Bley, *Kolonialherrschaft*, 43; Gewald, "Colonization," 195; Pool, *Samuel Maharero*, 115.

102. NAN/ZBU J.XII.d.9, vol. 1, "Leutwein—Samuel," Windhoek, 20 December 1894, 65–66, quoted in Pool, *Samuel Maharero*, 117.

103. Leutwein, "Leutwein an AAKA," 24 February 1904.

104. NAN/ZBU J.XIII.b.6, vol. 3, "Leutwein an Reichskanzler," Windhoek, 13 December 1894, 167–68, quoted in Pool, *Samuel Maharero*, 117.

105. See especially Gewald, "Colonization," 189–90.

106. *Koloniales Jahrbuch*, vol. 2, 1889, quoted in Drechsler, *"Let Us Die Fighting,"* 27.

107. Pool, *Samuel Maharero*, 120–23; Gewald, "Colonization," 193.

108. Gewald, *Towards Redemption*, 83; Pool, *Samuel Maharero*, 120.

109. NAN/ZBU A.I.a.2, vol. 1, "Friedrich von Lindequist: Bericht betr.

Arbeiten der Südgrenze des Hererolandes," Windhoek, 19 January 1895, quoted in Pool, *Samuel Maharero*, 121–22.

110. NAN/ZBU A.I.A.2, vol. 1, "Leutwein an Samuel Maharero," Gibeon, 5 February 1895, quoted in Pool, *Samuel Maharero*, 122.

111. Gewald, *Towards Redemption*, 1996; Gewald, "Religion, Labour and Resistance"; Gewald, "Colonization," 2000; Gewald, "Herero Genocide"; Gewald, *Words Cannot Be Found*.

112. Gewald, "Colonization," 194.

113. Bley, *Kolonialherrschaft*, 56; Gewald, *Towards Redemption*, 105–7.

114. Gewald, "Colonization," 194–95.

115. Leutwein, *Elf Jahre*, 82.

116. Ibid.

117. BArchB R 1001/2101, Carl Weiss, "Eingabe in Windhoek," 7 February 1896, 3. See also Gewald, *Towards Redemption*, 106.

118. BArchB R 1001/2101, Hermann Sander, "Eingabe in Windhoek," 6 January 1896, 27.

119. BArchB R 1001/2101, Ferdinand Otto, "Eingabe in Windhoek," 6 January 1896, 28.

120. Gewald, *Towards Redemption*, 107.

121. Leutwein, *Elf Jahre*, 97–99.

122. Gewald, *Towards Redemption*, 108.

123. Ibid.

124. Leutwein, *Elf Jahre*, 126.

125. Gewald, *Towards Redemption*, 111; Gewald, "Colonization," 198.

126. Leutwein, *Elf Jahre*, 126.

127. Gewald, "Colonization," 196–97; Pool, *Samuel Maharero*, 165; Rizzo, *Gender and Colonialism*, 55.

128. RMG Chronicle, quoted in Gewald, *Towards Redemption*, 112.

129. Leutwein, *Elf Jahre*, 127–29.

130. Gewald, *Towards Redemption*, 113; Rizzo, *Gender and Colonialism*, 56.

131. Rizzo, *Gender and Colonialism*, 56.

132. Ibid.

133. Gewald, "Colonization," 198–99.

134. Ibid., 201.

135. Bley, *Kolonialherrschaft*, 134–35; Gewald, *Towards Redemption*, 143.

136. Gewald, *Towards Redemption*, 144.

137. Leutwein, "Leutwein an AAKA," September 1904. See also Gewald, *Towards Redemption*, 145. Emphasis added.

138. Leutwein, *Elf Jahre*, 429.

139. Moyd, *Violent Intermediaries*, 115–47.

140. Gewald, "Colonization," 203.

141. Ibid., 204; Pool, *Samuel Maharero*, 186.

142. Historians are increasingly skeptical that Samuel Maharero ever formally conspired to revolt against the imperial government. See especially Pool, *Samuel Maharero*, 184–87; Gewald, *Towards Redemption*, 178–91; and Zimmerer and Zeller, *Genocide in German South-West Africa*.

143. Samudzi, "Capturing German South West Africa," 47–52.

144. Leutwein, *Elf Jahre*, 428–30.

145. Leutwein, "Leutwein an AAKA," 24 February 1904.

146. Leutwein, *Elf Jahre*, 429.

147. Stoler and Cooper, "Between Metropole and Colony," 6.

148. Gewald, *Towards Redemption*, 38.

149. VEM/RMG 1.404, Johannes Olpp, "Beitrag zur Missionsgeschichte des Witbooistammes," 1897.

150. BArchB, R151-F, "Die Rechtlichen Verhältnisse der Eingeborenen, Abgesehen von der Gerichtsbarkeit," W.III. A1, Reichskolonialamt 3. Verordnungsentwürfe, 8 January 1907.

151. Witbooi, "152. Witbooi an Leutwein."

CHAPTER 5

1. BArchB R 1001/2058, Carl Becker, "Eingabe: Annullierung seiner Ehe mit einer Rehebother," 1 September 1909, 193–94.

2. BArchB R 1001/2058, *Verordnung des Reichskanzlers, betreff die Selbstverwaltung in Deutsch-Südwestafrika*, 28 January 1909, 1–9.

3. Ibid.

4. BArchB R 1001/2058, Becker, "Eingabe," 1 September 1909, 194.

5. Ibid.

6. Ibid.

7. BArchB R 1001/2058, Dr. Wilhelm Külz, *Die Selbstverwaltung für Deutsch-Südwestafrika* (Bückeburg, 1909), 52.

8. Zimmerer and Zeller, *Völkermord*.

9. Leutwein, *Elf Jahre*, 429.

10. Walther, *Creating Germans Abroad*.

11. Hintrager, "9. Mischehenverbot 1905 und Frauenfrage," 73–80.

12. Krüger, *Kriegsbewältigung*, 23–24.

13. Anderson, *Imagined Communities*, 149.

14. BArchB R 1001/2057, Consul Reimer, "Bericht von Konsul Reimer an die Auswärtiges Amt," 16 October 1908, 175–76.

15. BArchB R 1001/2057, Reimer, "Bericht an die Auswärtiges Amt," 16 October 1908, 176.

16. Ibid., 176–77.

17. Rohrbach, *Deutsche Kolonialwirtschaft, Südwest-Afrika*, 21.

18. Hyslop, "White Working-Class Women," 65.

19. Aitken, *Exclusion and Inclusion*, 109–17.

20. Guettel, *German Expansionism*, 143.

21. Wildenthal, *German Women for Empire*; Aitken, *Exclusion and Inclusion*.

22. BArchB R 1001/1220, Tecklenburg, "Erlass Nr. 710 an die AA—Kolonial Abteilung," 17 July 1905, 36.

23. Ibid.

24. BArchB R 1001/1220, "Einziehung von Vermögen Eingeborener im südwestafrikanischen Schutzgebiet," 26 December 1908, 72. See especially paragraphs 1, 3, subsections 4 and 5, 7, and 10.

25. BArchB R 1001/2118, Tecklenburg, "Bericht an die Auswärtiges Amt—Kolonial Abteilung," 3 July 1905, 154.

26. Steinmetz, *Devil's Handwriting*, 205.

27. BArchB R 1001/1220, Tecklenburg, "Erlass Nr. 710," 33–36.

28. Schuckmann, "Eine Programmrede des Gouverneurs," 467–68.

29. "Die Erziehung."

30. "Verordnung des Gouverneurs" (18 August), 1181–82. See also Cohen, "'Natives.'"

31. BArchB R 1001/1220, "Deutsche Schutzgebiete. Die Einziehung von Eingeborenen-Land," *Kölnische Zeitung*, 11 January 1906, 113.

32. "Verordnung des Gouverneurs" (18 August), 1181.

33. BArchB R 1001/1139, "Verordnung des Gouverneurs von Deutsch-Südwestafrika, betr. Die Paßpflicht der Eingeborenen," *Deutsches Kolonialblatt* 18 (18 August 1907):1882–84.

34. Steinmetz, *Devil's Handwriting*, 211.

35. "Verordnung des Gouverneurs" (18 August), 1181–82.

36. BArchB R 1001/5423, Tecklenburg, "Bericht an die AAKA," 68–69. See also Guettel, *German Expansionism*, 141–42.

37. BArchB R 1001/5420, Wilhelm Solf, "Rede," 2 May 1912, 73.

38. "Verordnung des Gouverneurs" (18 August), 1181–82.

39. "Verfügung des Kolonialamts";
"Verordnung des Gouverneurs" (22
March).

40. BArchB R 1001/1218,"Zur
Verhandlung steht die Frage der Schaf-
fung von Eingeborenen Reservaten im
Hererolande," 14 November 1902, 183–85.

41. BArchB R 1001/1218, "Tecklenburg Bericht an die Kaiser Wilhelm II," 7
April 1898.

42. BArchB R 1001/1218, Sitzung, "Zur
Verhandlung steht die Frage der Schaf-
fung von Eingeborenen Reservaten im
Hererolande," 14 November 1902, 183–85.

43. Steinmetz, *Devil's Handwriting*,
209.

44. National Archives of Namibia
(NAN), Kaislerliches Bizirksamt Wind-
hoek (BWI) 34, E.I.c (1), Bericht Nr. 40,
Omaruru Distrikt, 3 January 1908, 141.

45. Rohrbach, "Südwestafrika nach
dem Kriege," 166.

46. "Settler Lyric," ca. 1910, in
Hintrager, *Südwestafrika in der deutschen
Zeit*, 86–87.

47. Liliencron, "Die Frauenfrage in
den Kolonien."

48. Smidt, "'Germania führt die
deutsche Frau,'" 430–31.

49. Ibid.

50. Pierard, "Transportation," 318.

51. Kolonial-Wirtschaftliches Komitee, *Kolonial-Handels-Adressbuch*, 32.

52. *Kolonie und Heimat* (July 1914): 8.
See also Pierard, "Transportation," 319.

53. Leutwein, *Elf Jahre*, 232–34.

54. Rohrbach, *Deutsche Kolonialwirtschaft, kulturpolitische Grundsatze*.

55. Külz, "Colonial Administration
Speech," 392.

56. Wildenthal, *German Women for
Empire*; O'Donnell, Bridenthal, and
Reagin, *Heimat Abroad*.

57. Wildenthal, *German Women for
Empire*, 9.

58. Brockmann, *Die deutsche Frau*, iv.

59. Ibid., 2. See also Wildenthal, "'She
Is the Victor.'"

60. Liliencron, *Krieg und Frieden*,
299. See also Wildenthal, *German
Women for Empire*, 139.

61. Eckenbrecher, "Die deutsche Frau
und die Kolonien."

62. Gerstenberger, *Truth to Tell*,
64–99.

63. Neugebohrn, "Wie können die
Frauen," 8.

64. Niessen-Deiters, "Rassenreinheit!," 8.

65. See Wildenthal, *German Women
for Empire*; Smidt, "'Germania führt die
deutsche Frau'"; O'Donnell, "Colonial
Women Question"; O'Donnell, "Home,
Nation, Empire."

66. Wildenthal, "'She Is the Victor,'"
384.

67. Brockmann, *Die deutsche Frau*, 7.

68. Karow, *Wo sonst der Fuß des
Kriegers trat*.

69. Ibid., 33. See also Reagin, "Imagined *Hausfrau*," 81.

70. Karow, *Wo sonst der Fuß des
Kriegers trat*, 128.

71. Frenssen, *Peter Moors*, 195.

72. BArchB R 1001/1153, "Die Buren-
frage in Südafrika betreffend," 22 March
1905, 54–65.

73. Ibid., 60.

74. Walther, *Creating Germans
Abroad*, 64–68.

75. BArchB R 1001/1522, Dr. Göring,
"Bericht an Fürst von Bismarck," 15 May
1887, 75.

76. BArchB R 1001/1170–83, Ansied-
lungverhältnisse in Deutsch
Südwestafrika, 1903–1927.

77. Bley, *South-West Africa*, 122.

78. Leutwein, *Elf Jahre*, 414–15.

79. BArchB R 1001/1152, Leutwein,
"Germans in S.W. Africa: Germans and

Boer Settlers," *Cape Times*, 18 March 1903, 172.

80. Politisches Archiv des Auswärtigen Amt (hereafter PAAA) 14796, Kaiser Wilhelm II, "Telegram."

81. Ullrich, *Die nervöse Grossmacht*, 187–88. See also Rosenbach, *Das deutsche Reich*.

82. PAAA 14788, W. H. Burns, "Grandma's Request," 15 April 1900, 9–10.

83. PAAA 14788, Burns, "Grandma's Request," 10.

84. PAAA 14788, "German-Born Roman Catholic," "Letter to Count von Bülow," 10 May 1900, 14–15.

85. PAAA 14796, Schellendorff, "Deutschlands Interessen," 13 January 1900.

86. PAAA 14796, "Ein Patriot," "Briefe an die Reichskanzler," 3 December 1900.

87. Cape Town Archival Repository (hereafter CAP)/GH 35/140, Local Correspondence RE, Rising of Natives in German Southwest Africa.

88. CAP/GH 35/140, Inspector Edensor, "Telegram: Dutchmen in German Southwest Africa," 16 September 1905.

89. BArchB R 1001/1152, Conrad Rust, "Der Bur und das Deutschtum in Deutschsüdwestafrika," *Alldeutsche Blätter*, no. 23 (6 June 1903): 2–3.

90. BArchB R 1001/1149, "Die Bureneinwanderung nach Deutsch-Südwestafrika," *Alldeutscher Verband*, 23 April 1900.

91. Ibid.

92. BArchB R 1001/1152, "Zu der Boerenansiedelung in Deutsch-Westafrika," *Der Tag*, 6 September 1902.

93. BArchB R 1001/1151, "A Great Boer Trek to German West Africa," *African Review*, 21 September 1901.

94. BArchB R 1001/1148, "The Trek Movement," *Cape Times*, 22 February 1894.

95. Ibid.

96. Leutwein, *Elf Jahre*, 414.

97. Ibid., 414–15. See also Bley, *South-West Africa*, 111.

98. Rohrbach, quoted in Leutwein, *Elf Jahre*, 412.

99. Ibid.

100. BArchB R 1001/1152, Captain Ludwig von Estorff, "Betrifft beabsichtigte Buren-Einwanderung," 14 November 1902.

101. BArchB R 1001/1153, Schuckmann, "Auf das Schreiben vom 26 February 1908," 9 March 1908.

102. BArchB R 1001/1154, Friedrich Deckert, "Brief an die AAKA," 25 April 1903.

103. BArchB R 1001/1154, Carl Hanke, "Brief an die AAKA," 5 January 1905.

104. BArchB R 1001/1461, Bernhard Dernburg, "The Boer States: German Duke's Aberrations," *Natal Mercury*, 15 June 1908, 97.

105. Weitz, *World Divided*, 236.

106. *SBVdR*, 1903–1904, vol. 1, 60th Sitzung, 17 March 1904, 1900. See also H. Smith, "Talk of Genocide," 107–8.

107. *SBVdR*, 1903–1904, vol. 1, 14th Sitzung, 17 March 1904, 1891.

108. Ibid.

109. *SBVdR*, 1903–1904, vol. 1, 60th Sitzung, 17 March 1904, 1897.

110. Ibid., 1896–1897.

111. *SBVdR*, 1903–1904, vol. 1, 14th Sitzung, 19 January 1904, 365. See also Hull, *Absolute Destruction*, 106.

112. *SBVdR*, 1903–1904, vol. 1, 60th Sitzung, 17 March 1904, 1891.

113. *SBVdR*, 1912, vol. 284, 128th Sitzung, 7 March 1907, 4365.

114. BArchB R 1001/2089, Trotha, "Kommando der Schutztruppe, J. Nr. 3737," 2 October 1904, 7.

115. *SBVdR*, 1903–1904, vol. 1, 60th Sitzung, 17 March 1904, 1903–1904.
116. *SBVdR*, 1910–1911, vol. 262, 99th Sitzung, 12 December 1910, 3595.
117. Hull, *Absolute Destruction*, 63.
118. Kuss, *German Colonial Wars*, 57. See also Mommsen, "Public Opinion and Foreign Policy."
119. Sobich, *"Schwarze Bestien, rote Gefahr."*
120. Short, *Magic Lantern Empire*, 134–35. See also Sperber, *Kaiser's Voters*, 203–64.
121. "Die Koloniale Lügenfabrik," quoted in Short, *Magic Lantern Empire*, 138.
122. *Fränkischer Kurier*, 7 January 1907, quoted in Short, *Magic Lantern Empire*, 138.
123. Dernburg, *Zielpunkte*, 5.
124. Ibid., 9.
125. Ibid.
126. Ibid., 20.
127. Sperber, *Kaiser's Voters*, 248–49.
128. BArchB R 1001/2058, Schuckmann, "Antwort: Auf die Eingabe vom 1 September 1909," 11 October 1909.
129. BArchB R 1001/2058, "Dernberg an Schuckmann," 11 December 1907.
130. Ibid.
131. Ibid.
132. Arendt, "Race-Thinking Before Racism," 73.
133. Ibid., 72–73.

CHAPTER 6

1. Zimmerer, *Deutsche Herrschaft*.
2. Krüger, *Kriegsbewältigung*, 112–14.
3. BArchB R 1001/2089, Trotha, "Kommando der Schutztruppe, J. Nr. 3737," 2 October 1904, 7.
4. Frenssen, *Peter Moors*, 6.
5. Weitz, *World Divided*, 212–13.
6. Lehmann, "Fraternity, Frenzy, and Genocide," 115–25. See also Kalb, "Reprinting German Colonial Settler Narratives."
7. Warncke, "Brief an Eltern," in *Briefe 1893–1904*, 224.
8. Dagmar Zumbrunn-Warncke, "Vorwort," in Warncke, *Briefe*, 4.
9. Ibid., 4–5.
10. Ibid., 6.
11. Warncke, "Brief an Eltern," in *Briefe 1893–1904*, 10.
12. Ibid., 13.
13. Ibid., 16–17.
14. Ibid., 22.
15. Ibid., 23.
16. Warncke, "Brief an Willi," in *Briefe 1893–1904*, 79.
17. Ibid.
18. Warncke, "Brief an Eltern," in *Briefe 1893–1904*, 21.
19. Ibid.
20. Thanks in large part to the collective interest of their readership, the editors of the *Neustrelitzer Zeitung* paid Warncke's father 50 marks for his letters. See Warncke, *Briefe 1893–1904*, 92.
21. Warncke, "Brief an *Neustrelitzer Zeitung*," in *Briefe 1893–1904*, 92–93.
22. Ibid., 92.
23. Warncke, "Brief an Vater," in *Briefe 1893–1904*, 217.
24. Ibid., 218.
25. Ibid.
26. Ibid., 220.
27. Ibid., 222.
28. Ibid., 217.
29. Ibid., 222.
30. Ibid., 222–23.
31. Warncke, "Brief an Eltern," in *Briefe 1893–1904*, 224.
32. Paul Warncke, note added to ibid., 226.

33. Hellwig, "AAKA an Dr. med. Paul Warncke," Nr. 6734, 10528, 12 May 1904, in Warncke, *Briefe 1893–1904*, 228.

34. "Einer von vielen," 234.

35. Ibid., 237.

36. Ibid., 238.

37. Rosenblad, *Adventure*, 5–9.

38. Ibid., 18.

39. Ibid., 21.

40. Ibid., 27.

41. Ibid., 34.

42. Ibid., 143.

43. Ibid., 144.

44. Ibid., 159.

45. Ibid.

46. NAN/ZBU, Farm Register, 1902: U.V.F.14. "Franzfontein."

47. Janson, "Aus dem Farmerleben in Südwest."

48. Krüger, *Kriegsbewältigung*, 72.

49. Ibid., 12.

50. Estorff, "Brief an Vater," 13 May 1894, quoted in Jenny, *Südwestafrika*, 52.

51. Estorff, *Wanderung und Kämpfe*.

52. Ibid., 20, 22.

53. Estorff, *Kriegserlebnisse in Südwestafrika*. See also Kuss, *German Colonial War*, 276.

54. Estorff, *Kriegserlebnisse in Südwestafrika*, 23–24.

55. Ibid., 33.

56. Crozier, "What Was Tropical?"

57. Janson, "Aus dem Farmerleben in Südwest," 3.

58. Crozier, "What Was Tropical?," 529. See also Campbell, *Race and Empire*.

59. Estorff, *Wanderungen und Kämpfe*, 116–17. See also Schaller, "'Ich glaube.'"

60. Estorff, *Wanderungen und Kämpfe*, 117.

61. *Die Kämpfe der deutschen Truppen*, 207.

62. Mehnert, *Kriegsgeschichten*, 3–5.

63. Mehnert, *Mit Schwert und Pflugschar*, 67.

64. Ibid., 67.

65. Ibid., 71.

66. Ibid., 76.

67. Mehnert, "1904 Afrika entgegen," in *Kriegsgeschichten aus Südwestafrika*.

68. Ibid., 73.

69. Mehnert, *Kriegsgeschichten*, 14–15.

70. Ibid., 16.

71. Mehnert, *Mit Schwert und Pflugschar*, 119.

72. Ibid., 126.

73. Schauroth, *Liebes Väterchen*, 2–3.

74. Ibid., 50.

75. Ibid., 51.

76. Ibid., 136.

77. *Meine Kriegserlebnisse*, 10.

78. Ibid., 11–12.

79. Ibid., 16, 49.

80. Ibid., 55.

81. Ibid.

82. Ibid., 61.

83. Ibid.

84. Ibid., 66.

85. Zollmann, *Koloniale Herrschaft*; Muschalek, *Violence as Usual*.

86. Muschalek, *Violence as Usual*, 28.

87. Ibid., 42.

88. In ibid., 135.

89. See especially Ocobock, "Spare the Rod, Spoil the Colony"; Zollmann, *Koloniale Herrschaft*; Muschalek, *Violence as Usual*, 130–57.

90. *Meine Kriegserlebnisse*, 127.

91. Breckenridge, "Allure of Violence," 689. See also Muschalek, *Violence as Usual*, 36–38.

92. BArchB R 1001/1181, H. Lane, "Eingabe an die Auswärtiges Amt—Kolonial Abteilung," 7 February 1912, 165.

93. Ibid.

94. BArchB R 1001/1174, Rud Erpf, "Eingabe an die Auswärtiges Amt—Kolonial Abteilung," 13 April 1907," 5–6.

95. BArchB R 1001/1175, Karl Freimüller, "Eingabe an die Auswärtges

Amt—Kolonial Abteilung," 7 November 1907, 55–56.

96. BArchB R 1001/1172, Karl Cremer, "Eingabe an die Auswärtiges Amt," 25 February 1913, 65.

97. BArchB R 1001/1170, Julius Asser, "Eingaben an die Auswärtiges Amt," 28 August 1907, 12.

98. BArchB R 1001/1172, J. Christ, "Eingaben an die Auswärtiges Amt," 30 October 1910, 42.

99. BArchB R 1001/1172, J. Christ, "Eingaben an die Auswärtiges Amt," 27 November 1910, 47.

100. BArchB R 1001/1174, Ludwig Eckstein, "Eingabe an die Auswärtiges Amt—Kolonial Abteilung," 24 June 1908, 62–63.

101. BArchB R 1001/1172, Johann Andrae, "Eingaben an die Auswärtiges Amt," 16 October 1907, 13.

102. BArchB R 1001/1172, Georg Andler, "Eingaben an die Auswärtiges Amt," 1 April 1908, 23.

103. "Program of the General German Congress," quoted in Short, *Magic Lantern Empire*, 67.

104. BArchB R 1001/1136, "Die Zukunft Deutsch-Südwestafrika," *Berliner Neueste Nachrichten*, 15 December 1901, 91–92.

105. Hesse, foreword to *Die Schutzverträge in Südwestafrika*.

106. Ibid., 5.

107. BArchB R 1001/1170, Johannes Apel, "Eingabe an die Auswärtiges Amt—Kolonial Abteilung," 12 January 1909, 476–77.

108. BArchB R 1001/1177, Walther Heinemann, "Eingabe an die Auswärtiges Amt—Kolonial Abteilung," 27 May 1912, 114–17.

109. Ibid., 114–15.

110. Ibid., 115–16.

111. BArchB R 1001/1174, Gustav Engelke, "Eingabe an die Auswärtiges Amt—Kolonial Abteilung," 6 June 1909, 77–78.

112. Ibid., 77.

113. Ibid., 77–78.

114. BArchB R 1001/1172, Otto Seyfarth, "Eingaben an die Auswärtiges Amt," 15 June 1907, 14.

115. "Official slogan" of the *Deutscher Kolonialverein*, Fitzpatrick, *Liberal Imperialism*, 193.

CONCLUSION

1. Krüss, "Südwest ist Gross," 3.

2. Weitz, "From the Vienna."

3. Poley, *Decolonization in Germany*; Klotz, "Weimar Republic"; Sluga, *Internationalism*; Pedersen, *Guardians*; Schilling, *Postcolonial Germany*; Wempe, *Revenants of the German Empire*.

4. Höpker, *Als Farmerin in Deutsch-Südwest*, 93.

5. Wempe, *Revenants of the German Empire*.

6. Schnee, *German Colonization Past and Future*.

7. Ibid., 49.

Bibliography

ARCHIVAL AND UNPUBLISHED MATERIALS

Bundesarchiv, Berlin-Lichterfelde (BArchB)
Deutsch Kolonialgesellschaft (R 8023): 170–75
Kaiserliches Gouvernement in Deutsch-Südwest-Afrika (R 151-F): 82688
Reichskolonialamt (R 1001): 1134e–44; 1145; 1147–53; 1154; 1170–83; 1204–6; 1218–19; 1220; 1462–63; 1466; 1468; 1470; 1483–91; 1500; 1522; 1532; 1537–38; 2057–58; 2089; 2092–96; 2101; 2103–4; 2111–17; 2121; 2151
Schutzgebiet Deutsche-Südwest Afrika (R 1002): 1104; 1117; 1414–15

Cape Town Archival Repository, Cape Town (CAR)
General Dispatches: Emigration of Natives from German Southwest Africa, 1902 (GH 23/50); Settlement of Boers in German Southwest Africa (GH 23/66); Herero Natives from German SWA Crossing into Cape Colony, 1906 (GH 23/82); Local Correspondence RE Rising of Natives in German Southwest Africa, 1905–6 (GH 35/140); Reports on German SWA Situation by Resident Magistrate in Walvis Bay, 1904 (GH 35/141); Recruiting of Boers for Service in German Southwest Africa, 1905 (GH 35/151); Immigration into German Southwest Africa, 1906 (GH 35/152); Position and Treatment of German Authorities in South Africa, 1905 (PMO 253)

Freie Universität zu Berlin—Universitätsbibliothek, Berlin
Deutsches Kolonialblatt

National Archives of Namibia, Windhoek (NAN)
Deutsch-Südwestafrikanische Zeitung
Kaiserliches Bezirksamt Windhoek (BWI): 34:E.I.c (1)
Südwestbote: Windhuker Nachrichten
Zentralbureau des Kaiserlichen Gouvernements (ZBU): A.I.a.2 Band 1; A.I.A.2 Band 1; W.II.D.16 Band 3; J.XIII.b.6 Band 3; J.XII.d.9 Band 1; U.V.F.14; Woermann-Linie, 1901

National Library of South Africa, Cape Town (NLSA)
Süd-Afrikanische-Zeitung

Politisches Archiv des Auswärtigen-Amt, Berlin (PAAA)
Afrika Generalia 13—Südafrika: 14706–17
Die englische Kolonialpolitik in Afrika: 16179
Frage einer Intervention der Mächte: 14786–88
Kundgebungen in Deutschland zu Gunsten Buren: 14796
Die Walfischbai. (Deutsch-englische Verhandlungen über Regelung der Walfischbai Grenzfrage durch ein Schiedsgericht): 14802–4

Staatsbibliothek zu Berlin—Preußischer
Kulturbesitz, Berlin (Stabi)
Deutsche Kolonialzeitung
Kolonie und Heimat: In Wort und Bild;
    Koloniales Jahrbuch

Vereinte Evangelische Mission—
Rheinische Missionsgesellschaft,
Wuppertal (VEM/RMG)
Kleinschmidt, Franz Heinrich (1.573);
    Hahn, Carl Hugo (1.575); Hahn,
    Carl Hugo—Schriftwechsel aus d.
    Nachlaß (1.576); Hahn, Carl Hugo,
    1841–1866 (1.577a–c); Rath,
    Johannes (1.581a); Carl Hugo
    Hahn: Bericht von 1845–1871
    (2.593); Herero-Aufstand (2.603);
    Missionarskonferenze im Herero-
    land: Protokolle (2.611); Vorträge
    und Aufsätze zu Südwestafrika
    (2.635a); Deutsche Kolonialbe-
    hörden in Südwestafrika: u.a.
    Fürsorge die Herero (2.660)

Wilson Library—University of
Minnesota, Twin Cities
Die Gartenlaube—Illustriertes
    Familienblatt
Globus: Illustrierte Zeitschrift für Länder-
    und Völkerkunde
Stenographische Berichte über die
    Verhandlungen des deutschen
    Reichstages

NEWSPAPERS AND PERIODICALS

Cape Argus
Deutsche Zeitung
Fränkischer Kurier
Frankfurter Zeitung
Kölnische Volkszeitung
Kölnische Zeitung
London Times
National Zeitung
Neustrelitzer Zeitung
Norddeutschen Allgemeinen Zeitung
Vossische Zeitung

PUBLISHED PRIMARY SOURCES

Adalbert, Heinrich. *Denkschrift über die
    Bildung einer deutschen Kriegsflotte.*
    Potsdam: Riegelschen, 1848.
"Dem Andenken zweier deutschen
    Eroberer." *Die Gartenlaube*, no. 14
    (1855): 185.
"An unsere Freunde und Leser!" *Die
    Gartenlaube* (1853): 1.
Andree, Karl. *Geographische Wanderun-
    gen.* 2 vols. Dresden: Rudolf
    Kuntze, 1859.
"Baumwolle in Afrika." *Globus: Illust-
    rierte Zeitschrift für Länder- und
    Völkerkunde* 3 (1863): 160.
"Die bengalische Provinz Assam." *Globus:
    Illustrierte Zeitschrift für Länder-
    und Völkerkunde* 18 (1870): 16.
Bohrdt, Hans. "Die Nordwestdeutsche
    Gewerbe- und Industrie Ausstel-
    lung zu Bremen." *Daheim* 26
    (1890): 682.
Brehm, Alfred. "Die deutsche Expedi-
    tion nach Mittelafrika und ihre
    Gegner." *Die Gartenlaube*, no. 5
    (1862): 74.
Brockmann, Clara. *Die deutsche Frau
    in Südwestafrika: Ein Beitrag zur
    Frauenfrage in unseren Kolonien.*
    Berlin: Ernst Siegfried Mittler und
    Sohn Königliche Hofbuchhand-
    lung, 1910.
Buchner, Max. "Reitochsen in Südwest-
    Afrika." *Die Gartenlaube* (1885):
    432–34.
———. "Wie lebt man auf einer Afrika-
    reise?" *Schorers Familienblatt* 5
    (1884): 232–35.
Bülow, Franz Joseph von. *Deutsch-
    Südwestafrika: Drei Jahre im Lande
    Hendrik Witbois.* Berlin: E. S.
    Mittler, 1896.
Büttner, Carl Gotthilf. "Deutschland
    und Angra Pequena." *Deutsche
    Kolonialzeitung* 1, no. 15 (1884):
    300–302.

————. *Das Hinterland von Walfischbai und Angra Pequena: Eine Übersicht der Kulturarbeit deutscher Missionare und der seitherigen Entwicklung des deutschen Handels.* Heidelberg: Carl Winter's Universitätsbuchhandlung, 1884.

————. "Die Missionsstation Otyimbingue in Damaraland." *Zeitschrift der Gesellschaft für Erdkunde zu Berlin* 20 (1885): 38–56.

————. "Über das Erbauen von Häusern für Europäer im Innern Afrikas." *Deutsche Kolonialzeitung* 1 (1887): 23.

"The Congo Free State." *Scottish Geographical Magazine* 1 (1885): 290–304.

Dernburg, Bernhard. *Zielpunkte des deutschen Kolonialwesens: Zwei Vorträge gehalten von Bernhard Dernburg.* Berlin: Mittler, 1907.

"Die deutschen Fremdenlegion und das Kap der guten Hoffnung." *Die Gartenlaube*, no. 3 (1857): 47.

Deutscher Kolonialverein. "Deutscher Kolonialverein." *Deutsche Kolonialzeitung* 21 (1884): 417.

"Deutsche Weihnachtsfeier in Californien." *Globus: Illustrierte Zeitschrift für Länder- und Völkerkunde* 28 (1863): 143.

"Deutschlands erster Kriegshafen." *Die Gartenlaube*, no. 8 (1883): 132–36.

Eckenbrecher, Margarethe von, et al. "Die deutsche Frau und die Kolonien." *Südwestbote: Windhuker Nachrichten*, 15 (October 1913): 1–18.

————. *Deutsch-Südwestafrika: Kriegs- und Friedensbilder.* Leipzig: Wilhelm Weicher, 1907.

Een, Thure Johan Gustav. *Memories of Several Years in South-Western Africa (1866–1871).* Windhoek: Namibia, 2004.

"Einer von vielen." *Landeszeitung*, no. 195, 21 August 1904. In Warncke, *Briefe 1893–1904*, 234.

"Eisenbahn über das Hochgebirge nach Chile." *Globus: Illustrierte Zeitschrift für Länder- und Völkerkunde* 18 (1870): 46.

"Die Erziehung der Eingeborenen zur Arbeit in Deutsch-Ostafrika." *Jahrbuch über die deutschen Kolonien* 1 (1908): 117–24.

Estorff, Ludwig von. *Kriegserlebnisse in Südwestafrika: Vortrag gehalten in der Militärischen Gesellschaft zu Berlin, 8.2.1911.* Berlin: Ernst Siegfried Mittler, 1911.

————. *Wanderung und Kämpfe in Südwestafrika, Ostafrika und Südafrika.* Windhoek: Privatdruck des Herausgebers, 1968.

Fabri, Friedrich. *Bedarf Deutschland der Colonien? Eine politisch-ökonomische Betrachtung.* Gotha: Perthes, 1879.

Feißkohl, Karl. *Ernst Keils publizistische Wirksamkeit und Bedeutung.* Stuttgart: Union Deutsche Verlagsgesellschaft, 1914.

Fenchel, Tobias. "Letter to Rhenish Mission." 25 January 1895. In Helmut Bley, *South-West Africa Under German Rule, 1894–1914*, 42. London: Heinemann, 1971.

François, Curt von. "59. Gespräch zwischen von François und Witbooi." 9 June 1892. In Witbooi, *Afrika den Afrikanern!*, 126–32.

————. *Deutsch-Südwest-Afrika: Geschichte der Kolonisation bis zum Ausbruch des Krieges mit Witbooi.* Berlin: Dietrich Reimer, 1899.

————. "Exposé Concerning the Southwest African Protectorate with Special Consideration of the Time Period from 1 October 1892 Until 30 September 1893" ["Denkschrift, bertreffend das südwestafrikanische Schutzgebiet unter besonderer Berücksichtigung des zeitraums vom 1. Oktober 1892 bis zum 30. September 1893"]. *Deutsches Kolonialblatt* 3 (1893): 17.

————. "François an AAKA." 12 April 1893. In Drechsler, *Aufstände in Südwestafrika*, 70.

Frenssen, Gustav. *Peter Moors Fahrt nach Südwest: Ein Feldzugsbericht.* Berlin: G. Grotesche, 1906.

"Fünfundzwanzig Jahre Deutsch-Südwestafrika: Zum Gedenken an den 1 Mai 1883." *Deutsche Kolonialzeitung* 18 (2 May 1908): 314.

"General Act of the Conference of Berlin Concerning the Congo." *American Journal of International Law* 3, no. 1, Supplement: Official Documents (January 1909): 7–25.

Gerstäcker, Friedrich Wilhelm. *Unter den Penhuenchen.* Wund: Münchhausen, o.D.

"Goldwäschereien in Finnland." *Globus: Illustrierte Zeitschrift für Länder- und Völkerkunde* 18 (1870): 320.

Göring, Heinrich Ernst. "8. Göring an Witbooi." 21 November 1885. In Heywood and Maasdorp, *Hendrik Witbooi Papers*, 11–12.

————. "24a. Göring an Witbooi." 20 May 1890. In Witbooi, *Afrika den Afrikanern!*, 85.

Hahn, Carl Hugo. *Grundzüge einer Grammatik des Hereró (im westlichen Afrika) nebst einem Wörterbuche.* Berlin: Wilhelm Hertz, 1857.

————. *Tagebücher 1837–1860.* 5 vols. Edited by Brigitte Lau. Windhoek: Archeia, 1985.

Hahn, Emma Sarah. *The Letters of Emma Sarah Hahn: Pioneer Missionary Among the Herero.* Edited by Dorothy Guedes. Windhoek: Namibia Scientific Society, 1992.

Hahn, Theophilus. "Die Buschmänner: Ein Beitrag zur südafrikanischen Völkerkunde." *Globus: Illustrierte Zeitschrift für Länder- und Völkerkunde* 18, nos. 5–10 (1870): 65–68, 81–85, 102–5, 140–43, 153–55.

Hesse, Hermann. *Die Schutzverträge in Südwestafrika: Ein Beitrag zur rechtsgeschichtlichen und politischen Entwickelung des Schutzgebietes.* Berlin: Wilhelm Süfferott, 1905.

Heywood, Annemarie, and Eben Maasdorp, eds. *The Hendrik Witbooi Papers.* Annotated by Brigitte Lau. Windhoek: Springwell, 1990.

Höpker, Lydia. *Als Farmerin in Deutsch-Südwest: Was ich in Afrika erlebte.* Minden: W. Köhler, 1936.

Hundeshagen, Friedrich. *Die deutsche Auswanderung als Nationalsache, insbesondere die Auswanderung des Proletariats.* Frankfurt am Main: Heinrich Ludwig Brönner, 1849.

"In den Steppen von Afrika." *Die Gartenlaube* (1871): 11–13.

Jaeger, F., and L. Waibel. "Beiträge zu Landeskultur von Südwestafrika." *Mitteilungen aus deutschen Schutzgebieten* 14, nos. 1 and 2 (1920–21): 1–80.

Janson, Hubert. "Aus dem Farmerleben in Südwest." *Kolonie und Heimat: Im Wort und Bild* 1, no. 23 (1907/8): 3. In Walther, *Creating Germans Abroad*, 29–30.

Jung, Karl Emil. "Deutschlands Colonialbestrebungen: Deutsche an der Westküste von Afrika." *Die Gartenlaube*, no. 37 (1884): 609–17.

Die Kämpfe der deutschen Truppen in Deutsch-Südwestafrika. Vol. 1, *Der Feldzug gegen die Hereros.* Berlin: Mittler, 1907.

Karow, Maria. *Wo sonst der Fuß des Kriegers trat: Farmerleben in Südwest nach dem Kriege.* Berlin: Mittler, 1909.

Keil, Ernst, ed. *Der Leuchtthurm: Monatsschrift zur Unterhaltung und Belehrung für das deutsche Volk.* Vols. 2–5. Leipzig: Kiel, 1846–50.

Kirchhoff, Alfred. "Deutsch-Afrika." *Deutsche Kolonialzeitung* 1, no. 17 (1884): 333–35.

Kleinschmidt, Franz Heinrich. *Jonker Afrikaner und Missionar Kleinschmidt: Zwischen Rehoboth und Otjimbingwe; Tagebuch, Briefe, Berichte, 1839–1864.* Wether: W. Moritz, 1855.

Kolonial-Wirtschaftliches Komitee. *Kolonial-Handels-Adressbuch.* Berlin: Mittler, 1914.

"Die Kongokonferenz zu Berlin." *Über Land und Meer* 53, no. 14 (1884–85): 307.

Krüss, James. "Südwest ist Gross." In *Heimat Südwest: Ein Lesebuch für Sudwestafrika*, edited by Tilla Kellner, 3. Hannover: Hermann Schroedel Verlag, 1969.

Külz, Wilhelm. "Colonial Administration Speech." *Kolonialzeitschrift* 13, no. 25 (21 June 1912): 392. In Lora Wildenthal, *German Women for Empire, 1884–1945*, 103. Durham: Duke University Press, 2001.

———. *Die Selbstverwaltung für Deutsch-Südwestafrika.* Berlin: Wilhelm Süsserott, 1909.

"Die Lage im Hererolande." *Deutsche Kolonialzeitung* 17 (1 September 1887): 532–33.

Leutwein, Theodor. "96b. Leutwein an Witbooi." 5 May 1894. In Witbooi, *Afrika den Afrikanern!*, 179–80.

———. "108a. Leutwein an Witbooi." 21 August 1894. In Witbooi, *Afrika den Afrikanern!*, 197.

———. "110. Leutwein an Witbooi." 9 February 1894. In Heywood and Maasdorp, *Hendrik Witbooi Papers*, 121–23.

———. *Elf Jahre Gouverneur in Deutsch Südwestafrika.* Berlin: Siegfried Mittler und Sohn, 1907.

———. *Die Kämpfe mit Hendrik Witboi 1894 und Witboi Ende.* Leipzig: R. Voigtländer Verlag, 1912.

———. "Leutwein an AAKA." 24 February 1904. In Drechsler, *Aufstände in Südwestafrika*, 148.

———. "Leutwein an AAKA." September 1904. In Helmut Bley, *South-West Africa Under German Rule, 1894–1914*, 139–40. London: Heinemann, 1971.

Liliencron, Adda von. "Die Frauenfrage in den Kolonien." *Kolonie und Heimat* (1908/9). In Walther, *Creating Germans Abroad*, 46.

———. *Krieg und Frieden: Erinnerungen aus dem Leben einer Offiziersfrau.* Berlin: R. Risenschmidt, 1912.

———. *Reiterbriefe aus Südwest: Briefe und Gedichte aus dem Feldzuge in Südwest-Afrika in den Jahren 1904–1906.* Leipzig, 1907.

List, Friedrich. *Das nationale System der politischen Oekonomie.* Stuttgart: J. G. Cotta'sche Verlag, 1841.

Marvin, H. "English-Africa: Should Boers and Germans Dominate?" Reprinted as "Deutschland, England und Süd-Afrika." *Deutsche Kolonialzeitung* 16 (13 April 1888): 122–23.

Mehnert, Gottreich Hubertus. *Kriegsgeschichten aus Südwestafrika: Eine Liebeserklärung an ein Land und seine Menschen.* Windhoek: Glanz & Gloria, 2005.

———. *Mit Schwert und Pflugschar in Sachsen und Südwestafrika: Anekdoten und Geschichten eines Südwester Pioniers.* Windhoek: Glanz & Gloria, 2007.

Meine Kriegserlebnisse in Deutsch Südwestafrika. Minden: W. Köhler, 1907.

"Ein Morgen auf der Götterburg der Athener." *Die Gartenlaube*, no. 8 (1869): 123.

Neisser, Eugen. "Das Leben und Treiben der Eingeborenen." In *Deutschland und seine Kolonien im Jahre 1896: Amtlicher Bericht über die erste Deutsche Kolonial-Ausstellung*, edited by Gustav Meinecke and Rudolf Hellgrewe, 25–42. Berlin: Dietrich Reimer, 1897.

"Die neue Aera der Colonialpolitik." *Die Gartenlaube*, no. 49 (1884): 805–6.

Neugebohrn. "Wie können die Frauen Südwestafrikas die Bestrebungen des kolonialen Frauenbundes unterstützen?" *Kolonie und Heimat* 3 (1909/10): 8.

Niessen-Deiters, Leonore. "Rassenreinheit!" *Kolonie und Heimat* 36 (1911–12): Nachrichten.

Olpp, Johannes. "Beitrag zur Geschichte des Witbooistammes, für die Barmer Missionsgesellschaft." In Witbooi, *Afrika den Afrikanern!*, iii.

———. "Zur Charakteristik der Namas (Namaquas)." *Berichte der RMG* 32 (1876): 78. In Steinmetz, *Devil's Handwriting*, 119.

Poschinger, Hermann von. *Fürst Bismarck und die Parlamentarier*. 3 vols. Breslau: Trewendt, 1894–96.

Prager, Erich. *Die deutsche Kolonialgesellschaft 1882–1907*. Berlin: Dietrich Heimer, 1908.

Preuss, Eduard. *Kolonialerziehung des deutschen Volkes: Leitende Ideen und Material*. Berlin: Alexander Duncker, 1907.

Radowitz, Joseph von. *Reden für die deutsche Nation: Stenographischer Bericht über die Verhandlungen der deutschen constituirenden Nationalversammlung zu Frankfurt am Main*. Frankfurt am Main: Sauerländer, 1848.

Ratzel, Friedrich. *Anthropogeographie: Grundzüge der Anwendung der Erdkunde auf die Geschichte*. Stuttgart: Engelhorn, 1882.

Riegel, Herman. *Ein Hauptstück von unserer Muttersprache, der allgemeine deutsche Sprachverein und die Errichtung einer Reichsanstalt für die deutsche Sprache*. Braunschweig: C. A. Schwetschke und Sohn, 1888.

"Robinsons Insel—eine deutsche Ansiedelung." *Die Gartenlaube*, no. 14 (1869): 224.

Rohden, L. von. *Geschichte der Rheinischen Missions-Gesellschaft*. Barmen: D. B. Wiemann, 1871.

Rohlfs, Gerhard. *Quer durch Afrika: Reise vom Mittelmeer nach dem Tschad-See und zum Golf von Guinea*. Leipzig: Brockhaus, 1874.

Rohrbach, Paul. *Der deutsche Gedanke in der Welt*. Düsseldorf: Langewiesche Verlag, 1912.

———. *Deutsche Kolonialwirtschaft, kulturpolitische Grundsatze für die Rassen und Missionsfragen*. Berlin: Buchverlag der "Hilfe," 1909.

———. *Deutsche Kolonialwirtschaft, Südwest-Afrika*. Vol. 1. Berlin: Buchverlag der "Hilfe," 1907.

———. "Südwestafrika nach dem Kriege." In *Jahrbuch über die deutschen Kolonien I.*, vol. 1, edited by Karl Schneider, 156–66. Essen: G. D. Baedeker, 1908.

Rosenblad, Eberhard. *Adventure in South West Africa, 1894–1898*. Windhoek: Namibia Scientific Society, 2004.

Rupp, Erwin. *Soll und Haben in Deutsch-Südwest-Afrika*. Berlin: Dietrich Reimer, 1904.

Schauroth, Erich von. *Liebes Väterchen: Briefe aus dem Namaaufstand 1905–1906*. Windhoek: Glanz & Gloria, 2008.

Schnee, Heinrich. *German Colonization Past and Future: The Truth About the German Colonies*. London: George Allen and Unwin, 1926.

Schöneberg, Heinrich. "Berichte der RMG 10," 16, 1853: 241. In Steinmetz, *Devil's Handwriting*, 241.

Schuckmann, Bruno von. "Eine Programmrede des Gouverneurs." *Deutsches Kolonialblatt* 10 (15 May 1908): 467–68.

Simonsfeld, Heinrich. *Die Deutschen als Colonisatoren in der Geschichte*. Hamburg: Richter, 1885.

Sturz, Johann. *Kann und soll ein Neu-Deutschland geschaffen werden und auf welche Weise?* Vol. 1, *Ein Vorschlag zur Verwertung der deutschen Auswanderung im nationalen Sinne.* Berlin: Nicolai, 1862.

Tabel, Werner. "Die Literatur der Kolonialzeit Südwestafrikas: Memoiren berühmter Persönlichkeiten, Teil 3: Curt von Francois." In Werner Tabel et al., *Afrikanischer Heimatkalender 1983*, 78. Windhoek: Informationsausschuss der Evangelisch-Lutherischen Kirche in Namibia, 1983.

"Die Transvaal-Republik im Kafferlande." *Die Gartenlaube* (1855): 14.

Treitschke, Heinrich von. "Die ersten Versuche deutscher Kolonialpolitik." In *Aufsätze, Reden und Briefe*, edited by Karl Martin Schiller, 555–66. Meersburg: Hendel, 1929.

"Unser Programm." *Deutsche Kolonialzeitung* 1 (1884): 1–2.

Vedder, Heinrich. *Das alte Südwestafrika: Südwestafrikas Geschichte bis zum Tode Mahareros 1890.* Berlin: Martin Warneck, 1934.

"Verfügung des Kolonialamts betr. die Verwertung fiskalischen Farmlandes in Südwestafrika." *Deutsches Kolonialblatt* 18 (28 May 1907): 604–5.

"Verordnung des Gouverneurs von Deutsch-Südwestafrika, betr. Bildung von Wildreservaten in dem südwestafrikanischen Schutzgebiet." *Deutsches Kolonialblatt* (22 March 1907): 428–29.

"Verordnung des Gouverneurs von Deutsch-Südwestafrika, betr. Maßregeln zur Kontrolle der Eingeborenen." *Deutsches Kolonialblatt* (18 August 1907): 1181–82.

Volz, B., ed., *Leitfaden für den Unterricht in der Geographie von Prof. H. A. Daniel.* 176th ed. Halle an der Saale: Waisenhaus, 1891.

"Vom Vorgebirge der Guten Hoffnung." *Globus: Illustrierte Zeitschrift für Länder- und Völkerkunde* 18 (1870): 208.

Warburg, Otto. "Die deutsche Kolonialausstellung: Die Ausstellung der aus unseren Kolonien exportierten Produkte und deren Bewertung in der Industrie im Tropenhaus der Kolonialausstellung." *Deutsche Kolonialzeitung* 39 (26 September 1896): 307–9.

Warncke, Hans. *Briefe 1893–1904 von Hans Warncke alias "Hans Waffenschmied" aus Windhuk und Hamakari.* Edited by Dagmar Zumbrunn-Warncke. Windhoek: Kuiseb Verlag, 2014.

Warneck, Gustav. "Die christliche Mission und die überseeische Politik." *Allgemeine Missions-Zeitschrift* 28 (1901): 161–80.

Weber, Ernst von. *Die Erweiterung des deutschen Wirtschaftsgebietes und die Grundlegung zu überseeischen deutschen Staaten.* Leipzig: Twietmeyer, 1879.

———. *Vier Jahre in Afrika.* Leipzig: Brockhaus, 1878.

"Wie soll man kolonisieren? Von einem alten Praktiker." *Deutsche Kolonialzeitung* 1, no. 17 (1884): 337–41.

Wigand, Georg. *Die beiden deutschen Reichsverfassungen: Nebst der Denkschrift mit Belehrungen und Erläuterungen.* Leipzig: Georg Wigand, 1849.

Wigard, Franz, ed. *Reden für die deutsche Nation: Stenographischer Bericht über die Verhandlungen der deutschen constituirenden Nationalversammlung zu Frankfurt a.M.* Vol. 1. Frankfurt am Main: Sauerländer, 1848.

Witbooi, Hendrik. "14. Witbooi an Göring vom Hornkranz." 23 March 1889. In Witbooi, *Afrika den Afrikanern!*, 60–61.

———. "20. Witbooi an Olpp." 3 January 1990. In Witbooi, *Afrika den Afrikanern!*, 73–77.

———. "25. Witbooi an Göring." 29 May 1890. In Witbooi, *Afrika den Afrikanern!*, 86.

———. "26. Witbooi an Maharero." 30 May 1890. In Witbooi, *Afrika den Afrikanern!*, 91–92.

———. "68. Witbooi an die Engländer in Walfischbucht." 4 August 1892. In Witbooi, *Afrika den Afrikanern!*, 143–48.

———. "97. Witbooi an Leutwein." 6 May 1894. In Witbooi, *Afrika den Afrikanern!*, 180–81.

———. "111. Witbooi an Leutwein." 3 September 1894. In Witbooi, *Afrika den Afrikanern!*, 199–200.

———. "152. Witbooi an Leutwein." 14 November 1904. In Heywood and Maasdorp, *Hendrik Witbooi Papers*, 158–59.

———. *Afrika den Afrikanern! Aufzeichnungen eines Nama-Häuptlings aus der Zeit der deutschen Eroberung Südwestafrikas 1884 bis 1894.* Munich: J. H. W. Dietz, 1982.

Wolf, Eugen. *Vom Fürsten Bismarck und seinem Haus: Tagebuchblätter.* 2nd ed. Berlin: Egon Fleischel, 1904.

"Zur Charakteristik der Namas (Namaquas)." *Berichte der RMG* 32, no. 3 (1876): 81–82.

SECONDARY SOURCES

Aitken, Robbie. *Exclusion and Inclusion: Gradations of Whiteness and Socio-Economic Engineering in German Southwest Africa, 1881–1914.* Bern: Peter Lang, 2007.

Aitken, Robbie, and Eve Rosenhaft, eds. *Black Germany: The Making and Unmaking of a Diaspora Community, 1884–1960.* Cambridge: Cambridge University Press, 2013.

Ames, Eric, Marcia Klotz, and Lora Wildenthal, eds. *Germany's Colonial Pasts.* Lincoln: University of Nebraska Press, 2005.

Anderson, Benedict R. *Imagined Communities: Reflections on the Origin and Spread of Nationalism.* London: Verso, 1991.

Applegate, Celia. *A Nation of Provincials: The German Idea of Heimat.* Berkeley: University of California Press, 1990.

Arendt, Hannah. *The Origins of Totalitarianism.* New York: Harcourt Brace, 1951.

———. "Race-Thinking Before Racism." *Review of Politics* 6, no. 1 (1944): 36–73.

Bachmann, Klaus. *Genocidal Empires: German Colonialism in Africa and the Third Reich.* Berlin: Peter Lang, 2018.

Bade, Klaus. *Friedrich Fabri und der Imperialismus in der Bismarckzeit: Revolution-Depression-Expansion.* Freiburg: Atlantis Verlag, 1975.

Baranowski, Shelley. *Nazi Empire: German Colonialism and Imperialism from Bismarck to Hitler.* Cambridge: Cambridge University Press, 2011.

Barth, Dieter. *Zeitschrift für Alle.* Münster: Institut für Publizistik der Universität Münster, 1974.

Belgum, Kristen. *Popularizing the Nation: Audience, Representation, and the Production of Identity in "Die Gartenlaube," 1853–1900.* Lincoln: University of Nebraska Press, 1998.

Berman, Nina. *Orientalismus, Kolonialismus und Moderne: Zum Bild des Orients in der deutschsprachigen Kultur um 1900.* Stuttgart: M & P, 1997.

Best, Jeremy. "Godly, International, and Independent: German Protestant Missionary Loyalties Before World War I." *Central European History* 47, no. 3 (2014): 585–611.

———. *Heavenly Fatherland: German Missionary Culture Between Globalization and Nationalism.* Toronto: University of Toronto Press, 2021.

Blackler, Adam A. "From Boondoggle to Settlement Colony: Hendrik Witbooi and the Evolution of Germany's Imperial Project in Southwest Africa, 1884–1894." *Central European History* 50 (2017): 449–70.

———. "The Language of Empire: Aspiring German Colonists and the *Heimat* Ideal." In Pugach, Pizzo, and Blackler, *After the Imperialist Imagination*, 59–79.

Bley, Helmut. *Kolonialherrschaft und Sozialstruktur in Deutsch-Südwestafrika.* Hamburg: Leibniz-Verlag, 1968.

———. *South-West Africa Under German Rule, 1894–1914.* London: Heinemann, 1971.

Bochert, Christian. "The Witboois and the Germans in South West Africa: A Study of Their Interaction Between 1863 and 1905." MA thesis, University of Natal, 1980.

Bowersox, Jeff. "Boy's and Girl's Own Empires: Gender and the Uses of the Colonial World in Kaiserreich Youth Magazines." In Perraudin and Zimmerer, *German Colonialism and National Identity*, 57–68.

———. "Neuer Lebensraum in unseren Kolonien: Die Berliner Kolonialausstellung von 1933." In Heyden and Zeller, ". . . Macht und Anteil an der Weltherrschaft," 177–84.

———. *Raising Germans in the Age of Empire: Youth and Colonial Culture, 1871–1914.* Oxford: Oxford University Press, 2013.

Breckenridge, Keith. "The Allure of Violence: Men, Race and Masculinity on the South African Goldmines, 1900–1950." *Journal of Southern African Studies* 24, no. 4 (1998): 669–93.

Brehl, Medardus. "Das Drama spielte sich auf der dunklen Bühne des Sandfeldes ab." In Zimmerman and Zeller, *Völkermord in Deutsch-Südwestafrika*, 86–96.

Brogiato, Heinz Peter. "Wissen ist Macht—Geographisches Wissen ist Weltmacht": Die schulgeographischen Zeitschriften im deutschsprachigen Raum (1800–1945) unter besonderer Berücksichtigung des Geographischen Anzeigers.* Trier: Geographisches Gesellschaft Trier, 1998.

Buch, Hans Christoph. "'No One Wanders Under Palm Trees Unpunished': Goethe and Humboldt." In *Cosmos and Colonialism: Alexander von Humboldt in Cultural Criticism*, edited by Rex Clark and Oliver Lubrich, 231–39. New York: Berghahn, 2012.

Campbell, Chloe. *Race and Empire: Eugenics in Colonial Kenya.* Manchester: Manchester University Press, 2012.

Campt, Tina M. *Other Germans: Black Germans and the Politics of Race, Gender, and Memory in the Third Reich.* Ann Arbor: University of Michigan Press, 2005.

Canis, Konrad. *Bismarcks Außenpolitik 1870 bis 1890: Aufstieg und Gefährdung.* Paderborn: Schöningh, 2004.

Ciarlo, David. *Advertising Empire: Race and Visual Culture in Imperial Germany.* Cambridge: Harvard University Press, 2011.

———. "Picturing Genocide in German Consumer Culture, 1904–10." In Perraudin and Zimmerer, *German Colonialism and National Identity*, 69–89.

Cohen, Cynthia. "'The Natives Must First Become Good Workmen': Formal Educational Provision in German South West and East Africa Compared." *Journal of Southern African Studies* 19, no. 1 (1993): 115–34.

Confino, Alon. *The Nation as a Local Metaphor: Württemberg, Imperial Germany, and National Memory, 1871–1918.* Chapel Hill: University of North Carolina Press, 1997.

Conrad, Sebastian. *German Colonialism: A Short History.* Cambridge: Cambridge University Press, 2008.

———. *Globalisierung und Nation im deutschen Kaiserreich.* Munich: C. H. Beck, 2006.

Cooper, Frederick, and Ann Laura Stoler, eds. *Tensions of Empire: Colonial Cultures in a Bourgeois World.* Berkeley: University of California Press, 1997.

Crozier, Anna. "What Was Tropical About Tropical Neurasthenia? The Utility of the Diagnosis in the Management of British East Africa." *Journal of the History of Medicine and Allied Sciences* 64, no. 4 (2009): 518–48.

Dickinson, Edward Ross. "The German Empire: An Empire?" *History Workshop Journal* 66 (2008): 129–62.

Di Maio, Irene S., ed. *Gerstäcker's Louisiana: Fiction and Travel Sketches from Antebellum Times Through Reconstruction.* Baton Rouge: Louisiana State University Press, 2006.

Drechsler, Horst. *Aufstände in Südwestafrika.* East Berlin: Dietz, 1984.

———. *"Let Us Die Fighting": The Struggle of the Herero and Nama Against German Imperialism (1884–1915).* London: Zed Press, 1980.

Eckert, Andreas. "Afrikanische Nationalisten und die Frage der Menschenrechte." In *Moralpolitik:*

Geschichte der Menschenrechte im 20. Jahrhundert, edited by Stefan-Lundwig Hoffmann, 312–36. Göttingen: Wallstein, 2010.

———. *Herrschen und Verwalten: Afrikanische Bürokraten, Staatliche Ordnung und Politik in Tansania, 1920–1970.* Munich: R. Oldenbourg, 2007.

Eggers, Maureen Maisha. "Knowledges of (Un-)Belonging: Epistemic Change as a Defining Mode for Black Women's Activism in Germany." In Lennox, *Remapping Black Germany,* 33–45.

Eley, Geoff. "Empire by Land or Sea? Germany's Imperial Imaginary, 1840–1945." In Naranch and Eley, *German Colonialism in a Global Age,* 19–45.

El-Tayeb, Fatima. *Schwarze Deutsche: Der Diskurs um "Rasse" und nationale Identität 1890–1933.* Frankfurt am Main: Campus, 2001.

Engel, Lothar. *Kolonialismus und Nationalismus im deutschen Protestantismus in Namibia 1907–1945: Beiträge zur Geschichte der deutschen evangelischen Mission und Kirche im ehemaligen Kolonial- und Mandatsgebiet Südwestafrika.* Bern: Peter Lang, 1976.

———. "Die Stellung der Rheinischen Missionsgesellschaft zu den politischen und gesellschaftlichen Verhältnissen: Südwestafrikas und ihr Beitrag zur dortigen kirchlichen Entwicklung bis zum Nama-Herero-Aufstand 1904–1907." PhD diss., Hamburg, 1972.

Fanon, Frantz. *The Wretched of the Earth.* New York: Grove, 1963.

Fitzpatrick, Matthew. *Liberal Imperialism in Germany: Expansionism and Nationalism, 1848–1884.* New York: Berghahn, 2008.

———. "Narrating Empire: 'Die Gartenlaube' and Germany's

Nineteenth-Century Liberal Expansionism." *German Studies Review* 30, no. 1 (February 2007): 97–120.

———. "The Pre-History of the Holocaust? The *Sonderweg* and the *Historkierstreit* Debates and the Abject Colonial Past." *Central European History* 41 (2008): 477–503.

Florvil, Tiffany N., and Vanessa D. Plumly, eds. *Rethinking Black German Studies: Approaches, Interventions and Histories.* London: Peter Lang, 2018.

Gerstenberger, Katharina. *Truth to Tell: German Women's Autobiographies and Turn-of-the-Century Culture.* Ann Arbor: University of Michigan Press, 2000.

Gerwarth, Robert, and Stephan Malinowski. "Hannah Arendt's Ghost: Reflections on the Disputable Path from Windhoek to Auschwitz." *Central European History* 42 (2009): 279–300.

Gewald, Jan-Bart. "Colonization, Genocide and Resurgence: The Herero of Namibia, 1890–1933." In *People, Cattle and Land: Transformations of a Pastoral Society in Southwestern Africa*, edited by Michael Bollig and Jan-Bart Gewald, 187–225. Cologne: R. Köppe, 2000.

———. "The Herero Genocide: German Unity, Settlers, Soldiers, and Ideas." In *Die (koloniale) Begegnung: AfrikanerInnen in Deutschland (1880–1945), Deutsche in Afrika (1880–1918)*, edited by Marianne Bechhaus-Gerst and Reinhard Klein-Arendt, 109–27. Frankfurt am Main: Peter Lang, 2003.

———. *Herero Heroes: A Socio-Political History of the Herero of Namibia, 1890–1923.* Athens: Ohio University Press, 1999.

———. "Religion, Labour and Resistance in Namibia—II—The Road of the Man Called Love and the Sack of Sero: The Herero-German War and the Export of Herero Labour to the South African Rand." *Journal of African History* 40, no. 1 (1999): 21–40.

———. *Towards Redemption: A Sociopolitical History of the Herero of Namibia Between 1890 and 1923.* Leiden: Research School CNWS, 1996.

———. *Words Cannot Be Found: German Colonial Rule in Namibia; An Annotated Reprint of the 1918 Blue Book.* Leiden: Brill, 2003.

Grimmer-Solem, Erik. *Learning Empire: Globalization and the German Quest for World Status, 1875–1919.* Cambridge: Cambridge University Press, 2019.

Grosse, Pascal. *Kolonialismus, Eugenik, und bürgerliche Gesellschaft in Deutschland 1850–1918.* Frankfurt: Campus, 2000.

———. "What Does German Colonialism Have to Do with National Socialism? A Conceptual Framework." In Ames, Klotz, and Wildenthal, *Germany's Colonial Pasts*, 115–34.

Gründer, Horst. *Geschichte der deutschen Kolonien.* Stuttgart: Schöningh, 2012.

Guettel, Jens-Uwe. *German Expansionism, Imperial Liberalism, and the United States, 1776–1945.* Cambridge: Cambridge University Press, 2012.

Hamouda, Fayçal. *Der Leipziger Verleger Ernst Keil und seine "Gartenlaube."* Leipzig: Edition Hamouda, 2014.

Hartmann, Wolfram. "Sexual Encounters and Their Implications on an Open and Closing Frontier: Central Namibia from the 1840s to 1905." PhD diss., Columbia University, 2002.

Henrichsen, Dag. *Herrschaft und Alltag im vorkolonialen Zentralnamibia:*

Das Herero- und Damaraland im 19. Jahrhundert. Windhoek: Basler Afrika Bibliographien Namibia Resource Center, 2011.

Herre, Franz. *Friedrich Wilhelm IV: Der andere Preußenkönig.* Berlin: Casimir Katz Verlag, 2007.

Heyden, Ulrich van der, and Joachim Zeller, eds. *". . . Macht und Anteil an der Weltherrschaft": Berlin und der deutsche Kolonialismus.* Münster: Unrast, 2005.

Hintrager, Oskar. "9. Mischehenverbot 1905 und Frauenfrage." In Hintrager, *Südwestafrika in der Deutschen Zeit,* 73–80. Munich: Kommission Verlag, 1955.

———. *Südwestafrika in der deutschen Zeit.* Munich: R. Oldenbourg, 1955.

Hochman, Erin R. *Imagining a Greater Germany: Republican Nationalism and the Idea of Anschluss.* Ithaca: Cornell University Press, 2016.

Honeck, Misch, Martin Klimke, and Anne Kuhlmann, eds. *Germany and the Black Diaspora: Points of Contact, 1250–1914.* New York: Berghahn, 2013.

Hull, Isabel V. *Absolute Destruction: Military Culture and the Practices of War in Imperial Germany.* Ithaca: Cornell University Press, 2005.

———. "Military Culture and the Production of 'Final Solutions' in the Colonies: The Example of Wilhelminian Germany." In *The Specter of Genocide: Mass Murder in Historical Perspective,* edited by Robert Gellately and Ben Kiernan, 141–62. Cambridge: Cambridge University Press, 2003.

Hyslop, Jonathan. "White Working-Class Women and the Invention of Apartheid: 'Purified' Afrikaner Nationalist Agitation for Legislation Against 'Mixed' Marriages, 1934–9." *Journal of African History* 36, no. 1 (1995): 57–81.

Jaeger, Jens. "Colony as *Heimat?* The Formation of Colonial Identity in Germany Around 1900." *German History* 27, no. 4 (2009): 467–89.

Jenny, Hans. *Südwestafrika: Land zwischen den Extremen.* Stuttgart: Kohlhammer, 1966.

Kalb, Martin. *Environing Empire: Nature, Empire, and the Making of German Southwest Africa.* New York: Berghahn, forthcoming.

———. "Reprinting German Colonial Settler Narratives in Namibia Today." In *Archiving Colonialism: Culture, Space and Race,* edited by Yu-Ting Huang and Rebecca Weaver-Hightower, 221–37. New York: Routledge, 2018.

Kallaway, Peter. "German Lutheran Missions, German Anthropology and Science in African Colonial Education." In *Empire and Education in Africa: The Shaping of a Comparative Perspective,* edited by Peter Kallaway and Rebecca Swartz, 205–34. New York: Peter Lang, 2016.

Kennedy, Katharine. "African Heimat: German Colonies in Wilhelmine and Weimar Reading Books." *Internationale Schulbuchforschung* 24 (2002): 1–26.

Kiernan, Ben. *Blood and Soil: A World History of Genocide and Extermination from Sparta to Darfur.* New Haven: Yale University Press, 2007.

Klotz, Marcia. "The Weimar Republic: A Postcolonial State in a Still-Colonial World." In Ames, Klotz, and Wildenthal, *Germany's Colonial Pasts,* 135–47.

Koch, Marcus. *Nationale Identität im Prozess nationalstaatlicher Orientierung: Dargestellt am Beispiel Deutschlands durch die Analyse der Familienzeitschrift "Die Gartenlaube" von 1853–1890.* Frankfurt am Main: Lang, 2003.

Krüger, Gesine. "The Golden Age of the Pastoralists: Namibia in the 19th Century." In Zimmerer and Zeller, *Genocide in German South-West Africa*, 3–18.

———. *Kriegsbewältigung und Geschichts-bewußtsein: Realität, Deutung und Verarbeitung des deutschen Kolonial-kriegs in Namibia; 1904 bis 1907.* Göttingen: Vandenhoeck & Ruprecht, 1999.

Kundrus, Birthe. "From the Periphery to the Center: On the Significance of Colonialism for the German Empire." In Müller and Torp, *Imperial Germany Revisited*, 253–65.

———. "Die Kolonien—'Kinder des Gefühls und der Phantasie.'" In *Phantasiereiche: Zur Kulturge-schichte des deutschen Kolonialismus*, edited by Birthe Kundrus, 7–18. Frankfurt am Main: Campus, 2003.

———. "Kontinuitäten, Parallelen, Rezeptionen: Überlegungen 'Kolo-nialisierung' des Nationalsozialismus." *Werkstatt Geschichte* 15 (2006): 45–62.

———. *Moderne Imperialisten: Das Kaiserreich im Spiegel seiner Kolo-nien.* Cologne: Böhlau, 2003.

———. *Phantasiereich: Zur Kulturges-chichte des deutschen Kolonialismus.* Frankfurt am Main: Campus, 2003.

Kuss, Susanne. *German Colonial Wars and the Context of Military Violence.* Cambridge, MA: Harvard University Press, 2017.

Langbehn, Volker, and Mohammad Salama, eds. *German Colonialism: Race, the Holocaust, and Postwar Germany.* New York: Columbia University Press, 2011.

———. "Introduction: Reconfiguring German Colonialism." In Langbehn and Salama, *German Colonialism*, ix–xxxi.

Lau, Brigitte. "Kleine Zusammenfassung zur Dokumentation des Ortsnamen 'Windhoek.'" *Mitteilungen der Südwestafrikanischen Wissenschaft-lichen Gesellschaft* 29 (1988): 124–25.

———. *Namibia in Jonker Afrikaner's Time.* Windhoek: Documentary Publications, 1987.

———. "The Oppressed as Oppressors—Unresolved Issues of Namibian Historiography." In *Africa Seminar Collected Papers*, vol. 5, edited by A. Spiegel, 59–81. Cape Town: Centre for African Studies, Univer-sity of Cape Town, 1985.

Lehmann, Jörg. "Fraternity, Frenzy, and Genocide in German War Litera-ture, 1906–1936." In Perraudin and Zimmerer, *German Colonialism and National Identity*, 115–25.

Lekan, Thomas. "German Landscape: Local Promotion of the *Heimat* Abroad." In O'Donnell, Bridenthal, and Reagin, *Heimat Abroad*, 141–66.

Lennox, Sara, ed. *Remapping Black Germany: New Perspectives on Afro-German History, Politics, and Culture.* Amherst: University of Massachusetts Press, 2016.

Lerp, Dörte. *Imperiale Grenzräume: Bevölkerungspolitiken in Deutsch-Südwestafrika und den östlichen Provinzen Preußens 1884–1914.* Frankfurt am Main: Campus, 2016.

Loth, Heinrich. *Die christliche Mission in Südwestafrika: Zur destruktiven Rolle der Rheinischen Missionsgesell-schaft beim Prozess der Staatsbildung in Südwestafrika (1842–1893).* Berlin: Akademie, 1963.

———. *Kolonialismus unter der Kutte.* Berlin: Dietz, 1960.

Lührs, Wilhelm. "Vor hundert Jahren—die Nordwestdeutsche Gewerbe-und Industrieausstellung." *Bremisches Jahrbuch* 69 (1990).

Madley, Benjamin. *An American Geno-cide: The United States and the California Indian Catastrophe,*

1846–1873. New Haven: Yale University Press, 2016.

———. "From Africa to Auschwitz: How German South West Africa Included Ideas and Methods Adopted and Developed by the Nazis in Eastern Europe." *European History Quarterly* 33, no. 3 (2003): 429–64.

———. "Patterns of Frontier Genocide, 1803–1910: The Aboriginal Tasmanians, the Yuki of California, and the Herero of Namibia." *Journal of Genocide Research* 6 (June 2004): 167–92.

Martin, Peter. *Schwarze Teufel, edle Mohren: Afrikaner in Bewußtein und Geschichte der Deutschen*. Hamburg: Junius, 1993.

Maxwell, Alexander, and Sacha E. Davis. "Germanness Beyond Germany: Collective Identity in German Diaspora Communities." *German Studies Review* 39, no. 1 (2016): 1–15.

Mazón, Patricia, and Reinhild Steingröver, eds. *Not So Plain as Black and White: Afro-German Culture and History, 1890–2000*. Rochester: University of Rochester Press, 2005.

Meissner, Hans-Otto. *Durch die sengende Glut der Sahara: Die Abenteuer des Gerhard Rohlfs*. Stuttgart: Klett, 1982.

Menzel, Gustav. *C. G. Büttner, Missionar, Sprachpolitiker und Politiker in der deutschen Kolonialbewegung*. Wuppertal: Verlag der Vereinigten Evangelischen Mission, 1995.

———. *Die Rheinische Mission: Aus 150 Jahren Missionsgeschichte*. Wuppertal: Vereinte Evangelische Mission, 1978.

———. "Widerstand und Gottesfurcht": Hendrik Witbooi—eine Biographie in zeitgenössischen Quellen. Cologne: Rüdiger Köppe, 2000.

Michael, Theodor. 2017. *Black German: Afro-German Life in the Twentieth Century*. Translated by Eve

Rosenhaft. Liverpool: Liverpool University Press.

Mogk, Walter. *Paul Rohrbach und das "Grössere Deutschland": Ethischer Imperialismus im Wilhelminischen Zeitalter; Ein Beitrag zur Geschichte des Kulturprotestantismus*. Berlin: W. Goldmann, 1972.

Mommsen, Wolfgang J. "Public Opinion and Foreign Policy in Wilhelmian Germany, 1897–1914." *Central European History* 24, no. 4 (1991): 381–401.

Morgan, Stephen. "Shepherds of a Dying Flock: The Rhenish Mission, the Herero, and German Colonial Conquest in South-West Africa." PhD diss., University of Notre Dame, 2014.

Moses, A. Dirk. *Empire, Colony, Genocide: Conquest, Occupation, and Subaltern Resistance in World History*. New York: Berghahn, 2008.

———. "Hannah Arendt, Imperialisms, and the Holocaust." In Langbehn and Salama, *German Colonialism*, 72–92.

Moyd, Michelle. *Violent Intermediaries: African Soldiers, Conquest, and Everyday Colonialism in German East Africa*. Athens: Ohio University Press, 2014.

Müller, Sven Oliver, and Cornelius Torp, eds. *Imperial Germany Revisited: Continuing Debates and New Perspectives*. New York: Berghahn, 2011.

Murphy, Mahon. *Colonial Captivity During the First World War: Internment and the Fall of the German Empire, 1914–1919*. Cambridge: Cambridge University Press, 2018.

Muschalek, Marie. *Violence as Usual: Policing and the Colonial State in German Southwest Africa*. Ithaca: Cornell University Press, 2019.

Naranch, Bradley. "Beyond the Fatherland: Colonial Visions, Overseas

Expansion, and German Nationalism, 1848–1885." PhD diss., Johns
Hopkins University, 2006.

———. "Global Proletarians, Uncle
Toms, and Native Savages: Popular
German Race Science in the Eman-
cipation Era." In Honeck, Klimke,
and Kuhlmann, *Germany and the
Black Diaspora*, 169–86.

———. "Inventing the *Auslandsdeutsche*:
Immigration, Colonial Fantasy, and
German Identity, 1848–71." In
Ames, Klotz, and Wildenthal,
Germany's Colonial Pasts, 21–40.

Naranch, Bradley, and Geoff Eley, eds.
*German Colonialism in a Global
Age*. Durham: Duke University
Press, 2014.

Nipperdey, Thomas. *Deutsche Geschichte
1866–1918*. Vol. 2. Munich: C. H.
Beck, 1990.

Nyhart, Lynn K. *Modern Nature: The
Rise of the Biological Perspective in
Germany*. Chicago: University of
Chicago Press, 2009.

Ocobock, Paul. "Spare the Rod, Spoil
the Colony: Corporal Punishment,
Colonial Violence, and Genera-
tional Authority in Kenya,
1897–1952." *International Journal of
African Historical Studies* 45, no. 1
(2012): 29–56.

O'Donnell, Krista. "The Colonial
Women Question: Gender, National
Identity, and Empire in the German
Colonial Society's Female Emigra-
tion Program, 1896–1914. PhD diss.,
SUNY Binghamton, 1995.

———. "Home, Nation, Empire: Domestic Germanness and Colonial
Citizenship." In O'Donnell, Bridenthal, and Reagin, *Heimat Abroad*,
40–57.

O'Donnell, Krista, Renate Bridenthal,
and Nancy Reagin, eds. *The Heimat
Abroad: The Boundaries of Germanness*. Ann Arbor: University of
Michigan Press, 2005.

Oermann, Nils Ole. *Mission, Church and
State Relations in South West Africa
Under German Rule (1884–1915)*.
Stuttgart: Franz Steiner, 1999.

Oguntoye, Katharina. *Eine afro-deutsche
Geschichte: Zur Lebenssituation von
Afrikanern und Afro-Deutschen in
Deutschland von 1884 bis 1950*.
Berlin: Hoho Verlag Christine
Hoffmann, 1997.

Olusoga, David, and Casper W.
Erichsen. *The Kaiser's Holocaust:
Germany's Forgotten Genocide and
the Colonial Roots of Nazism*.
London: Bloomsbury House, 2010.

Opitz, Katharina, Katharina Oguntoye,
and Dagmar Schultz, eds. *Farbe
bekennen: Afro-deutsche Frauen
auf den Spuren ihrer Geschichte*.
Berlin: Orlanda Freuenverlag,
1986.

Osterhammel, Jürgen. *Die Verwandlung
der Welt: Eine Geschichte des 19.
Jahrhunderts*. Munich: C. H. Beck,
2009.

Paletschek, Sylvia. "Popular Presenta-
tions of History in the Nineteenth
Century: The Example of *Die
Gartenlaube*." In *Popular Historiog-
raphies in the 19th and 20th
Centuries*, edited by Sylvia
Paletschek, 34–53. New York:
Berghahn, 2011.

Pedersen, Susan. *The Guardians: The
League of Nations and the Crisis of
Empire*. Oxford: Oxford University
Press, 2015.

Perras, Arne. *Carl Peters and German
Imperialism, 1856–1918: A Political
Biography*. Oxford: Clarendon
Press, 2004.

Perraudin, Michael, and Jürgen
Zimmerer. *German Colonialism
and National Identity*. New York:
Routledge, 2011.

———. "Introduction: German Colonialism and National Identity." In
Perraudin and Zimmerer, *German*

Colonialism and National Identity, 1–6.

Pierard, Richard. "The Transportation of White Women to German Southwest Africa, 1898–1914." *Race and Class* 12 (1971): 317–22.

Platt, Kristin, ed. *Reden von Gewalt*. Munich: Wilhelm Fink Verlag, 2002.

Poley, Jared. *Decolonization in Germany: Weimar Narratives of Colonial Loss and Occupation*. Bern: Peter Lang, 2005.

Pommerin, Reiner. *"Sterilisierung der Rheinlandbastarde": Das Schicksal einer farbigen deutschen Minderheit 1918–1937*. Düsseldorf: Droste, 1997.

Pool, Gerhard. *Samuel Maharero*. Windhoek: Gamsberg, 1991.

Porter, Brian. *When Nationalism Began to Hate: Imagining Modern Politics in Nineteenth-Century Poland*. Oxford: Oxford University Press, 2000.

Prein, Philipp. "Guns and Top Hats: African Resistance in German Southwest Africa, 1907–1915." *Journal of Southern African Studies* 20, no. 1 (1994): 99–121.

Pugach, Sara. *Africa in Translation: A History of Colonial Linguistics in Germany and Beyond, 1814–1945*. Ann Arbor: University of Michigan Press, 2012.

Pugach, Sara, David Pizzo, and Adam A. Blackler, eds. *After the Imperialist Imagination: Two Decades of Research on Global Germany and Its Legacies*. London: Peter Lang, 2020.

Rash, Felicity. *German Images of the Self and the Other: Nationalist, Colonialist, and Anti-Semitic Discourse, 1871–1918*. New York: Palgrave Macmillan, 2012.

Reagin, Nancy. "The Imagined *Hausfrau*: National Identity, Domesticity, and Colonialism in Imperial Germany." *Journal of Modern History* 73, no. 1 (2001): 54–86.

Reimann-Dawe, Tracey. "Time, Identity, and Colonialism in German Travel Writing on Africa, 1848–1914." In Perraudin and Zimmerer, *German Colonialism and National Identity*, 21–32.

Rizzo, Lorena. *Gender and Colonialism: A History of Kaoko in North-Western Namibia, 1870s–1950s*. Basel: Basler Afrika Bibliographien, 2012.

Rosenbach, H. *Das deutsche Reich, Großbritannien und der Transvaal (1896–1902)*. Göttingen: Vandenhoeck and Ruprecht, 1993.

Said, Edward. *Orientalism*. New York: Random House, 1979.

Samudzi, Zoe. "Capturing German South West Africa: Racial Production, Land Claims, and Belonging in the Afterlife of the Herero and Nama Genocide." PhD diss., University of California San Francisco, 2021.

Sandler, Willeke. "Colonial Education in the Third Reich: The Witzenhausen Colonial School and the Rendsburg Colonial School for Women." *Central European History* 49, no. 2 (2016): 181–207.

———. *Empire in the Heimat: Colonialism and Public Culture in the Third Reich*. Oxford: Oxford University Press, 2018.

Sartre, Jean-Paul. *On Genocide: And a Summary of the Evidence and the Judgments of the International War Crimes Tribunal*. Boston: Beacon Press, 1968.

Schaller, Dominik J. "'Ich glaube, dass die nation als solche vernichtet werden muss': Kolonialkrieg und Völkermord in 'Deutsch-Südwestafrika' 1904–1907." *Journal of Genocide Research* 6, no. 3 (2004): 397–98.

Schilling, Britta. *Postcolonial Germany: Memories of Empire in a Decolonized Nation*. Oxford: Oxford University Press, 2015.

Schultz, Hans-Dietrich. *Die deutschsprachige Geographie von 1800 bis 1970: Ein Beitrag zur Geschichte ihrer Methodologie*. Berlin: Geographisches Institut der Freien Universität, 1980.

———. *Die Geographie als Bildungsfach im Kaiserreich: Zugleich ein Beitrag zu ihrem Kampf um die preußische höhere Schule von 1870–1914 nebst dessen Vorgeschichte und teilweiser Berücksichtigung anderer deutscher Staaten*. Osnabrück: Selbstverlag des Fachgebietes Geographie im Fachbereich Kultur- und Geowissenschaften der Universität Osnabrück, 1989.

Schultz, Hans-Dietrich, and Peter Brogiato. "Die 'Gesellschaft für Erdkunde zu Berlin' und Afrika." In Heyden and Zeller, ". . . *Macht und Anteil an der Weltherrschaft*," 87–94.

Scott, James C. *Seeing Like a State: How Certain Schemes to Improve the Human Condition Have Failed*. New Haven: Yale University Press, 1998.

Short, John Phillip. *Magic Lantern Empire: Colonialism and Society in Germany*. Ithaca: Cornell University Press, 2012.

Sluga, Glenda. *Internationalism in the Age of Nationalism*. Philadelphia: University of Pennsylvania Press, 2013.

Smidt, Karen Boge. "'Germania führt die deutsche Frau nach Südwest': Auswanderung, Leben, und soziale Konflikte deutscher Frauen in der ehemalige Kolonie Deutsch-Südwestafrika, 1884–1920; Eine sozial- und frauengeschichtliche Studie." PhD diss., Otto-von-Euericke-Universität Magdeburg, 1995.

Smith, Helmut Walser. *The Continuities of German History: Nation, Religion, and Race Across the Long 19th Century*. New York: Cambridge University Press, 2008.

———. "The Talk of Genocide, the Rhetoric of Miscegenation: Notes on Debates in the German Reichstag Concerning Southwest Africa, 1904–14." In *The Imperialist Imagination: German Colonialism and Its Legacy*, edited by Sara Friedrichsmeyer, Sara Lennox, and Susanne Zantop, 107–24. Ann Arbor: University of Michigan Press, 1998.

Smith, Woodruff D. *The German Colonial Empire*. Chapel Hill: University of North Carolina Press, 1978.

———. *The Ideological Origins of Nazi Imperialism*. New York: Oxford University Press, 1986.

Snyder, Edward. "Work Not Alms: The Bethel Mission to East Africa and German Protestant Debates of Eugenics, 1880–1933." PhD diss., University of Minnesota, 2013.

Sobich, Frank Oliver. *"Schwarze Bestien, rote Gefahr": Rassismus und Antisozialismus im deutschen Kaiserreich*. Frankfurt am Main: Campus, 2006.

Sperber, Jonathan. *The European Revolutions, 1848–1851*. Cambridge: Cambridge University Press, 2005.

———. *The Kaiser's Voters: Electors and Elections in Imperial Germany*. Cambridge: Cambridge University Press, 2009.

Sperling, Walter. "Zur Darstellung der deutschen Kolonien im Erdkundeunterricht (1890–1914) mit besonderer Berücksichtigung der Lehrmittel." *Internationale Schulbuchforschung* 11, no. 4 (1989): 387–410.

Steinmetz, George. *The Devil's Handwriting: Precoloniality and the*

German Colonial State in Qingdao, Samoa, and Southwest Africa. Chicago: University of Chicago Press, 2007.

———. "The First Genocide of the Twentieth Century and Its Postcolonial Afterlives: Germany and the Namibian Ovaherero." *Journal of the International Institute* (2005). https://www.umich.edu/news/MT /NewsE/10_05/steinmetz.html.

Stoecker, Helmuth. *Drang nach Afrika.* Berlin: Akademie, 1977.

Stoler, Ann Laura. "Sexual Affronts and Racial Frontiers: European Identities and the Cultural Politics of Exclusion in Colonial Southeast Asia." In *Becoming National: A Reader*, edited by Geoff Eley and Grigor Suny, 286–324. Oxford: Oxford University Press, 1996.

Stoler, Ann Laura, and Frederick Cooper. "Between Metropole and Colony: Rethinking a Research Agenda." In Cooper and Stoler, *Tensions of Empire*, 1–56.

Strandmann, H. Pogge von. "Consequences of the Foundation of the German Empire: Colonial Expansion and the Process of Political-Economic Rationalization." In *Bismarck, Europe, and Africa: The Berlin Africa Conference 1884–1885 and the Onset of Partition*, edited by Stig Förster, Wolfgang Mommsen, and Ronald Robinson, 105–20. Oxford: Oxford University Press, 1988.

———. "Domestic Origins of Germany's Colonial Expansion Under Bismarck." *Past and Present* 42, no. 1 (1969): 140–59.

Torp, Cornelius. "The 'Coalition of 'Rye and Iron' Under the Pressure of Globalization: A Reinterpretation of Germany's Political Economy Before 1914." *Central European History* 43 (2010): 401–27.

Townsend, Mary. *The Rise and Fall of Germany's Colonial Empire, 1884–1918.* New York: H. Fertig, 1966.

Trüper, Ursula. *The Invisible Woman: Zara Schmelen, African Mission Assistant at the Cape and in Namaland.* Basel: Basler Afrika Bibliographien, 2006.

Ullrich, Volker. *Die nervöse Grossmacht: Aufstieg und Untergang des deutschen Kaiserreichs, 1871–1918.* Berlin: Fischer Verlag, 1997.

Unangst, Matthew. "Men of Science and Action: The Celebrity of Explorers and German National Identity, 1870–1895." *Central European History* 50 (2017): 305–27.

Vedder, Heinrich. *The Native Tribes of South West Africa.* Cape Town: Frank Cass, 1966.

Vick, Brian E. *Defining Germany: The 1848 Frankfurt Parliamentarians and National Identity.* Cambridge, MA: Harvard University Press, 2002.

———. "Imperialism, Race, and Genocide at the *Paulskirche*: Origins, Meanings, Trajectories." In Perraudin and Zimmerer, *German Colonialism and National Identity*, 9–20.

Wallace, Marion. *A History of Namibia: From the Beginning to 1990.* New York: Columbia University Press, 2011.

Walther, Daniel Joseph. *Creating Germans Abroad: Cultural Policies and National Identity in Namibia.* Athens: Ohio University Press, 2002.

———. "Gender Construction and Settler Colonialism in German Southwest Africa, 1894–1914." *Historian* 66, no. 1 (2004): 1–18.

Wehler, Hans-Ulrich. *Bismarck und der Imperialismus.* Cologne: Kiepenheuer u. Witsch, 1969.

Weitz, Eric D. "From the Vienna to the Paris System: International Politics and the Entangled Histories of

Human Rights, Forced Deportations, and Civilizing Missions." *American Historical Review* 113, no. 5 (2008): 1313–43.

———. *A World Divided: The Global Struggle for Human Rights in the Age of Nation-States*. Princeton: Princeton University Press, 2019.

Wempe, Sean Andrew. *Revenants of the German Empire: Colonial Germans, Imperialism, and the League of Nations*. Oxford: Oxford University Press, 2019.

Werner, Wolfgang. "A Brief History of Land Dispossession in Namibia." In "Namibia: Africa's Youngest Nation March." Special issue, *Journal of Southern African Studies* 19, no. 1 (1993).

Wildenthal, Lora. *German Women for Empire, 1884–1945*. Durham: Duke University Press, 2001.

———. "'She Is the Victor': Bourgeois Women, Nationalist Identities, and the Ideal of the Independent Woman Farmer in German Southwest Africa." In *Society, Culture, and the State in Germany, 1870–1930*, edited by Geoff Eley, 371–95. Ann Arbor: University of Michigan Press, 1997.

Wolfe, Patrick. "Settler Colonialism and the Elimination of the Native." *Journal of Genocide Research* 8, no. 4 (2006): 387–409.

Zantop, Susanne. *Colonial Fantasies: Conquest, Family and Nation in Precolonial Germany, 1770–1870*. Durham: Duke University Press, 1997.

Zeller, Joachim. *Genocide in German South-West Africa: The Colonial War of 1904–1908 and Its Aftermath*. Monmouth, Wales: Merlin Press, 2008.

Zimmerer, Jürgen. "The Birth of the Ostland Out of the Spirit of Colonialism: A Postcolonial Perspective on the Nazi Policy of Conquest and Extermination." *Patterns of Genocide* 39, no. 2 (2005): 197–219.

———. "Colonialism and the Holocaust: Towards an Archaeology of Genocide. In *Genocide and Settler Society: Frontier Violence and Stolen Indigenous Children in Australian History*, edited by A. Dirk Moses, 49–76. New York: Berghahn Books, 2004.

———. *Deutsche Herrschaft über Afrikaner: Staatlicher Machtanspruch und Wirklichkeit im kolonialen Namibia*. 3rd ed. Münster: LIT, 2004.

———. "Die Geburt des 'Ostlandes' aus dem Geiste des Kolonialismus: Die nationalsozialistische Eroberungs- und Beherrschungspolitik in (Post-)Kolonialer Perspektive." *Sozial.Geschichte: Zeitschrift für historische Analyse des 20. and 21. Jahrhunderts* 19 (2004): 10–43.

———. *Kein Platz an der Sonne: Erinnerungsorte der deutschen Kolonialgeschichte*. Frankfurt am Main: Campus, 2013.

———. "Krieg, KZ und Völkermord in Südwestafrika: Der erste deutsche Genozid." In Zimmerer and Zellner, *Völkermord in Südwestafrika*, 45–63.

———. *Von Windhuk nach Auschwitz? Beiträge zum Verhältnis von Kolonialismus und Holocaust*. Berlin: Lit-Verlag, 2011.

Zimmerer, Jürgen, and Joachim Zeller, eds. *Genocide in German South-West Africa: The Colonial War of 1904–1908 in Namibia and Its Aftermath*. Monmouth, Wales: Merlin Press, 2008.

———, eds. *Völkermord in Deutsch-Südwestafrika: Der Kolonialkrieg*

(1904–1908) in Namibia und seine Folgen. Berlin: C. H. Links, 2004.

Zimmerman, Andrew. *Alabama in Africa: Booker T. Washington, the German Empire, and the Globalization of the New South*. Princeton: Princeton University Press, 2010.

———. *Anthropology and Antihumanism in Imperial Germany*. Chicago: University of Chicago Press, 2001.

Zimmermann, Klaus, and Birte Kellermeier-Rehbein, eds. *Koloniale und postkoloniale Linguistik*. Bremen: Institut für Deutsche Sprache, 2015.

Zollmann, Jakob. *Koloniale Herrschaft und ihre Grenzen: Die Kolonialpolizei in Deutsch-Sudwestafrika 1894–1915*. Göttingen: Vandenhoeck and Ruprecht, 2010.

Index

Italicized page references indicate illustrations. Endnotes are referenced with "n" followed by the endnote number.

Milton Keynes UK
Ingram Content Group UK Ltd.
UKHW010012221123
433005UK00007B/347